3D DATA ACQUISITION FOR BIOARCHAEOLOGY, FORENSIC ANTHROPOLOGY, AND ARCHAEOLOGY

3D DATA ACQUISITION FOR BIOARCHAEOLOGY, FORENSIC ANTHROPOLOGY, AND ARCHAEOLOGY

Edited by

NORIKO SEGUCHI
BEATRIX DUDZIK

ELSEVIER

ACADEMIC PRESS
An imprint of Elsevier

Academic Press is an imprint of Elsevier
125 London Wall, London EC2Y 5AS, United Kingdom
525 B Street, Suite 1650, San Diego, CA 92101, United States
50 Hampshire Street, 5th Floor, Cambridge, MA 02139, United States
The Boulevard, Langford Lane, Kidlington, Oxford OX5 1GB, United Kingdom

Notices
Knowledge and best practice in this field are constantly changing. As new research and experience broaden our understanding, changes in research methods, professional practices, or medical treatment may become necessary.

Practitioners and researchers must always rely on their own experience and knowledge in evaluating and using any information, methods, compounds, or experiments described herein. In using such information or methods they should be mindful of their own safety and the safety of others, including parties for whom they have a professional responsibility.

To the fullest extent of the law, neither the Publisher nor the authors, contributors, or editors, assume any liability for any injury and/or damage to persons or property as a matter of products liability, negligence or otherwise, or from any use or operation of any methods, products, instructions, or ideas contained in the material herein.

Library of Congress Cataloging-in-Publication Data
A catalog record for this book is available from the Library of Congress

British Library Cataloguing-in-Publication Data
A catalogue record for this book is available from the British Library

ISBN: 978-0-12-815309-3

For information on all Academic Press publications visit our website at https://www.elsevier.com/books-and-journals

Publisher: Stacy Masucci
Acquisition Editor: Elizabeth Brown
Editorial Project Manager: Ana Claudia A. Garcia
Production Project Manager: Bharatwaj Varatharajan
Cover Designer: Miles Hitchen

Typeset by TNQ Technologies

Contents

Contributors

Will Archer
Department of Human Evolution, Max Planck Institute for Evolutionary Anthropology, Leipzig, Germany; Department of Archaeology, University of Cape Town, Cape Town, South Africa

Beatrix Dudzik
Department of Anatomy, DeBusk College of Osteopathic Medicine, Lincoln Memorial University, Harrogate, TN, The United States of America

Yoshinori Kawakubo
Department of Anatomy and Anthropology, Faculty of Medicine, Saga University, Saga, Japan

Mary-Margaret Murphy
Department of Anthropology, The University of Montana, Missoula, MT, The United States of America

Kengo Ohno
Department of Forensic Medicine, Faculty of Medicine, Saga University, Saga, Japan

Anna M. Prentiss
Department of Anthropology, The University of Montana, Missoula, MT, The United States of America

Darya Presnyakova
Department of Early Prehistory and Quaternary Ecology, University of Tübingen, Schloss Hohentübingen, Tübingen, Germany

Stefan Schlager
Department of Biological Anthropology, Albert-Ludwigs University Freiburg, Freiburg, Germany

Noriko Seguchi
Faculty of Social and Cultural Studies, Kyushu University, Fukuoka, Japan; Department of Anthropology, The University of Montana, Missoula, MT, The United States of America

Shiori Yonemoto
The Kyushu University Museum, Kyushu University, Fukuoka, Japan

CHAPTER ONE

Introduction

Noriko Seguchi[1,2] Beatrix Dudzik[3], Mary-Margaret Murphy[2], Anna M. Prentiss[2]
[1]Faculty of Social and Cultural Studies, Kyushu University, Fukuoka, Japan
[2]Department of Anthropology, The University of Montana, Missoula, MT, The United States of America
[3]Department of Anatomy, DeBusk College of Osteopathic Medicine, Lincoln Memorial University, Harrogate, TN, The United States of America

Introduction

Advances in three-dimensional (3D) technology have impacted biological anthropology, archaeology, and geometric morphometric (GM) research in many ways related to the virtual preservation of skeletal and archaeological collections. 3D digitizing and imaging methods are now enabling researchers to expand and improve biological anthropological, forensic anthropological, and archaeological research. Various analytical methods for understanding shape and morphological diversification have been innovated. The 3D approach is becoming a significant toolkit in biological/forensic anthropology and archaeology.

Anthropological research into the evolution of shapes using GM analysis has a long history (Bookstein, 1991; Rohlf and Marcus, 1993) and in recent years has become a critical tool in biological anthropology (McKeown and Jantz, 2005; McKeown and Schmidt, 2013). Throughout the history of anthropology, craniofacial morphology has been intensely studied by biological anthropologists (Howells, 1973, 1996; Slice et al., 2005; Williams and Slice, 2010). For example, the analysis of ancient populations through the investigation of craniofacial variation has been used widely. It is considered to be an effective and informative way to understand population relationships and modern population structure and to infer relationships in the past (i.e., Hanihara, 1996; Brace et al., 2001, 2006, 2014; Seguchi et al., 2011; Schmidt and Seguchi, 2014, 2016). Because of the neutrality of craniofacial traits and structures (Relethford, 2004a, 2004b; Weaver et al., 2007; Von Cramon-Taubadel, 2009, 2011; 2019; Betti et al., 2009, 2010; Relethford, 2010), statistical analysis of craniofacial shapes (morphometrics) are used for assigning membership to certain human populations

3D Data Acquisition for Bioarchaeology, Forensic Anthropology, and Archaeology
ISBN: 978-0-12-815309-3
https://doi.org/10.1016/B978-0-12-815309-3.00001-2

and for identification in the fields of biological and forensic anthropology. Biological anthropology has focused on not just research on population history and structure using neutral craniofacial morphology but also on the study of functional morphology, such as masticatory stress or climate adaptation (Harvati and Weaver, 2006; Fukase et al., 2015; Ohno et al., 2016; Nathan et al., 2018). These aspects recently have been investigated by anthropologists using shape analysis with 3D technology. 3D measuring techniques and 3D imaging are now opening up new possibilities in the study of population history and structure and functional morphology.

Moreover, valuable 3D data from human mummified and skeletal remains (e.g., "Ötzi," "Kennewick individual," *Ardipithecus*, *Homo naledi*, etc.) captured by computed tomography (CT) and scanning magnetic resonance imaging (MRI) from various archaeological sites during the last decades have spurred the continuing growth of cutting edge scientific research. 3D data have been used to conduct more accurate reconstruction and are providing many new insights on issues such as causes of death, diseases the individuals suffered from, and so on.

Morphometric studies in archaeology using 3D scanning have begun to appear in the archaeological literature, especially associated with lithic tool studies, such as Paleo-Indian projectile point tip shapes using GM (Buchanan and Collard, 2010) and phylogenetic studies of projectile points (Shott, 2011a, 2011b). It is clear that the current advanced research on lithic technology is dependent on access to 3D scanning technology for GM analysis.

Additionally, 3D scanning offers an opportunity to recognize and to quantify morphological variability of artifacts, including convexity and twist and scar patterns that are difficult or impossible to recognize under normal optical conditions (Bretzke and Conard, 2012). This can result in the ability to collect sophisticated data observations, and it provides enhanced visual perspectives on artifacts made from rough materials, such as patterns of scars (Scholts et al., 2012) and pictorial line drawings that are difficult to observe without access to 3D images (Prentiss et al., 2015).

Although crania have many homologous landmarks, archaeological artifacts such as lithics and potteries have few homologous landmarks. Therefore, utilization of semilandmarks has been developed. 3D scanning has proved useful in research not only in biological anthropology (including bioarchaeology and forensic anthropology) but also in archaeology.

Difficulty of utilization of 3D technology

Learning how to acquire useful 3D model data, as well as manipulation and familiarization with 3D virtual data and the virtual environment, will be beneficial for the fields of biological anthropology, bioarchaeology, forensic anthropology, and archaeology. Although the 3D methods and techniques are extremely attractive to many anthropologists, technologies such as high-resolution 3D images created from CT and MRI are difficult to use for nonmedical researchers because the devices are expensive, require specialized training to operate, and require expensive software programs. In addition, materials such as mummified remains are usually stationary and cannot be removed from their research institution. For the analysis of shape and functional morphology, biological and forensic anthropologists have started to use portable 3D digitizers and portable laser 3D surface scanners. Laser scanners have a wide price range, from more affordable devices of around $5000 to expensive laser and white light scanner devices that are more than $50,000 (Kuzminsky and Gardiner, 2012). Researchers have been able to start using inexpensive devices to create images in cases where they lack access to the highest quality 3D surface scanners. Devices usually come with software used to view, process, and manipulate the scans, but it requires extensive training to create 3D images. It is time-consuming to learn how to create proper 3D models using these devices in comparison to traditional 2D measurements.

There are plenty of published articles that discuss and use 3D digitizers and 3D scanners for studies in the field of biological anthropology. However, such articles usually focus on GM analysis and elliptical Fourier analysis (i.e., Garvin and Ruff, 2012; Scholts et al., 2011; Thayer and Dobson, 2010). These articles are often difficult for beginners to follow and also may not specifically describe details of data acquisition and processing techniques (Kuzminsky and Gardiner, 2012). In addition, academic articles do not mention the difficulties beginners may encounter; for example, how to set up a cranium or a long bone in a stable manner, how to determine which materials may cause difficulties in the capture of images, and what kinds of surface processing should be chosen. Beginners often wish to use several free software packages for processing models, collecting landmarks, and GM analysis. It can be difficult to master how to use free software packages without someone's help unless participating in 3D research networks/groups. If students choose 3D projects without a 3D-equipped lab with advisors to direct them, they may end up spending many years trying to figure out all of the 3D processes needed to analyze their data. Helping to save others from the above challenges we have faced is the driving force behind writing this handbook.

This handbook covers two 3D technologies: (1) the 3D digitizer and (2) the 3D scanner. We mainly focus on craniofacial data acquisition and data analysis, but in one chapter, we also cover 3D data acquisition and analysis of archaeological artifacts. As a handbook for the collection and processing of 3D scanned data, this book provides a tool for scholars and students interested in pursuing research projects with 3D models. This handbook explores the best practices of data acquisition methods for recording landmark and semilandmark data on fragile archaeological human remains and archaeological artifacts. This book will enhance the reader's understanding of GM by introducing the technology used for virtual model processing protocols, alignment methods, data acquisition techniques, basic technological protocols, and variations in research design within different subfields of biological anthropology and archaeology.

Advancements in three-dimensional technologies

A brief description of three-dimensional digitizers

To capture cranial shape in quantifiable dimensions, biological anthropology has traditionally applied straightforward osteometric measurement tools such as sliding and spreading calipers. Measurement tools typically can be used in the field and in the lab. Although manual measurements are considered to be as reliable in the field as in the lab, because manual measurements do not require a complex laboratory, yet advanced training and experience is still necessary when skeletal material is measured in situations that do not offer the amenities of a laboratory, such as sturdy, fixed tables, chairs, and artificial lighting (Bass, 2005; Hale et al., 2014). Craniofacial measurements by spreading and coordinate calipers do not require the complex stabilization of crania but are rather time-consuming. This leads to data collection trips in the field becoming rather costly. But during the last few decades, a new method has been introduced: 3D landmark point data collection.

3D landmark data by Microscribe (Revware, Raleigh, NC, USA) digitizers have been accepted as the primary tools of applied 3D coordinate analysis within biological anthropology (Ousley and McKeown, 2001). Data collected with a digitizer can be composed of individual points and scribed curves or arcs as referenced in 3Skull (Current version is 1.76, Ousley, 2014) and applied by Williams and Slice (2010). In programs such as 3Skull, the interface prompts the user to collect a series of traditional cranial landmarks as defined by Howells (1973), Martin (1956) and the updated Data Collection Procedures for Forensic Skeletal Material 2.0 (Langley et al., 2016), in the same order for each cranium. If the cranium is damaged, or not all landmarks are desired, the user can skip these during the collection process. Landmark location can also be recorded using Excel and can be made up of a combination of landmarks desired by the user, or newly defined points, but the user must take care to record desired landmarks in the same order for all crania in a data set.

The stylus of the digitizer will record the x, y, and z location of each landmark relative to an arbitrary 0, 0, 0 axis located in the base of the digitizer. Euclidean distances calculated from 3D digitized point data have the advantage of being proximate to the caliper-based two-dimensional (2D) craniometrics that were used before the advent of digitized methods and continue to be taught and used where equipment for scanning and digitizing is not available. Comparatively, digitized data are dimensionally advanced over 2D craniometrics as they provide distance information between any combination of landmarks in multiple planes. In contrast to the traditional 2D morphometric method, which disassociates the geometric relationships between individual measurements, 3DGM (3-Dimensional geometrics morphometrics) maintain the geometric relationship and information that lies in the association of groups or configurations of landmarks (Von-Cramon-Taubadel, 2019).

Traditional 2D measurements/morphometrics provide limited information about the geometric positions and structures. However, this allows data recorded with a digitizer to be merged with large-scale databases of linear measurements, such as the world-wide craniofacial data set collected by W.W Howells (Howells, 1973, 1996), the UMMA—University of Michigan Museum of Anthropology data set (Brace and Hunt, 1990; Brace et al., 2001, 2006), and Hanihara's world-wide craniometrics data set (Hanihara, 1996). Distances between a pair of landmarks (craniofacial measurements defined by Martin (1956), Howells (1973), or Brace and Hunt, 1990; Brace et al., 2001; 2006) can be computed using different software (Ohno et al., 2016).

At this time, smaller-scale 3D archaeological and forensically relevant craniofacial databases are available and open to all to include archaeological examples and the Forensic 3D database, supplied by 3D-ID (Slice and Ross, 2009). Unfortunately, not all academic spheres share the ideology that sharing data is mutually beneficial, and some researchers maintain the professional belief that their own database should not be publicly shared.

A brief description of scanned data within medical sciences and biological anthropology

The scanning of data (surface laser scans, CT, MRI) imports real objects into a 3D virtual environment and involves a broad range of digital capture and processing techniques. However, scanning methods exhibit unique limitations. The data may accumulate potential errors at the various stages of capture, alignment, and reconstruction. Capture error in 3D scanning can happen with any interaction during the scanning process that interferes with accurate reproduction of the surface (Shearer, 2017). First, movement can cause error in all forms of surface scanning. Second, medical imaging formats are sensitive to high-density materials and metallic elements. Third, alignment and reconstruction are capable of moderating the degree of error found in a scan-based model. However, that moderation can be either positive or negative depending on the execution of the scan collection and the processes applied to the raw data to output mesh models (Murphy, 2015).

Medical imaging provides many modes of data collection. CT is used with high frequency for both direct patient data collection and for the collection of research samples. This is due to a balance of factors of cost, availability, and the existing variations of technology that are available to medical researchers. To provide a select few examples, CT scans have been used to create and analyze 3D representations of skeletal samples, as carried out by Mahfouz et al. (2007), who created CT scans of nearly all individuals in the William M. Bass Donated Skeletal Collection at the University of Tennessee. A large percentage of the individuals that make up the Bass collection have known medical histories, cause of death, and other biologically relevant information on file, which provides huge research potential for biological and forensic anthropologists. Edgar and Berry (2016) created a searchable database of decedent CT scans taken at autopsy from the University of New Mexico Health Sciences Center Office of the Medical Investigator, which has huge implications for forensic anthropological research, including potential for topics of trauma, age-at-death, and sex estimation. Additionally, Gunz et al. (2009) combined CT scans with thin-plate spline data to reconstruct fossil hominid crania, demonstrating the possibilities of archaeological and paleoanthropological remains and fossils.

Benefits of 3D measurements

When these new methods were introduced and adapted in the field of anthropology, it raised the simple question of whether data captured by traditional methods could be combined with data acquired by new methods (i.e., multiple devices and multiple observers). Using a 3D digitizer, one can easily collect both 2D linear measurement data and 3D coordinate data within a time that is short when compared with the use of conventional calipers. Compared with data collection by a 3D digitizer, collecting 3D scan data and processing/creating virtual 3D models are more time-consuming. However, once 3D scan data have been acquired, researchers are able to analyze the geometric structure of a specimen visually on the 3D mesh models anytime.

The sensitivity of advanced technological methods arguably makes up for the increased data complexity in light of the better, cheaper, faster, and more readily available computational power to handle them. However, that is assuming that advanced methods in practice offer significant improvements in accuracy commensurate to stated benchmarks. Reliability of digitized landmarks and comparing landmark selection in direct and digital environments have been addressed by researchers in medical and anthropological fields (Abdel Fatah et al., 2014; Hale et al., 2014; Jantz et al., 2013; Olszewski et al., 2006, 2007, 2010, 2013; Ross and Williams, 2008; Ross et al., 2010; Slice et al., 2005; Shearer et al., 2012; Sholts et al. 2010, 2011a, 2011b; Wong et al., 2008). Training and experience have an impact on the relative accuracy of the collected data (Shearer, 2017). Although several dozen studies have been published on the topic of evaluation of the precision, accuracy, and repeatability of landmark data on 3D models (Robinson and Terhune, 2017; Shearer et al., 2017), their conclusions usually caution us to combine and use data that were acquired by multiple observers with multiple devices.

Sharing databases

One of the best features of data created by 3D technology is that one can share and transmit physical information as just data. We propose collaborative efforts that offer the advantages of researchers sharing, cooperating remotely, and combining data sets. This permits the development of large databases to be shared with other researchers as 3D virtual data are accumulated.

Additionally, capturing geometric and shape data from skeletal remains and archaeological artifacts ensures digital curation of morphological information, and it can be used to preserve and document materials in museum. On the night of September 2, 2018, Brazil's oldest museum, the National Museum of Brazil in Rio de Janeiro, caught fire, and a large part of the collection in the building was destroyed. The Paleo-American remains excavated from Lagoa Santa were also lost in the fire. If 3D data by CT scanner or surface scanner were captured and uploaded to cloud technologies, copies of important data sets could be backed up and stored in additional digital locations. Furthermore, 3D and scan data can be used in conjunction with 3D printing technologies to reproduce skeletal models, and 3D printed reproductions can be used indefinitely for anthropological and medical research and education, as preservation of biological material would no longer be an issue. This also applies to situations in which human remains will undergo repatriation. If permission is granted and CT scan and surface scans are allowed to be collected before reburial or repatriation, researchers will be able to study the morphology of materials long after remains are returned. Moreover, ethical issues associated with dissemination of 3D models must be discussed among anthropologists.

To share databases, a standard protocol for data collecting and processing is required. As long as collection and processing of samples has a statistically insignificant impact on deviation from the original "true" sample, these data are very valuable to the advancement of the study of human skeletal remains and archaeological artifacts. At the current time, it is possible to choose from several methods to capture information from skeletal remains and artifacts.

Currently, a researcher at Stanford University has started a project entitled "Building a skeletal collection from medical imaging data: Volumetric reproductions of human skeletal materials using 3D Printing technologies" (Algee-Hewitt, personal communication). This researcher is amassing a repository of cranial CT scans from various world populations that will ultimately be used to create 3D models that can be used for morphological analysis. The scans and 3D data will be curated in the Stanford Digital Repository and 3D printed models will be produced to initiate the construction of a 3D printed skeletal collection that represents various world populations of different age and socioeconomic cohorts.

Benefits of this volume: the contents of each chapter

The benefits and importance of this volume are driven by the growth and innovations in current biometric research. The examples in this book are primarily of human crania. Therefore, we will focus the discussion mainly on 3D craniofacial data collection, analysis, and application in subsequent chapters. This book also provides an additional chapter about the application of GM on archaeological stone artifacts.

Many researchers have recently published methods in which qualitative osteological features are treated in a quantitative statistical methodology using digital data (Abdel Fatah et al., 2014; Dudzik and Jantz, 2016; Garvin and Ruff, 2012; Jantz et al., 2013; Pinto et al., 2013; Saso et al., 2011; Schlager and Ruedell, 2015; Schlager et al., 2018; Schimidt and Seguchi, 2016; Sholts et al., 2011a; Williams and Slice, 2010; and many others). What many of these studies overlook is the importance of standards of practice. The researcher should exercise caution and careful planning, and the potential for error should be discussed for further quantitative statistical application of 3D scan data.

In summary, recent technology with the capacity to sense, collect, and process large scale data and render 3D information has expanded significantly. This push has been fueled as greater processing, and computational powers have become more ubiquitous and less expensive with modern computers. The result is greater research access to advanced data collection technologies with the potential to change the ways researchers collect and interact with samples (Smith and Strait, 2008). Digital data collection creates a data sample that is static over time. Depending on the selected technology, scanning methods theoretically permit the most complete capture of skeletal or archaeological artifact data currently possible; shape, scale, variations in coloration, physical texture of the surface, bone density, even the ability to reproduce physical models of scanned crania without the risks associated with casting.

Development and testing of robust statistical methods as defined by Huber (1981) to apply to analyses of 3D surface data are under way (Abdel Fatah et al., 2014; Archer et al., 2017; Jantz et al., 2013; Mahfouz et al.,

2007; Petaros et al., 2017; Profico et al., 2018; Schlager and Ruedell, 2015; Schlager et al., 2018). For now, an imposing challenge is the consideration of the source and the consistency with which 3D surface data are collected, processed, and applied. Because researchers may lack exposure and experience working with 3D technologies, this volume provides some solutions and suggestions.

In Chapter 2 (Murphy and Seguchi), the protocols of image data collection and processing are provided. Chapter 2 offers "digital model sample—collection and processing protocol." When working with 3D model data, it is important to cultivate an understanding of manipulation and familiarization with virtual data and the virtual environment. The method of data capture and model processing varies greatly between technologies and different equipment. This means that important decisions need to be made to assure that models and data collected are useful for the intended research. This chapter provides a section concerning data management and file formats, proprietary and open source formats and conversion, and finally, processing the data from the model sample into useful form.

Chapter 3 (Ohno and Kawakubo) introduces "three-dimensional investigations of fragile archaeological human remains." This chapter describes a case study in Japan in which all archaeological and skeletal materials are fragile and curators give limited permission and access to human remains in their collection. The authors' experiences and problem-solving are useful for researchers who may share similar challenges. These same experiences can be applied to any researcher who may need to assuage the concerns of those who manage and maintain collections in order to be granted access. The chapter covers how to mark landmarks on crania when pencil use is not permitted, as well as describes digitizing devices and how to set up a cranium on a stable surface. This chapter also provides the equations for computing missing coordinate data using mirror reversing.

Chapter 4 (Dudzik) introduces "landmark and semilandmark data collection using digitizers and data processing." This chapter summarizes some of the approaches and software used to preprocess direct digitizer landmark data to allow for statistical analysis. This chapter is devoted to describing data collection protocol to include commonly used approaches for coordinate data collection of physical specimens between single and multiple observers and how to address collaboration between observers. This chapter describes how data acquisition is carried out on physical models using a direct digitizer (e.g., Microscribe) and how data can be stored for later analysis.

Chapter 5 (Murphy) describes "landmark and semilandmark data collection using 3D virtual model and data processing." This chapter summarizes some of the approaches and software used to preprocess direct digitizer landmark data to allow for statistical analysis. Additionally, statistical analyses available that can perform comparisons and predictions are described. This chapter describes both direct digitizer landmark/semilandmark point processing and data processing from Stratovan (digital) data. This section discusses 3D data alignment options and choosing the best alignment method based on various circumstances. In addition, this chapter describes how data acquisition is carried out on virtual models using Stratovan checkpoint software (Stratovan Corporation, Davis, CA) and how data can be stored for later analysis.

Chapter 6 (Seguchi, Murphy, and Yonemoto) explores "validity assessment—validity testing of mixed data by multiple devices, methods, and observers." This chapter outlines validity testing of the use of mixed data, where a sample is comprised of data collected using more than one type of technology. It examines observer error between landmark data acquisition using a Microscribe and landmark data acquisition using the Stratovan Checkpoint program on 3D mesh models. It discusses the conclusion that landmark data have a sufficiently low "margin of error" and that both types can be used in a well-designed experiment. It also discusses the conclusion that semilandmark data have a significant intraobserver error on the "difficult" curve types collected by Microscribe. This chapter demonstrates that the difficulty of visualization and collection using Microscribe is markedly higher compared with the virtual data collection method. Virtual data collection results in a truer more accurate set of data for analysis.

Chapter 7 (Schlager) provides "3D data analysis using R—3D data processing, shape analysis, and surface manipulations in R." This chapter is a practical introduction to working with 3D mesh and coordinate data in R, a powerful and open source software toolkit. This software is capable due to a package-based system of a vast array of 3D data work parts. For most new users, however, R can have a daunting learning curve. Reading and working through this chapter grounds the reader in software and syntax with realistic examples of 3D data. This tutorial gives an introduction into landmark-/surface-mesh-based statistical shape analysis in R—tailored for bioarchaeologists and anthropologists. Starting with importing raw data, the tutorial describes dealing with missing and erroneous data, introduces basic statistical analyses, and provides examples for semiautomatically transferring semilandmarks defined on a template throughout a sample. Extensive examples using the Yacchi skull sample from Kumejima, Okinawa, Japan (Fukumine et al., 2001) and code snippets are provided to allow the reader to easily replicate the analyses. The chapter relates to other chapters in the book with suggested project work flows.

Chapter 8 (Archer and Presnyakova) explores archaeological application and consideration of three dimensional geometric morphometrics (3DGM) to stone artifacts. GM has thus far only been applied successfully to a limited range of stone artifact forms due to the unique morphological characteristics of lithics and the substantial variability within many tool types. Subsequently, there are a number of potential pitfalls in adapting 3D approaches for usage in stone artifact analyses. In this chapter, some basic considerations in the application of 3DGM to stone artifacts are discussed. The potential effects of orientation error when applying 3DGM to actual archaeological assemblages are illustrated.

In our conclusion, Chapter 9 (Dudzik, Seguchi, Murphy, and Prentiss) gives a brief summary of major points covered in the book and provides recommendations for the use of 3D technology in biological anthropology and archaeology in future.

The chapters in this book illustrate how to acquire useful 3D model data, instructions for preprocessing using different types of data and technologies, guidelines for sample analyses, and case studies to help the reader become familiar with virtual data and how to navigate the virtual environment. The best practices outlined in subsequent chapters are adaptable for use in various subdisciplines of biological anthropology and archaeology, including bioarchaeology, forensic anthropology, and lithic analysis.

References

Abdel Fatah, E.E., Shirley, N.R., Jantz, R.L., Mahfouz, M.R., 2014. Improving sex estimation from crania using a novel three-dimensional quantitative method (report). Journal of Forensic Sciences 59 (3), 10.

Archer, W., Pop, C.M., Rezek, Z., Schlager, S., Lin, S.C., Weiss, M., Dogand, T., Desta, D., McPherron, S.P., 2017. A geometric morphometric relationship predicts stone flake shape and size variability. Archaeological and Anthropological Sciences 6 (38), 1945–1954. https://doi.org/10.1007/s12520-017-0517-2.

Bass, W.M., 2005. Human Osteology: A Laboratory and Field Manual. Missouri Archaeological Society, Springfield, MO.

Betti, L., Balloux, F., Amos, W., Hanihara, T., Manica, A., 2009. Distance from Africa, not climate, explains within-population phenotypic diversity in humans. Proc. R. Soc. B 276, 809–814.

Betti, L., Balloux, F., Hanihara, T., Manica, A., 2010. The relative role of drift and selection in shaping the human skull. American Journal of Physical Anthropology 141, 76–82.

Bookstein, F.L., 1991. Morphometric Tools for Landmark Data: Geometry and Biology. Cambridge University Press.
Brace, C.L., Hunt, D.K., 1990. A Nonracial Craniofacial Perspective on Human Variation: A(ustralia) to Z(uni). American Journal of Physical Anthropology 82, 341–360.
Brace, C.L., Nelson, A.R., Seguchi, N., Oe, H., Sering, L., Pan, Q., Li, Y., Tumen, D., 2001. Old World sources of the first New World human inhabitants: a comparative craniofacial view. The Proceedings of the National Academy of Sciences of the United States of America 98 (17), 10017–10022.
Brace, C.L., Seguchi, N., Quintyn, C.B., Fox, S.C., Nelson, A.R., Sotiris, K.M., Pan, Q., 2006. The questionable contribution of the Neolithic and the Bronze Age to European craniofacial form. The Proceedings of the National Academy of Sciences of the United States of America 103 (1), 242–247.
Brace, C.L., Seguchi, N., Nelson, A.R., Pan, Q., Umeda, H., Wilson, M., Brace, M.L., 2014. The Ainu and Jomon Connection. In: Owsley, D., Jantz, L.R. (Eds.), Kennewick Man: The Scientific Investigation of an Ancient American Skeleton. Texas A&M Press, College Station, pp. 463–471.
Bretzke, K., Conard, N.J., 2012. Evaluating variability in lithic assemblages using 3D models of stone artifacts. Journal of Archaeological Science 39, 3741–3749.
Buchanan, B., Collard, M., 2010. A geometric morphometrics-based assessment of blade shape differences among paleoindian projectile point types from western north America. Journal of Archaeological Science 37, 350–359.
Dudzik, B., Jantz, R.L., 2016. Misclassifications of hispanics using fordisc 3.1: comparing cranial morphology in asian and hispanic populations. Journal of Forensic Sciences. https://doi.org/10.1111/1556-4029.13123.
Edgar, H., Berry, S.D., 2016. Facilitating forensic research in multiple fields using a unique computed tomography dataset. NIJ award 2016-DN-BX-0144. Evolution: Education and Outreach 4, 435–445.
Fukase, H., Ito, T., Ishida, H., 2015. Geographic variation in nasal cavity form among three human groups from the Japanese Archipelago: ecogeographic and functional implications. American Journal of Human Biology. https://doi.org/10.1002/ajhb.22786.
Fukumine T., Doi N., Ishida H., Zukeran C., Sensui S., Saso A., and Higa T., Human skeletal remains from the Yacchi-no-Gama and Kanjinbaru grave sites. In: Okinawa Prefectural Archaeological Center (Ed),Yacchi-no-Gama, Kanjinnbaru Grave Sites. Okinawa Prefectural Archaeological Center Research Report, No. 6, 2001, Okinawa, Japan, 345–385. (in Japanese)
Garvin, H.M., Ruff, C.B., 2012. Sexual dimorphism in skeletal browridge and chin morphologies determined using a new quantitative method. American Journal of Physical Anthropology 147 (4), 661–670.
Gunz, P., Mitteroecker, P., Neubauer, S., Weber, G.W., Bookstein, F.L., 2009. Principles for the virtual reconstruction of hominin crania. Journal of Human Evolution 57 (1), 48–62.
Hale, A.R., Honeycutt, K.K., Ross, A.H., 2014. A geometric morphometric validation study of computed tomography–extracted craniofacial landmarks. Journal of Craniofacial Surgery 25 (1), 231–237.
Hanihara, T., 1996. Comparison of craniofacial features of major human groups. American Journal of Physical Anthropology 99, 389–412.
Harvati, K., Weaver, T.D., 2006. Human cranial anatomy and the differential preservation of population history and climate signatures. The Anatomical Record B 288A, 1225–1233.
Howells, W.W., 1973. Cranial Variation in Man; a Study by Multivariate Analysis of Patterns of Difference Among Recent Human Populations. Peabody Museum of Archaeology and Ethnology, Harvard University, Cambridge, MA.

Howells, W.W., 1996. Howells' craniometric data on the internet. American Journal of Physical Anthropology 101, 441–442.
Huber, P.J., 1981. Robust Statistics. Wiley, New York.
Jantz, R., Mahfouz, M., Shirley, N.R., Abdel Fatah, E., 2013. Improving Sex Estimation from Crania Using 3-dimensional CT Scans. U.S. Department of Justice. https://www.ncjrs.gov/pdffiles1/nij/grants/240688.pdf.
Kuzminsky, S.C., Gardiner, M.S., 2012. Three-dimensional laser scanning: potential uses for museum conservation and scientific research. Journal of Archaeological Science, Journal of Archaeological Science 39, 2744–2751.
Langley, N.R., Jantz, L.M., Ousley, S.D., Jantz, R.L., Milner, G., 2016. Data Collection Procedures for Forensic Skeletal Material 2.0. University of Tennessee and Lincoln Memorial University.
Mahfouz, M.R., Merkl, B.C., Abdel Fatah, E.E., Booth, R., Argenson, J.N., 2007. Automatic methods for characterization of sexual dimorphism of adult femora: distal femur. Computer Methods in Biomechanics and Biomedical Engineering 10 (6), 447–456.
Martin, R., 1956. Lehrbuch der Anthropologie, Revised third ed.
McKeown, A.H., Schmidt, R.W., 2013. Geometric morphometrics. In: DiGangi, E.A., Moore, M.K. (Eds.), Research Methods in Human Skeletal Biology. Academic Press, pp. 325–359.
McKeown, A.H., Jantz, R.L., 2005. Comparison of coordinate and craniometric data for biological distance studies. In: Slice, D.E. (Ed.), Modern Morphometrics in Physical Anthropology. Springer, Boston, MA, pp. 215–230.
Murphy, M.M., 2015. Validity of Landmark Selection Given Different 3D Scan Processing Parameters: Landmark Location on 3D Models of Yacchi Crania. University of Montana, Missoula.
Nathan, E., Holton, N.E., Piche, A., Yokley, T.R., 2018. Integration of the nasal complex: implications for developmental and evolutionary change in modern humans. American Journal of Physical Anthropology. https://doi.org/10.1002/ajpa.23466.
Ohno, K., Kawakubo, Y., Kuraoka, A., 2016. Re-evaluation of temporal changes in alveolar protrusion in Japan according to two newly introduced craniometric angles. Anthropological Science 124 (1), 63–72.
Olszewski, R., Cosnard, G., Macq, B., Mahy, P., Reychler, H., 2006. 3D CT-based cephalometric analysis: 3D cephalometric theoretical concept and software. Neuroradiology 48 (11), 853–862.
Olszewski, R., Tanesy, O., Cosnard, G., Zech, F., Reychler, H., 2010. Reproducibility of osseous landmarks used for computed tomography based three-dimensional cephalometric analyses. Journal of Cranio-Maxillofacial Surgery 214–221.
Olszewski, R., Frison, L., Wisniewski, M., Denis, J.M., Vynckier, S., Cosnard, G., Zech, F., Reychler, H., 2013. Reproducibility of three-dimensional cephalometric landmarks in cone-beam and low-dose computed tomography. Clinical Oral Investigation 17, 285. https://doi.org/10.1007/s00784-012-0688-2.
Olszewski, R., Zech, F., Cosnard, G., Nicolas, V., Macq, B., Reychler, H., 2007. Three-dimensional computed tomography cephalometric craniofacial analysis: experimental validation in vitro. International Journal of Oral and Maxillofacial Surgery 828–833. Denmark.
Ousley, S., McKeown, A., 2001. Human remains: conservation, retrieval and analysis: proceedings of a conference held in Williamsburg, VA, Nov. 7–11th 1999. In: Williams, E. (Ed.), BAR International Series. Archaeopress, pp. 173–184.
Ousley, S.D., 2014. Threeskull. Version 1.76.

Petaros, A., Garvin, H.M., Sholts, S.B., Schlager, S., Wärmländer, S.K.T.S., 2017. Sexual dimorphism and regional variation in human frontal bone inclination measured via digital 3d models. Legal Medicine 29 (2017), 53–61. Volume 3, edited by Karl Sailer. Gustav Fischer Verlag, Stuttgart.

Pinto, S.D., Cesar Jr., R., Urbanová, P., 2013. Analysis of supraorbital margins in human skull for characterization of sexual dimorphism. In: Cuadros-Vargas, A., Cayllahua Cahuina, E.J.Y. (Eds.), SIBGRAPI (The Conference on Graphics, Patterns, and Images). SIBGRAPI, Arequipa Peru, pp. 1–4.

Prentiss, A.M., Walsh, M., Barnett, K.D., Murphy, M.-M., Kuenstle, J., 2015. The coarse volcanic rock industry at Rio Ibanez 6 west, Aisén region, Patagonian Chile. Lithic Technology 40 (2), 112–127.

Profico, A., Schlager, S., Valoriani, V., 2018. Reproducing the internal and external anatomy of fossil bones: two new automatic digital tools. American Journal of Physical Anthropology 00, 1–8. https://doi.org/10.1002/ajpa.23493.

Relethford, J.H., 2004a. Boas and beyond: migration and craniometric variation. American Journal of Human Biology 16, 379–386.

Relethford, J.H., 2004b. Global patterns of isolation by distance on genetic and morphological data. Human Biology 76, 499–513.

Relethford, J.H., 2010. Population-specific deviations of global human craniometric variation from a neutral model. American Journal of Physical Anthropology 142, 105–111.

Robinson, C., Terhune, C.E., 2017. Error in geometric morphometric data collection: combining data from multiple sources. American Journal of Physical Anthropology 164, 62–75. https://doi.org/10.1002/ajpa.23257.

Rohlf, F.J., Marcus, L.F., 1993. A revolution in morphometrics. TREE 8, 129.

Ross, A.H., Williams, S., 2008. Testing repeatability and error of coordinate landmark data acquired from crania. Journal of Forensic Sciences 53 (4), 782–785.

Ross, A.H., Slice, D.E., Williams, S.E., 2010. Geometric Morphometric Tools for the Classification of Human Skulls. U.S. Department of Justice. https://www.ncjrs.gov/pdffiles1/nij/grants/231195.pdf.

Saso, A., Matsukawa, S., Suwa, G., 2011. Comparative analysis of the glabellar region morphology of the late Pleistocene Minatogawa crania: a three-dimensional approach. Anthropological Science 119 (2), 113–121.

Schlager, S., Profico, A., Vincenzo, F.D., Manzi, G., 2018. Retrodeformation of fossil specimens based on 3D bilateral semi-landmarks: implementation in the R Package "Morpho". PLoS One 13 (3) e0194073.

Schlager, S., Ruedell, A., 2015. Analysis of the human osseous nasal shape-population differences and sexual dimorphism: human Osseous Nasal Shape. American Journal of Physical Anthropology 157 (4). https://doi.org/10.1002/ajpa.22749.

Schmidt, R.W., Seguchi, N., 2014. Jomon Culture and the peopling of the Japanese archipelago: advancements in the fields of morphometrics and ancient DNA. Japanese Journal of Archaeology 2 (2014), 34–59.

Schmidt, R.W., Seguchi, N., 2016. Craniofacial variation of the Xiongnu nomads of Mongolia reveals their possible origins and population history. Quaternary International 405, 110–121.

Scholts, S.B., Stanford, D.J., Flores, L.M., Warmlander, S.K.T.S., 2012. Flake scar patterns of clovis points analyzed with a new digital morphometrics approach: evidence for direct transmission of technological knowledge across early north America. Journal of Archaeological Science 39, 3018–3026.

Seguchi, N., McKeown, A., Schmidt, R.W., Umeda, H., Brace, C.L., 2011. An alternative view of the peopling of South America: Lagoa Santa in craniometric perspective. Anthropological Science 119, 21–38.

Shott, M.J., 2011a. History written in stone: evolutionary analysis of stone tools in archaeology. Evolution: Education and Outreach 4, 435–445.

Shearer, B.M., Cooke, S.B., Halenar, L.B., Reber, S., Plummer, J.E., Delson, E., Tallman, M., 2017. Evaluating causes of error in landmark-based data collection using scanners. PLoS One 12 (11), e0187452.

Shearer, B.M., Sholts, S.B., Garvin, H.M., Wärmländer, S.K.T.S., 2012. Sexual dimorphism in human browridge volume measured from 3D models of dry crania: a new digital morphometrics approach. Forensic Science International 222 (1–3), 400.e401–400.e405.

Scholts, S.B., Flores, L., Walker, P., Warmlander, S., 2011a. Comparison of coordinate measurement precision of different landmark types on human crania using a 3D laser scanner and a 3D digitizer: implications for applications of digital morphometrics. International Journal of Osteoarchaeology 21 (5), 535–543.

Scholts, S.B., Walker, P.L., Kuzminsky, S.C., Miller, K.W.P., Wärmländer, S.K.T.S., 2011b. Identification of group affinity from cross- sectional contours of the human midfacial skeleton using digital morphometrics and 3D laser scanning technology. Journal of Forensic Sciences 56 (2), 333.

Scholts, S.B., Wärmländer, S.K.T.S., Flores, L.M., Miller, K.W.P., Walker, P.L., 2010. Variation in the measurement of cranial volume and surface area using 3D laser scanning technology. Journal of Forensic Sciences 55 (4), 871–876.

Shott, M.J., 2011b. History Written in Stone: Evolutionary Analysis of Stone Tools in Archaeology.

Slice, D., McKeown, A., Jantz, R., 2005. Comparison of Coordinate and Craniometric Data for Biological Distance Studies. Modern Morphometrics in Physical Anthropology. Springer US, pp. 215–230.

Slice, D.E., Ross, A.H., 2009. 3D-ID: Geometric Morphometric Classification of Crania for Forensic Scientists. http://www.3d-id.org.

Smith, N.E., Strait, S.G., 2008. PaleoView3D: from specimen to online digital model. Palaeontologia Electronica 11 (2), 1.00.

Thayer, Z.M., Dobson, S.D., 2010. Sexual dimorphism in chin shape: implications for adaptive hypotheses. American Journal of Physical Anthropology 143 (3), 417–425.

Von Cramon-Taubadel, N., 2009. Congruence of individual cranial bone morphology and neutral molecular affinity patterns in modern humans. American Journal of Physical Anthropology 140, 205–215.

Von Cramon-Taubadel, N., 2019. Multivariate morphometrics, quantitative genetics, and neutral theory: development a "modern synthesis" for primate evolutionary morphology. Evolutionary Anthropology 2019, 1–13. https://doi.org/10.1002/evan.21761.

Von Cramon-Taubadel, N., 2011. The relative efficacy of functional and developmental cranial modules for reconstructing global human population history. American Journal of Physical Anthropology 146, 83–93.

Williams, S.E., Slice, D.E., 2010. Regional shape change in adult facial bone curvature with age. American Journal of Physical Anthropology 143 (3), 437–447.

Weaver, T.D., Roseman, C.C., Stringer, C.B., 2007. Were Neandertal and modern human cranial differences produced by natural selection or genetic drift? Journal of Human Evolution 53, 135–145.

Wong, J.Y., Oh, A.K., Ohta, E., Hunt, A.T., Rogers, G.F., Mulliken, J.B., Deutsch, C.K., 2008. Validity and reliability of craniofacial anthropometric measurements of 3D digital photogrammetric images. The Cleft Palate-Craniofacial Journal 45 (3), 232–239.

CHAPTER TWO

Digital model sample—Scanning and processing protocol

Mary-Margaret Murphy[1], Noriko Seguchi[1,2]
[1]Department of Anthropology, The University of Montana, Missoula, MT, The United States of America
[2]Faculty of Social and Cultural Studies, Kyushu University, Fukuoka, Japan

Introduction

When working with three-dimensional (3D) model data, it is important to cultivate an understanding of manipulation and familiarization with virtual data and the virtual environment. The method of data capture and model processing varies greatly between technologies and different equipment. This means that important decisions need to be made to assure that models and data collected from models are useful for the intended research. The sample collection decisions made in a large medical imaging facility will be very different than those made for a single researcher working at remote locations with a portable desktop 3D laser scanner. This chapter introduces the virtual environment, software and file formats, standard alignment and orientation—continuing from this information to the use of surface scanning equipment for capturing surfaces to be processed into 3D models. We focus primarily on open source software. This chapter concludes with a section concerning data management and file formats; proprietary and open source formats and conversion; and finally processing the data from the model sample into useful form.

The virtual environment—introduction

What are virtual data?

Virtual data are a large category of data representation that uses computer software or graphing to create a visual representation of a unit, sample, or population. Underpinning virtual data is real data of some format. The simplest virtualization of data is the scatter plot; where a data point is defined by the expression of the values of x and y axes simultaneously. Thinking about this, the value of virtualization for data representation is obvious on

3D Data Acquisition for Bioarchaeology, Forensic Anthropology, and Archaeology
ISBN: 978-0-12-815309-3
https://doi.org/10.1016/B978-0-12-815309-3.00002-4

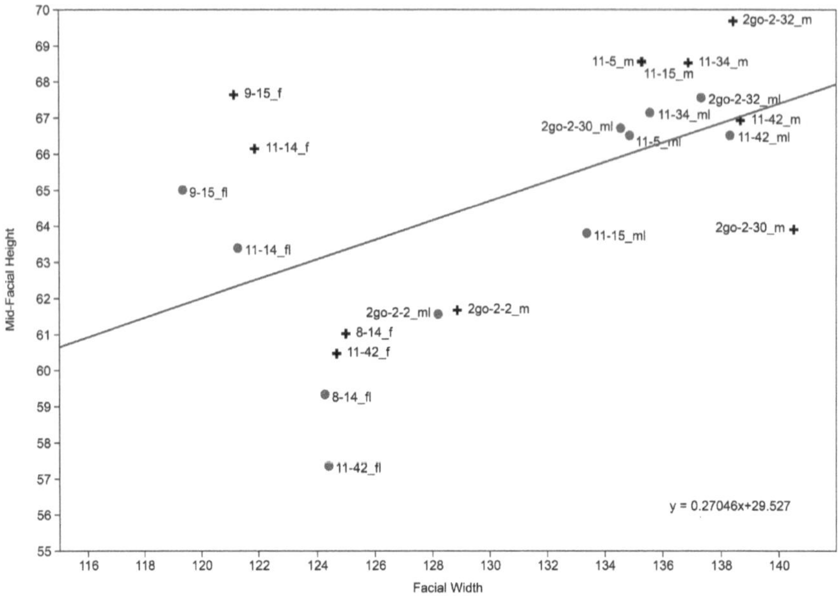

Figure 2.1 ***Scatterplot of facial width and height.*** This scatterplot is an example of two measures plotted together indicating the shape and direction of their relationship. This is the measure of midfacial height and facial width calculated from a data set of Microscribe and digitally derived landmarks of a sample of crania from Okinawa, Japan (Dudzik, 2013; Seguchi, 2010).

the level of plot data (Fig. 2.1). Although we use statistical and algorithmic functions to describe how the data behave, we are likely to see the extant patterns in such a representation.

Terms and definitions

What is a mesh model?

A 3D mesh model is a geometric object composed of ***vertices*** (points that taken alone are called a ***point cloud***) and ***faces*** distributed over the whole model. In a mesh or point cloud, we virtualize very dense and dimensional information that represents surfaces or objects. However complex these appear, they are still a collection of data points x, y, z.

This (Fig. 2.2) is a point cloud. It is a collection of points (vertices) in a 3D space. Taken together, these data are a representation of a multidimensional sampling of the surface of an object. A point cloud contains basic coordinate data that are used to represent an object in a digital environment.

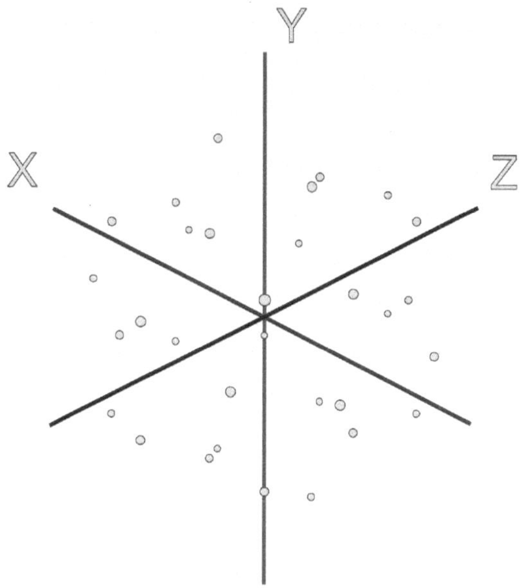

Figure 2.2 ***Simple point cloud.*** A simple point cloud for a dodecahedron generated as an automatic primitive in Meshlab software.

The file can still contain per-vertex information of attributes, such as color or texture, and the vector direction of the outward facing direction (***normal***). For comparison purposes, a point cloud can be used like a digital caliper against a mesh.

This (Fig. 2.3) is a mesh. It is comprised of a collection of points in 3D space. When connected by vectors, the mesh can include faces. As a whole, this mesh is a digital, multidimensional representation of an object. Point clouds and meshes can be converted back and forth and compared with each other. So long as the attributes are contained in the per-vertex information, color and normal vectors can be maintained when converting from point cloud to mesh and vice versa. However, a mesh can store more attributes, and that can be a greater advantage representing a sample object and a point cloud may be more suited to use as a comparative tool. Owing to the digital environment, a mesh can have a ***manifold*** state, an open or closed geometric state. Open manifold mesh objects are discontinuous in some way—having either an open void or surface regions that do not join together completely. An open manifold object can exist in a digital environment, but not a physical environment. To exist in a physical environment, and for the purposes of any 3D printing, an object must be in a

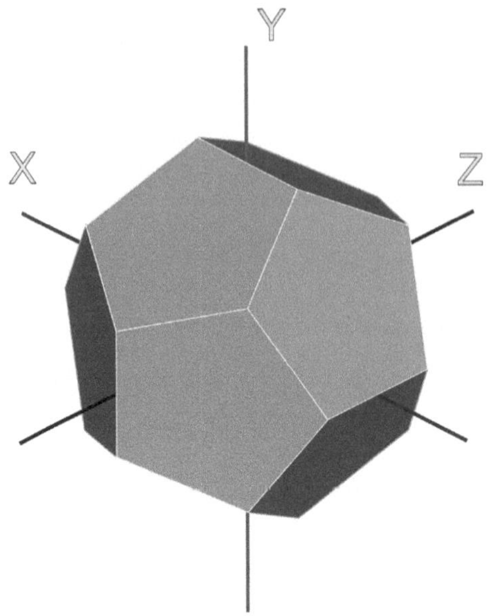

Figure 2.3 ***Simple mesh.*** A simple mesh of a dodecahedron generated as an automatic primitive in Meshlab software.

closed manifold geometric state (Cignoni and Scopigno, 2008; Jantz et al., 2013; Abdel Fatah et al., 2014).

How are real objects represented in a computer program?

3D files types can contain the information for a collection of landmark points in a delimited text file; this is the simplest type (Fig. 2.4). Coding in the file header tells software what data are contained in each delimited

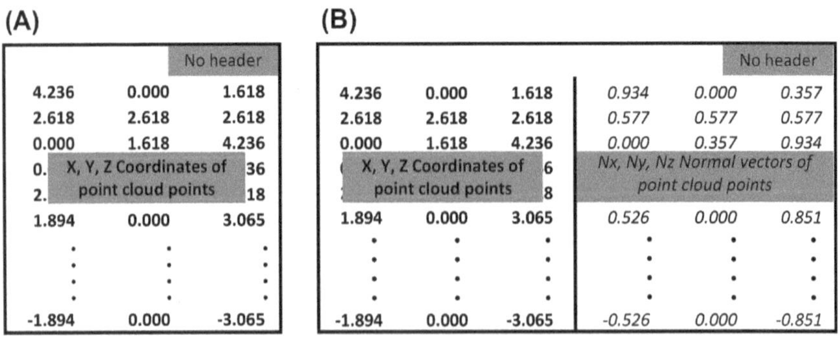

Figure 2.4 ***Notated point cloud file.*** The dodecahedron point cloud file with (A) no normal vectors and (B) normal vectors for all vertices. A point cloud file contains the minimum amount of data that can be used to represent 3D points in space.

column and some metadata about the file. After the header, data points are listed with their coordinate data. The file can also contain more information than just the coordinate location. Often in a sample, this type of file will include landmark identity, and sometimes more complex forms of 3D data.

As a 3D object increases in complexity and point density, reading and projecting the data encoded becomes more difficult. Not only the number of points (or *vertices* in a mesh) is much higher, but other descriptive parameters become important (Fig. 2.5). Faces are formed by vectors (edges) connecting proximal vertices. Both vertices and faces can have parameters known as normals—a vector direction perpendicular to the geometric position of the face or vertex. Most of the time, the normals will not be a concern during an analysis. However, they can become problematic during initial processing of mesh data from a scan.

Complex 3D objects require complex and specific software to be rendered (built for visual output) and to handle the rerendering required

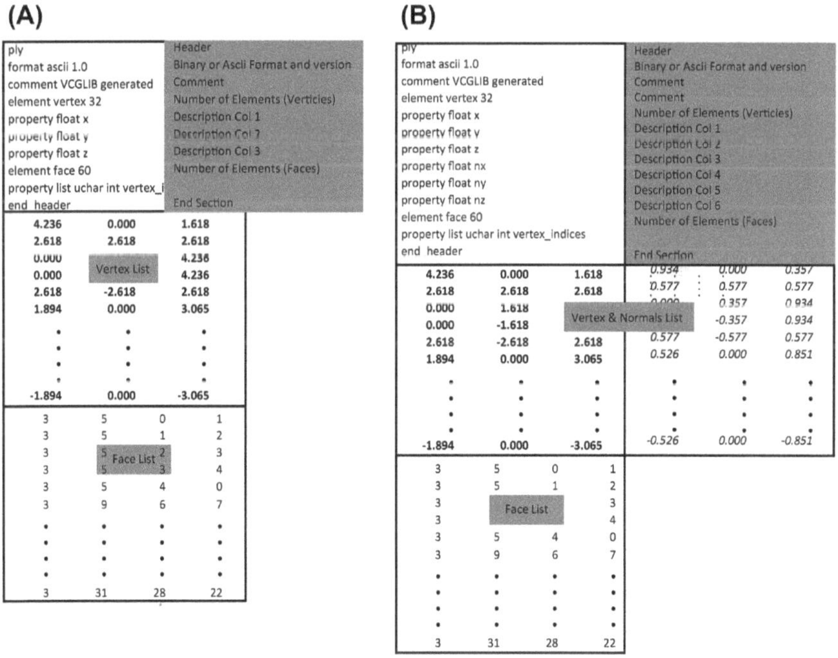

Figure 2.5 ***Notated simple *.ply file.*** The dodecahedron polygon (*.PLY) file with (A) no normal vectors and (B) normal vectors for all vertices. Below the list of X, Y, Z coordinates is the face parameters. The header contains formatting data and descriptions of the columns and number of elements.

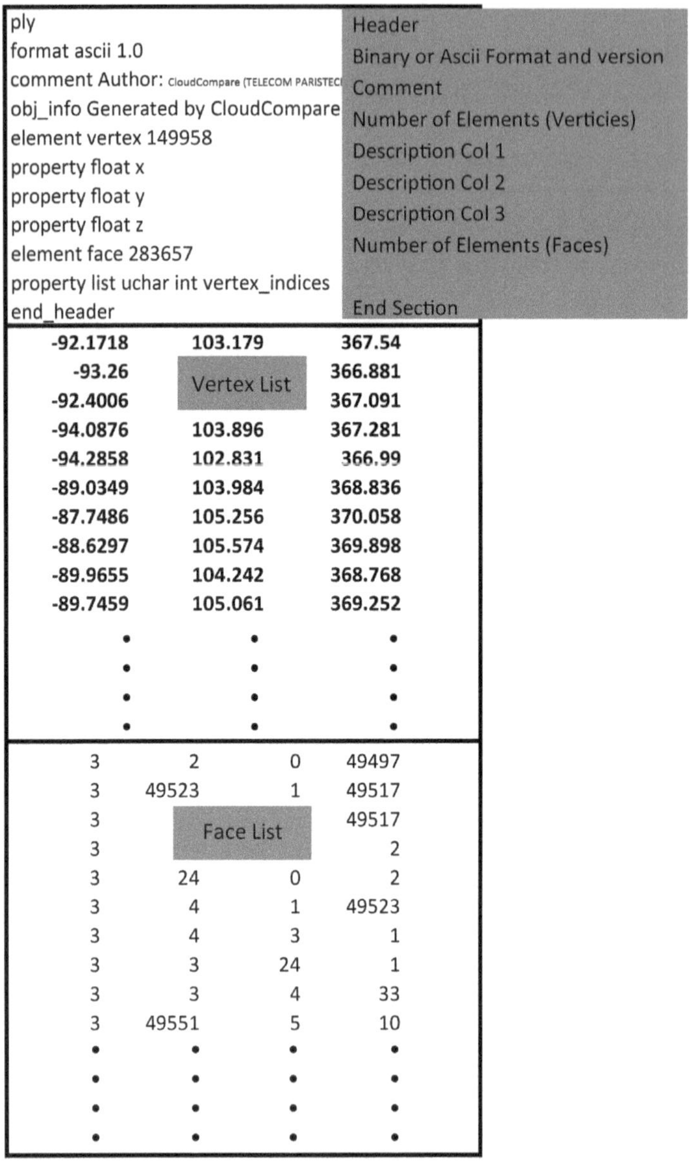

Figure 2.6 ***Notated complex *.ply file.***

to move and rotate a complex 3D objects in a digital space (Fig. 2.6). Consider that the position and orientation of each element must be recalculated for each movement of an object in a virtual space. This helps explain the reason older computer systems struggled with complex 3D renderings.

However, Windows (c) systems available at publishing include a 3D object app, which reflects the mainstream prevalence of digital models and 3D printing.

Software and file formats

What kinds of programs, and how do they facilitate working with virtual data?

What makes the use of 3D surface data possible for research is software for scan processing and data sampling that are specialized to the task. These programs are built to handle complex rendering to process raw scan data into whole complete representations. This section will cover information about several open source programs with tools for processing scan data and working with processed mesh models. The information for acquiring the open source software is included in the Supplementary Materials (2.1)

Meshlab software (Cignoni et al., 2008) is a straight-forward program that can be used to clean the surface scan data and process into mesh models—which is to select and delete the unwanted areas from scan files. The resulting mesh files were reformatted into ⋆.ply (polygon file) format.

This format is one of the available file formats, which can be handled by most 3D rendering software. This can be a matter of preference, or a factor of the information that is managed by the specific format. Two other common file types are ⋆.stl and ⋆.obj. STL (Stereolithography) files are used in most 3D printing applications, they do not retain texture (color) information. PLY and OBJ files retain a greater variety of information, including texture.

CloudCompare software (CloudCompare, 2.8, 2018) is a point cloud processor with areas of mesh surface functionality. Because point cloud contains slightly less complex data (no faces, face normals, or edges) CloudCompare uses this relative simplification to make large sample data such as building or topographical data.

Morpheus et al. (Slice, D.E., 2013) is a cross-platform, general purpose software package for morphometric analysis. Morpheus et al. facilitates the statistical 3D alignments, Bookstein alignment and Generalized Procrustes analysis (GPA) and allows visualization of landmarks and semilandmarks collected with Microscribe.

Geomagic software is a commercial software suite with a full constituent of mesh and point cloud capabilities. It combines industrially robust programs and protocol for creating, processing, and inspection. The industrial applications are overkill for biological and artifact models; but if it is available, it is worth spending time becoming familiar with the software. Owing to the price of the software, it may not be an option unless it is available through an institutional license.

Standard alignment and orientation

Scanned data (surface scan, CT, MRI) encompasses a broad range of digital capture and processing techniques that import real objects into a 3D virtual environment. Orientation differences between 3D digitizer coordinates, CT scans, and surface scanning technology present an issue regarding interoperability. It is possible to orient a subject object for 3D scanning in any direction, although consistency is recommended for multiple scans. This is true if for no other reason than the researcher's priori knowledge about the object. Orientation for comparison is important to dimensional data because significant differences in orientation can lead to weak statistical conclusions at the time of analysis if they have not been accounted for. Lele and Richtsmeier (2001) suggest that this to be due to any presumptive alignment taking place to the coordinate matrix of any set of coordinate data. To explain the deceptively difficult concepts that Lele and Richtsmeier highlight, consider two photographs of the same subject. One photograph is taken at alignment with the frontal aspect of the subject. The second photograph is taken with the subject rotated 10 degrees from frontal alignment. If it is presumed that the two photographs are the same subject, then this assumption would be rejected analytically without a large margin of error because the features would not express the same ratios and geometric relationships. This serves as a good warning against the possibility of spurious conclusions made from poorly understood or poorly aligned models.

Working with 3D data from various sources, a researcher must be concerned with data collected by different means—each of those having slight differences in orientation. The relationship between the coordinates of each set of points and each model is internally invariant. However, appropriately orienting all data for the multiple samples or various sources requires an understanding of the coordinate system of the sample units.

Orientation—Computed Tomography

CT scans are built from two-dimensional (2D) layers, each oriented as *(X, Y)* and building the *Z-plane* by stacking each successive layer. This is the global capturing orientation, which is parallel to the slices of a CT scan and independent from the resting orientation of the object undergoing scans. Surface scanning and coordinate digitization take in data in all dimensions simultaneously either dynamically or rotationally. If a cranium were to be placed on a single basal resting orientation and subjected to a CT scan and a surface scan, the resulting data would produce models that divided the X, Y, and Z planes differently (Fig. 2.7).

Medical imaging has available many modes of data collection. CT is used with a high frequency for both direct patient data collection and the collection of research samples. This owes to the balance of factors of cost, availability, and the available variation of the technology that are available to medical

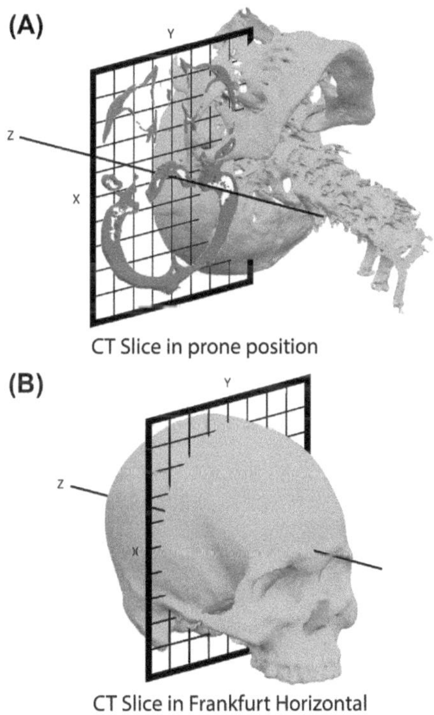

Figure 2.7 ***CT slices and coordinate system.*** (A) A model example of the slices of a CT scan in a "live" orientation. Each slice is a 2D representation of the plane transected by the CT particle beam. The 2D vectors defined in each slice are X and Y. When the slices are stacked together, the direction of the stacking becomes the Z vector. Changing the direction of the scan in relation to the subject being scanned changes the direction of the X, Y, and Z vectors (B) If a cranium is resting on the Frankfurt horizontal, X and Y dimension vectors become the lateral and the superior-posterior directions in relation to the cranium.

researchers. The slices of a CT scan to be converted into a 3D representation of a model, processed by separating the areas by the *voxel density,* which refers to the light or dark pixels produced on a sensor surface (X-ray film is an example of a sensor surface) converted to 3D by including the depth of the slice. The behavior of radioactive particles that pass through a given sample is reflected on the resulting image as light areas where fewer transmitted particles have passed through the subject, to darker areas indicating more transmitted particles. Bone tends to appear lighter than soft tissue due to a greater density that prevents most of the particles from reaching the detector. Observers must rely on training and experience to determine the settings that are most appropriate to the sample. Slice thickness, voxel density, and the radiographic tool are variable. Slices used could range from less than one to several millimeters thick. Features whose details fall between thicker slices will be difficult to interpret clearly and can carry high rates of error (Hale et al., 2014; Kim et al., 2012).

Orientation—three-dimensional digitizer

Anthropological training in the use of coordinate digitizer collection usually specifies a resting orientation of individual samples on the ***Frankfurt horizontal plane*** (Fig. 2.8) or resting on the basal portion of the skull. Protocol

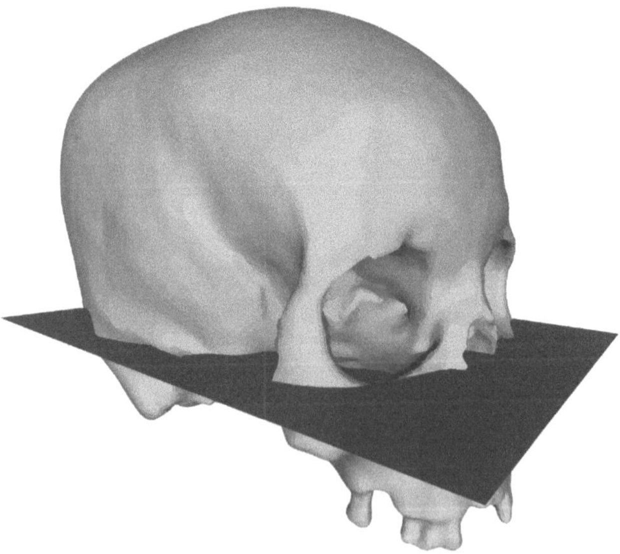

Figure 2.8 ***Frankfurt horizontal orientation.*** The plane indicates the Frankfurt horizontal intersecting the left and right porion landmark points and the left zygoorbitale landmark point.

for use of a secondary orientation is documented by Morpheus et al. (Slice, 2013) to make for an easier capture of basal or lateral landmarks within the work area of the digitizer arm. The alternative for cranial point sampling involves a flexible pedestal and mirror (Ousley, 2010). Strictly maintained uniformity of orientation is usually considered globally consistent enough to permit comparisons of samples collected by the same or multiple identically trained observers (Shearer et al., 2017). Observers using different resting orientations have problems making direct comparisons of landmark coordinates, as discussed by Ross and Williams (2008).

Orientation—surface scanner

Surface scanners create a dynamic orientation based on the object and scanning environment. Complex objects such as a skull necessitate capture of multiple orientations that are stitched together as described above. If the models were to be used for direct comparison or having coordinates collected without a standard alignment, the dynamic nature of scan collection can create exactly the problems that concerned Lele and Richtsmeier (2001).

Orientation—standard alignment

To reduce the problems with orientation with all methods, it is practical to apply as near as possible the same alignment to all methods. Some degree of variation will still occur, as it would occur for different observers or repeated measures by an observer on different days, so it is expected that the variation would be within an acceptable threshold. Software used to manipulate and generate 3D models uses an x, y, z virtual environment to render the models. If a model is moved in the environment, the changes in linear position (translation), rotation, or scale are recorded in a ***transformation matrix*** (Fig. 2.9).

Models of human crania built from surface scans or CT scans can be visually oriented to the Frankfurt horizontal plane by aligning the site of porion (the point on the human skull located at the upper margin of each external auditory meatus on the left and right lateral aspects of the cranium) with zygoorbitale (the lowest point of the inferior orbital margin). From here, the midline can be estimated for orientation from multiple structures.

A standard alignment is applied to the cranial models of each specimen by transformation matrix generated from manually transforming a primary

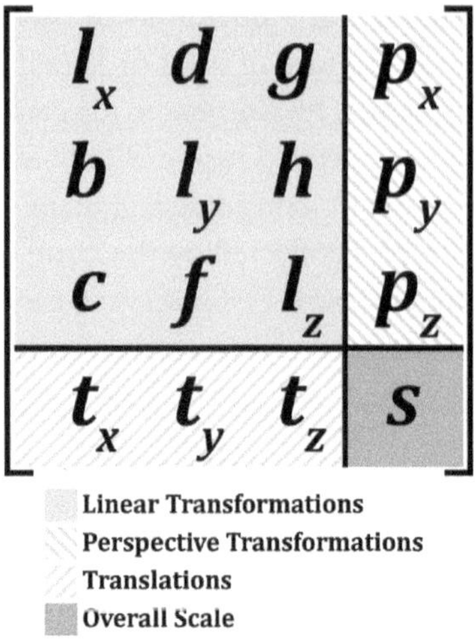

Figure 2.9 ***Transformation matrix structure (Rogers and Adams, 1990; Mortenson, 2007).*** Transformation matrix is represented in homogeneous coordinates, which due to their nature of representing an infinite projection of a point from the origin can be more easily applied to a coordinate than the Euclidean counterpart. This type of matrix can be used to represent all the necessary changes to the location of a point when transformation is applied. The changes to the location include translation, rotation, scale, and shear.

merged model *(Alpha)* in CloudCompare software (Girardeau-Montaut, 2014) as described above. The transformation matrix is saved, as it can be reapplied to models of that specimen generated from the primary merged model.

Collection

Surface scanner data collection

Laser and white-light 3D surface scanning are noninvasive and nonradiologic methods of capturing an object in three dimensions. Time-of-flight laser triangulation and fringe projection pattern are the primary capture methods used to recreate a 3D model of a real object. During a 3D surface scan, the object causes an interference with the laser light or fringe pattern projected from a primary origin. The interference is observed by the optical sensors of the scanner, which are offset from the projection origin, and the interference is interpreted into a set of 3D coordinates. The density of coordinates captured is dependent on the instrument and the settings selected by the observer. The actual process of capturing a scan with a 3D surface scanner will vary by the scanner.

A laser 3D surface scanner with an array of fine-tuned linear laser projections will capture a surface with a greater degree of detail than a single narrow-beam linear projection, which would have greater sensitivity than a wide-beam laser projection. The array also capitalizes on multiple projection angles, which offer a larger geometric sample from which to calculate triangulated distance.

Fringe pattern, or white-light 3D surface scans vary in color, pattern, and complexity. A single stationary surface capture involves the projection of one or more fringe patterns over a surface to calculate the surface shape by analysis of the deformation of the projected pattern. Increasing the number of patterns projected per stationary position increases the sample used to calculate the surface model. Multiple-offset optical sensors are also a common feature of white-light systems. Multiple optical sensors at offset angles from the projection origin increase the density of capture of complex surfaces by observing the projection from different angles determined by the offset.

Holes, cavities, and curvature can interfere with surface scans due to the nature of projection and observation methods that are used to determine the surface. A cavity, such as the eye orbits will typically exhibit internal reflection that distorts the laser or pattern projection. The geometric properties of a surface void are difficult for the optic sensor in terms of determining the dimensions and boundaries of these forms. Voids are characterized by edges and undercut dimensions that confound 3D scanners. Some problems can be overcome with careful capture and postprocessing. However, some problems in capture of surface variations are simply limitations of the technology. Multiple projections and acute sensor offset can improve the sensitivity with which borders and edges of a void are calculated but do not tend to improve the problems with internal reflection of a cavity. Unprocessed voids and cavities will result in a mesh model that is not in a closed manifold state.

Sources of error in collection of scan data

Theoretically, scanning technologies are capable of a very high degree of image resolution. However, all scanning methods still have limitations owing to the potential for variation and error at the various stages of capture, alignment, and reconstruction. Capture error in terms of 3D scanning has to do with any interaction during the scanning process that interferes with accurate reproduction of the surface. In most situations, sources of error can be detected and managed in scanning capture. But such sources must be identified in order to be controlled.

Movement can cause error in all forms of surface scanning. Medical imaging becomes blurred in an area where movement was not controlled. Stationary surface scanners struggle to interpret the variation in the information being collected during movement. Movement will change the positions of the scanner and the object in relationship to each other rapidly and repeatedly. This could happen faster than the scanner can capture and result in uncaptured areas. If the scanner does capture the surface during movement, the surface will appear disjointed and not continuous. Handheld scanners are moving during capture but still work under the assumption that the object is not moving. If the object being scanned with a handheld scanner is not stationary, the same problems as would be seen with movement for a stationary scanner will be experienced.

Medical imaging formats are sensitive to high-density materials and metallic elements. X-rays and magnetic resonance can only work where they are able to pass through the material. Differences in resistance of materials result in the variations that can be observed in medical imaging. Bone is more resistant than muscle and less resistant than titanium. On an X-ray, bone will have a lighter range of white value than healthy muscle tissue. A titanium medical device would have a lighter white value than bone. An X-ray focus directed through metal will not be able to pick out details on the other side of the metal because too much of the particle beam will be reflected by the metal. Magnetic resonance experiences interference from ferrous particles and any particles that can be excited by the magnetic field, resulting in deformations and artifacts.

Sources or error of surface

Objects are themselves the cause of problems with the accurate interpretation of their surface. The manner of interaction between the surface characteristics and scanning technologies dictates the degree of correspondence a 3D mesh file will have to the original object. Surface scanners have problems with high reflecting and transmitting surfaces (translucent or dark, in both instances, allowing light to pass through rather than be reflected back). Dental enamel is a good example of a surface that is difficult to capture with benchmark resolution. The characteristics of reflection and transmission (translucence) found in dental enamel cause the optic sensor to see defects and holes in the surface that do not exist on the real object.

Alignment and reconstruction are capable of moderating the degree of error found in a scan-based model; however, that moderation can be either positive or negative depending on the execution of the scan collection and the processes applied to the raw data to output mesh models.

Scan data collection error/resolution

To assume that advanced data collection technologies offer an improvement over their predecessors assumes that advanced methods collect data at a high degree of resolution and accuracy (Smith and Strait, 2008).

For example, the Z-Corp 3D scanner (3DSystems) used to collect the sample in this chapter processing example has a benchmark-capture resolution of 50 microns (= 0.05 mm), which should be more than sufficient to capture all but the finest foramina and surface irregularities expected to be found on the surface of a dry skull. This is not the case in practice. The human cranium is a complex object with surface characteristics that confound the optical sensors of surface scanners. In practice, the quality and accuracy of the surface that can be captured by 3D surface scanners will be reduced. However, when compared with handheld calipers, even a 100-micron resolution represents a much narrower margin of deviation.

Data capture

In preparation for scan collection, it will be necessary to determine that the scanning equipment is compatible with the sample. This will require tests to be done, unless previous work with the same sample type and scanner can be cited. Researching the background of either the type of sample, or the technology workspace can potentially uncover previous works that can save time in the data collection process. Previous published work involving the type of scanning technology can inform data collection research design decisions, even if that work involves different samples or different research questions.

If previous work is not applicable, the surface of the sample will need to be evaluated depending on the scanner type and the surface characteristics. Some scanning technology and scanning environments may require adapting the workflow plan to the particular sample and the possible application of surface treatments (Suggestions for surface treatments are included in the Supplementary Materials (2.2)).

Box 2.1

Scanning Workflow

This is a suggested workflow for the capture of surfaces using a 3D surface scanner. This workflow is for general guidelines as it is intended to be technology independent, rather than a specific set of instructions for a particular 3D surface scanner.

1. Prescan considerations
   a. Test scans
      i. Surface quality
         1. Reflection/refraction
         2. Translucence
         3. Contrast (light/dark)
      ii. Surface treatment (if needed)
         1. See report in Supplementary Materials (2.2)
      iii. Cavities, holes, convolutions, sharp edges
         1. White-light scanners will usually capture holes, cavities, and sharp edges better than a laser scanner, especially on light or reflective surfaces. The orbital area and the external auditory meatus of a cranium are examples.
         2. Convolutions are surprisingly often captured best by a single-camera versus Dual-camera system. This is surprising because dual-camera systems are generally better at capture of holes and cavities. Convolutions are different from a hole or cavity due to being obscured in direct view by other structures of the object, the posterior face of the frontal-temporal area of a cranium, for example.
      iv. Test scans of a type object (a unit of the sample that represents either a high degree of feature preservation or clear examples of the structures of interest) should be sufficient to determine which of the above issues a sample would need to be addressed to achieve quality scan capture.
2. Scan collection
   a. Follow protocol determined by test scans.
   b. Save copies of output in open source format.
3. Proceed to processing.

Collection—example

Technology collection and processing

We use the mesh images of the Yacchi-no-gamma materials (Okinawa Prefectural Archaeology Center, 2001) in this chapter. These images were captured by the Z-scanner 800. This is a handheld surface scanner that is moved around the subject object by the operator over the surface of interest.

Ideally, the subject object is static in position throughout the capture pass. The Yacchi-no-gamma crania were placed on a ***calibration surface*** and scanned in two passes (superior and inferior) for each of the cranial and mandibular elements. A calibration surface is part of the scanning environment that includes points or patterns that assist the scanner in determining the dynamic position in space. The calibration pattern does not change from scan to scan, or in position in space, so the scanner can calibrate against the pattern. Original raw scans include some areas within the scan environment that were not part of the skulls, which were captured in the scan passes, sometimes including the calibration patterns. This is a normal by-product of scanner interaction with the immediate scanning environment and can be advantageous when the extra scanned areas serve to calibrate and improve the alignment of the scan model. After a scan is captured, the unwanted areas can be removed from the mesh file produced by the scanner as part of processing.

Processing

Consider process levels, computational expense

In theory, the differences in landmark points selected among 3D models processed with different resolution should have statistically negligible differences among them and from landmark points collected using a 3D digitizer. If this proves to be accurate, it would support the use of a data conservative processing method for 3D mesh models, meaning one that results in a smaller file size for improved utility for users and computers. The rational for a smaller, more conservative file size comes down to the processing power, graphics hardware, and software rendering that working with 3D graphics requires. This must be considered concurrently with the importance of maintaining congruence with the original physical materials. Statistically significant differences that might occur between the landmark points for processing and selection methods based on 3D models of various sizes and resolutions would indicate the need for further research into methodological processes for the future application of 3D scan data. This is especially important in terms of the kind of archaeological sample presented in this project, which has by its nature a small sample size.

Technology

The processing of a 3D mesh should consider three parameters once the scan portions are aligned. Those parameters are vertex density, distribution, and quality. The first process parameter is analogous to resolution of an image. 3D mesh models are built from vertices interconnected to form faces. As the number of vertex and faces increases, as with image resolution, the mesh of a 3D model appears smoother. The distribution parameter describes the way in which the vertex spread over the mesh, randomly, uniformly, or decimated. The third parameter involves possible geometric states that virtual models can exist in so long as they are in an exclusively digital environment. A mesh model built from a 3D surface scan is not a true geometric solid. As an example, a sheet of paper represents a true geometric solid. It could be thought of in general as having a front and a back, from the perspective of 3D geometry, a sheet of paper has an outside surface and internal material in between. Even if a hole is punched through a sheet of paper, walls of the hole will maintain the outside surface and the solid state of the sheet. In virtual 3D rendering of a mesh model, a mesh will have an outer surface and an inner surface. The outer surface need not be complete or continuous to be rendered in a digital environment. Such a mesh model is defined as nonmanifold and can include models having overlapping, noncoincident (surfaces that overlap but do not touch or meet smoothly). Most software used for the manipulation of 3D mesh includes protocols to make a mesh model continuous and remove or repair any overlapping surfaces. Depending on the settings used, the mesh can be further made *watertight*, which repairs any places an incomplete mesh has a hole that exposes the inner faces. The results of the application of a watertight manifold process is an effectively solid model, and it is a requirement for a mesh model that will be used 3D printing, or computer-aided manufacture. The 3D mesh models used in this chapter example were processed to result in sets of models that were nonmanifold and sets that were watertight manifold to examine the surface accuracy and computational characteristics.

Processes for accurately rendering 3D meshes have undergone rapid evolution in the previous decade. Whereas once rendering of complex files was strictly the domain of high-powered purpose-configured systems—today both the processing power and the software are light and powerful enough for the computers available to the average consumer (Khazan et al., 2006; Girardeau-Montaut, 2015).

Density

The density of vertices of a mesh can be compared with the resolution of a 2D image. For a 2D image, the detail observable in a 600 dpi version versus a 72 dpi version is significant. The greater the number of vertices contained in a mesh (relative to the overall mesh), the greater degree of detail is expected. Geometrically, a larger number of vertices over a mesh must also mean that the variation between adjacent vertex is very low (small steps). Without looking further, this would seem to be a good thing. However, high density has some inherent problems.

A raw 3D surface scan is composed of multiple scanned angles, congruent areas guiding the reconstitution of the actual geometry. The congruent areas become overlapping areas, which will contain duplicate data. These overlaps could contain data from several sections with scanning created deviations increasing near the outer range of the scanned angle. These layers can become redundant, not actually conveying new data. They can also become inaccurate by retaining the data at the edge of a scanned angle where the scanning equipment can fail to compensate for distortion at the outer range of the field of view. All the redundant and distorted data have a further consequence of increasing the computational demands that a mesh puts on the software. For these reasons, a dense mesh should be processed to reduce the impact of redundant and distorted data, as well as the overall file size (Fig. 2.10).

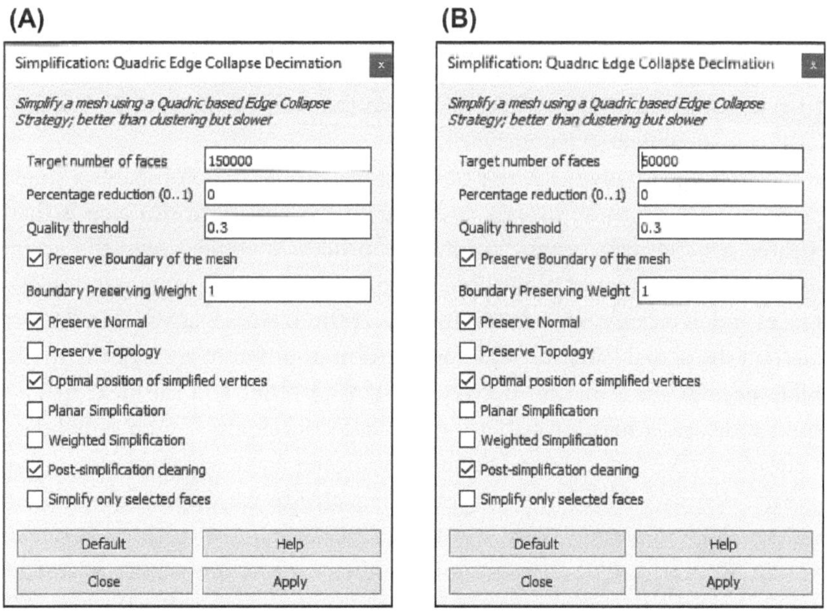

Figure 2.10 ***Meshlab (Cignoni et al., 2008) simplification setting.*** The settings applied to the aligned and joined hemispheres of the unprocessed models in the chapter example to affect the (A) high face count and (B) low face count process models.

Cleaning

The process of acquiring surface data to build a mesh model is never perfect. Every scanning system can be fooled into capturing artifacts and false-positive surfaces. Between the capture and analysis of a 3D mesh, these unwanted artifacts need to be removed. Areas of the scanning environment, unreferenced vertices, false-positive surfaces, and noncoincident surfaces that are captured can interfere with the accuracy of landmark selection and surface comparison. These problems also have computational consequences that keep a mesh file size larger than necessary and can sometimes create problems in processing algorithms.

Decimation

The process of ***decimation*** redistributes faces and vertices of a mesh so that complex areas are more dense (have a greater number of vertices and faces) and noncomplex areas are less dense. In the process of scan collection, vertices represent the points that are registered in the Euclidean space. The resulting distribution of vertices is a result of the scanning technology, rather than the complexity of the surface. Because of this, a scan should be collected at the highest practical resolution to capture the smallest feature of interest. Over an entire skull, the result is far more actual vertices than is necessary to produce an accurate digital version of a crania. The application of decimation makes it possible to reduce the number of vertices without sacrifice of quality and accuracy.

Decimation involves the use of a quadric model that compares a single vertex or edge to those nearest and records the variation; this step is then repeated for the next nearest point. The process is applied over the entire mesh resulting in a set of points that meets the criteria of a set target number of faces and vertices, with a distribution over the surface that varies in density based on the actual variation and convolution of different areas of the mesh. Differences in the variation between a starting point and the next nearest points indicates a high probability of surface complexity—such as bending or curving of the surface—and therefore indicates an area that would require a greater density of faces and vertices to characterize the shape of the original mesh model. Conversely, very low or no difference in the variation between the starting point and the closest points indicate a low probability of surface variation—a flat face of a cube, for example—and suggest that the area can be accurately rendered with fewer faces and vertices. The procedures for decimation implemented by the Meshlab software (Cignoni et al., 2008) use this quadric method with multiple iterations to develop a best fit representation of the original mesh model with a specified target number of faces.

There is an advantage of multiple iterations in that the potential for every seed, or initial starting point used for each iteration, having a very high or low complexity relative to the overall mesh and exerting a strong influence that introduces bias to more distance parts of the mesh is minimized (Hoppe, 1999). Once this has been applied, the areas of the faces over the mesh vary greatly depending on the degree of change over the surface at a given area of the mesh.

Processing example

The raw scan data for each cranium contributed by Seguchi (2010) must be processed to clean, align, and merge the superior and inferior views taken during scanning. Once merged, the scans can be further processed to remove extraneous data and correct scanning errors. At this point, the manifold version of the model will be made, which will produce a geometrically solid (or watertight) object. Although the nonmanifold models could not be rendered to a physical reproduction method, such as 3D printing, the landmarking process does not require that a model be manifold. Furthermore, each landmark collected will have a normalized vector perpendicular to the surface it defines.

There will be many options for processing scan data. Nearly all 3D scanners commercially available include software packages with mesh processing capabilities. In this chapter, the software focus is shifted from these scanner-specific proprietary packages to open source and non—scanner-specific software. This is consciously done with the mindset that the 3D lab space and scanner workstation may not always be available. Working with these separate software packages is a practical solution to this constraint.

Align scan segments

The superior and inferior components of the models were aligned by common geometry manually by the observer. This is step is done to minimize the difference between the models, which reduces the computational effort needed to perfect the final alignment. After this initial alignment, the Meshlab software (Cignoni et al., 2008) is directed to process the two components into an alignment with a small distance squared error (d^2) between overlapping components. After alignment, the d^2 average for all models was

Box 2.2

Model Processing Protocol

This is a suggested workflow for the processing of raw 3D surface scan data into mesh models. This workflow is for general guidelines as it is intended to be technology independent, rather than a specific set of instructions for a software package or 3D scanner software. Table 2.1 is an outline of the codebook for this section.

1. Sample
   a. Codebook
      i. Record the names of the sample unit
      ii. Record the number (total) and size of the raw scan files (aggregate—add up the file sizes of the partial scans)
      iii. Record the number of faces and vertices of the scans of each sample unit (aggregate—add up the total number)
2. Refine alignment of the sections of the raw scan to minimize the d^2 for overlapping areas.
   a. Codebook
      i. Record the d^2
3. Merge sections of the raw scans into a single model mesh file.
   a. Decide to make manifold
      i. Open manifold
      ii. Closed manifold
   b. Apply mesh processing
      i. Cleaning
      ii. Surface reconstruction
      iii. Decimation
   c. Codebook
      i. Record Manifold state
      ii. Record postprocessing computational
   d. Save new version of the merged and processed file
4. Align to single mesh model to predetermined global orientation Frankfurt horizontal plane* relates to human crania and will vary for different types of objects sampled. For crania the orientation applied is described in further chapters
   a. Align structures to a preselected plane
   b. Codebook
      i. Save the transformation matrix applied to the mesh
   c. Save new version of the merged and processed file
5. Save all versions to the appropriate naming convention and record the final file size for all versions

Table 2.1 Computational characteristics of raw models.

	Original pre-process parameters					Processed model (file size MB)		
	Model	**Faces**	**Vertices**	**Aligned (d^2)**	**File size (MB)**		**Model**	**File size (MB)**
1 2 3 4 5 6 7 8 . .	List of sample unit names or ID numbers referenced in the primary codebook	Number of faces and vertices are object parameters reported by 3D mesh editing software		The d^2 parameter is reported by 3D mesh editing software after alignment. Alternative parameters may be reported by some packages, but this number is important because it conveys the quality of the merged parts of the model.	File size is reported by software or OS. This represents part of the computational expense of a mesh. Larger files will place heavier computation demands and limits on a system.	1 2 3 4 5 6 7 8 . .	List of sample unit names or ID numbers referenced in the primary codebook	Processing is expected to reduce the file size of a mesh model. Minimally, the removal of redundant vertices reduces the total file size. Remeshing and decimation will also reduce the file size and decrease the computational demands cause by a mesh file.
		Faces	**Vertices**	**Aligned (d^2)**	**File size (MB)**		**Mean for models**	$\bar{x}$
Mean for sample		$\bar{x}$	$\bar{x}$	$\bar{x}$	$\bar{x}$		**Mean for sample** $\bar{x}$	4.9

Box 2.3

Processing Example Protocol

This section is an example workflow that was applied to the chapter example. Table 2.2 records the results of this processing workflow.

1. Sample
   a. Codebook
      i. Record the names of the sample unit
      ii. Record the number (total) and size of the raw scan files
      iii. Record the number of faces and vertices of the scans of each sample unit
2. Refine alignment of the sections of the raw scan to minimize the d^2 for overlapping areas
   a. Codebook
      i. Record the d^2
3. Merge sections of the raw scans into a single model mesh file
   a. Decide to make manifold
      i. Open manifold
      ii. Closed manifold
   b. Apply mesh processing
      i. Cleaning
      ii. Surface reconstruction
      iii. Decimation
   c. Codebook
      i. Record manifold state
      ii. Record postprocessing computational
   d. Save new version of the merged and processed file
4. Align to single mesh model to predetermined global orientation Frankfurt horizontal plane* relates to human crania and will vary for different types of objects sampled. For crania, the orientation applied is described in further chapters
   a. Align structures to a preselected plane
   b. Codebook
      i. Save the *transformation matrix* applied to the mesh
   c. Save new version of the merged and processed file
5. Save all versions to the appropriate naming convention and record the final file size for all versions

0.062127. The d^2 is included in tables 2.1 and 2.2, the latter lists the d^2 of the individual models in the chapter example.

With the maximum alignment of the top and bottom mesh models achieved, the two files can be digitally flattened into a single mesh file.

Table 2.2 Computational characteristics of raw models. This table indicates a mean file size of 6.58 MB for one clean hemisphere. This would indicate a high likelihood as merged, unprocessed mesh could average greater than 13 MB. The size of a file becomes an issue for 3D rendering as the file is dynamically read to reflect dimensions and movement in a semirealistic digital environment. This shows the file size reduction postprocessing for merged hemispheres for each processing parameter (Code: 1-HF, 2-HFNM, 3-LF, 4-LFNM). Of note is the reduction in files size to a maximum files size that is less than the smallest files size for a single hemisphere of the raw models.

		Original pre-process parameters							Processed model (file size MB)					
		Faces		Vertices		Aligned (d^2)	File size (MB)							
	Model	Top *.STL	Bottom *.STL	Top *.STL	Bottom *.STL		Top *.STL	Bottom *.STL		Model	1	2	3	4
1	2go-2-2_male	135,697	147,960	70,418	79,540	0.057746	7.1	6.5	1	2go-2-2_male	2.9	4.9	1	1.8
2	6go-6-6-male	134,594	NA	70,825	NA	NA	6.4	NA	2	6go-6-6-male	2.9	2.6	1	1
3	8-14_female	123,650	129,667	64,925	69,775	0.076798	6.2	5.9	3	8-14_female	2.9	2.6	1	1
4	11-5_male	136,570	137,711	71,262	74,563	0.07672	6.6	6.5	4	11-5_male	2.8	4.9	0.9	1.8
5	11-14_female	130,134	137,400	67,908	73,444	0.050739	6.6	6.2	5	11-14_female	2.8	4.9	0.9	1.8
6	11-15_male	144,021	141,576	75,325	75,868	0.056846	6.8	6.9	6	11-15_male	2.8	4.9	0.9	1.8
7	11-42 female	132,567	147,235	69,385	79,105	0.068469	7	6.3	7	11-42 female	2.9	3	1	1.1
8	2go-2-30_male	139,009	148,492	72,261	79,542	0.048818	7.1	6.6	8	2go-2-30_male	2.9	4.9	1	1.8
9	2go-2-32_male	140,304	155,535	73,605	83,869	0.078066	7.4	6.7	9	2go-2-32_male	2.9	4.9	1	1.8
10	7-12-Male	147,997	158,047	77,974	84,722	0.075532	7.5	7.1	10	7-12-male	2.9	4.9	1	1.8
11	9-15_female	122,513	130,734	64,651	70,120	0.047501	6.2	5.8	11	9-15_female	2.9	2.9	1	1
12	11-34_male	129,156	134,123	67,650	72,795	0.063547	6.4	6.2	12	11-34_male	2.8	3.1	0.9	1.2
13	11-42 male	139,581	NA	72,888	NA	NA	6.7	NA	13	11-42 male	2.7	2.7	2.7	2.7
★	11-19_female	133,777	136,790	69,530	73,952	0.06423	6.5	6.4	★	11-19_female	NA	NA	NA	NA
★	2-13_male	135,489	136,831	70,927	74,041	0.053619	6.5	6.5	★	2-13_male	NA	NA	NA	NA
★	2-16_female	135,939	138,288	71,035	74,570	0.051141	6.6	6.5	★	2-16_female	NA	NA	NA	NA
		Faces		**Vertices**		**Aligned (d^2)**	**File size (MB)**	**File size (MB)**	**Mean for models**		**2.72**	**3.80**	**1.24**	**1.76**
Mean for sample			138,046.2		73,215.83	0.062127	6.58	6.58	**Mean for sample**	2.3	**Min**	0.9	**Max**	4.9

★Some model files failed to resolve during this stage of processing due to indeterminate file corruption of the source file.

The flattened file retains the locations of all faces and vertices of the parent files. This can result in the retention of mesh defects. Defects can include isolated faces, unreferenced vertices, faces with inverted normals, and layers of mesh that overlap but do not intersect. These are problems that can result in a greater computational expense for analytical purposes and errors for placement of landmarks should the location intersect with a defect. Working with a large model file also affects research design by imparting a higher computational expense due to the file size. The rendering process used to project the visual equivalent of a 3D model in a digital environment must process large subsets of data within a single file as rapidly as possible, and without processing conflicting or corrupted data (Jantz et al., 2013).

Merge

After the superior and inferior views have been merged, the resulting file retains the raw information of both parent files. While working with a scan that exactly reflects the surface of the source would be considered a conservative approach, to use the size of files that result from raw data models is prohibitive due to the necessary computational thresholds and added time required by thresholds.

To mitigate the issue of file size and computational efficiency, it is sensible to consider the application of mesh processing methods that uniformly reduce the file size in a trade-off that minimally impacts the retention of accuracy.

Processing

Refining and aligning the raw scan files results in preprocess models with large areas of overlap that are redundant to the model and keep the mesh file size large. The average files size for each half of the raw scan files is 6.58 MB. Large files are undesirable because they slow down rendering and the application of any selection or analysis.

Processing the models produced two sets of two mesh models each. The processed models are reduced in size compared with the original raw scan files. The average size for the merged and processed mesh file is 2.3 MB, which is a reduction of at least 25% for each cranium. The high-face count models for each cranium are larger on average but still within a reasonable range for maintenance of detail contrasted to computational expense.

From the manifold and nonmanifold scan models, tertiary processing will be applied to create a sample set from each cranium of a research model for each of two processing criteria: high-face count and low-face count. The target number for faces is 150,000, determined by the mean number of faces of the primary models after the manifold step. The target number of faces used for the low-face count models is 50,000 faces (Jantz et al., 2013). Landmark collection follows the suggestions of Jantz et al. (2013) and Hsiao (1996) using selection planes that orient with the Frankfurt horizontal plane and the midsagittal plane to determine midline and lateral landmarks by their geometric description. The location of remaining landmarks lacking a geometric location will be determined and refined by visual assessment.

The methods in this chapter are designed to process a 3D mesh for optimization of file size and accuracy under one of two optimization frameworks (Fig. 2.11). One involves a random sampling of the surface (Kazhdan et al., 2006). The second applies an evaluation of the redundancy of the number of faces and vertices over a given area and by decimation reduces the density of both in areas and directions of low variation and maximizing the sampled density in areas of greater complexity (Hoppe, 1993).

Based on previous 3D cranial studies of CT scans (Saso et al., 2011; Jantz et al., 2013) and surface scans (Sholts et al. 2010, 2011; Shearer et al., 2012), the processing levels analogous to resolution were determined for each sample subset.150,000 faces (~75,000 vertices) were chosen for the

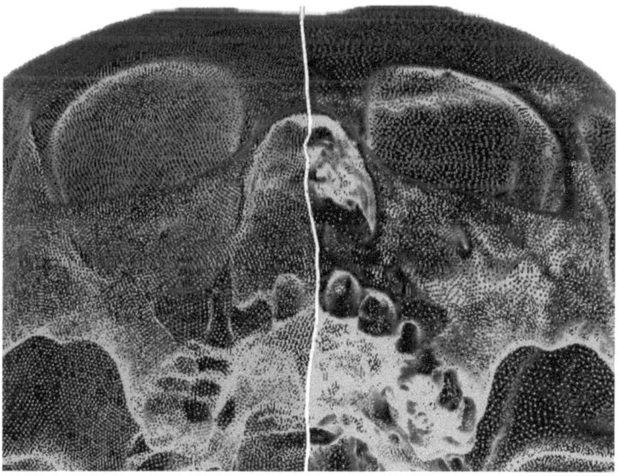

Figure 2.11 ***Random and decimated mesh.*** The two sides of the mesh model show two different mesh optimizations; the left side has vertices randomly and nearly uniformly over the surface of the mesh, and the right side has vertices distributed over the mesh with a greater density at the areas of high variation (curve, edge, cavity). Both versions capture the mesh accurately, but the decimated mesh can decrease the number of total vertices and still maintain a high degree of accuracy with a lower computational expense.

high-resolution random sampled models and 50,000 faces (~25,000 vertices) for the low-resolution decimation sampled models.

Conclusion

This chapter has introduced the virtual environment and many of the terms and concepts tied to working with the kind of data that 3D data capturing technologies and software make possible. Workflow and suggested practices for scan capture and model processing with 3D surface scanning technology help control and maintain the quality of research data. The next chapter will describe the set up and use of 3D contact digitizing with the Microscribe 3D Digitizer with fragile archaeological human remains and how data collected with the Microscribe can be applied in the anthropological research.

Supplementary data

Supplementary data related to this article can be found online at https://doi.org/10.1016/B978-0-12-815309-3.00002-4

References

Abdel Fatah, E.E., Shirley, N.R., Jantz, R.L., Mahfouz, M.R., 2014. Improving sex estimation from crania using a novel three- dimensional quantitative method. (report). Journal of Forensic Sciences 59 (3), 10.

Cignoni, P., Scopigno, R., 2008. Sampled 3D models for CH applications: a viable and enabling new medium or just a technological exercise? Journal on Computing and Cultural Heritage 1 (1), 1–23.

Cignoni, P., Callieri, M., Corsini, M., Dellepiane, M., Ganovelli, F., Ranzuglia, G., 2008. MeshLab: An Open-Source Mesh Processing Tool.

CloudCompare. Version 2.8 [GPL Software], 2018. Retrieved from http://www.cloudcompare.org/.

Dudzik, B., 2013. In: Dudzik, B. (Ed.), 3D Coordinate Landmarks from a Cranial Sample of the Yacchi-No-Gamma Osteological Materials, Kumejima, Okinawa, Japan. Unpublished.

Girardeau-Montaut, D., 2014. Cloud Compare - Open Source Project. http://www.cloudcompare.org: CloudCompare-Open Source Project.

Girardeau-Montaut, D., 2015. CloudCompare v2.6.1 User Manual. Retrieved from. http://www.cloudcompare.org/.

Hale, A.R., Honeycutt, K.K., Ross, A.H., 2014. A geometric morphometric validation study of computed tomography—extracted craniofacial landmarks. Journal of Craniofacial Surgery 25 (1), 231–237.

Hoppe, H., 1999. New quadric metric for simplifiying meshes with appearance attributes. In: Proceedings of the Conference on Visualization '99: Celebrating Ten Years. IEEE Computer Society Press, San Francisco, California, USA, pp. 59–66.

Hoppe, H., DeRose, T., Duchamp, T., McDonald, J., Stuetzle, W., 1993. Mesh optimization. In: Proceedings of the 20th Annual Conference on Computer Graphics and Interactive Techniques. ACM, Anaheim, CA, pp. 19–26.

Hsaio, T.H., Chang, H.P., Liu, K.M., 1996. Sex determination by discriminant function analysis of lateral radiographic cephalometry. Journal of Forensic Science 41 (5), 792–795.

Jantz, R., Mahfouz, M., Shirley, N.R., Abdel Fatah, E., 2013. Improving Sex Estimation from Crania Using 3-dimensional CT Scans. U.S. Department of Justice. https://www.ncjrs.gov/pdffiles1/nij/grants/240688.pdf.

Kazhdan, M., Bolitho, M., Hoppe, H., 2006. Poisson Surface Reconstruction.

Kim, M., Huh, K.-H., Yi, W.-J., Heo, M.-S., Lee, S.-S., Choi, S.-C., 2012. Evaluation of accuracy of 3D reconstruction images using multi-detector CT and cone-beam CT. Imaging Sci Dent 42 (1), 8.

Lele, S., Richtsmeier, J.T., 2001. An Invariant Approach to Statistical Analysis of Shapes. Chapman & Hall/CRC, Boca Raton, Fla.

Mortenson, M.E., 2007. Geometric Transformations for 3D Modeling. Industrial Press, New York.

Okinawa Prefectural Archaeology Center, 2001. Report No. 6. In: Yacchi Cave, Kanjin-Hara Tombs: The Report on the Archaeological Excavation in Conjunction with the Prefectural Project on Irrigation and Drainage. Okinawa Prefectural Archaeology Center, p. 436, (In Japanese).

Ousley, S.D., 2010. Threeskull. Version 2.0.

Rogers, D.F., Adams, J.A., 1990. Mathematical Elements for Computer Graphics. McGraw-Hill, New York.

Ross, A.H., Williams, S., 2008. Testing repeatability and error of coordinate landmark data acquired from crania*. Journal of Forensic Sciences 53 (4), 782–785.

Saso, A., Matsukawa, S., Suwa, G., 2011. Comparative analysis of the glabellar region morphology of the late Pleistocene Minatogawa crania: a three- dimensional approach. Anthropological Science 119 (2), 113–121.

Seguchi, N., 2010. 3D surface scans of a sample of crania from the Yacchi-no-gamma. Kumejima, Okinawa. In: Seguchi, N. (Ed.), Japan Osteological Collection. Unpublished.

Shearer, B.M., Sholts, S.B., Garvin, H.M., Wärmländer, S.K.T.S., 2012. Sexual dimorphism in human browridge volume measured from 3D models of dry crania: a new digital morphometrics approach. Forensic Science International 222 (1–3), 400.e401–400.e405.

Shearer, B.M., Cooke, S.B., Halenar, L.B., Reber, S.L., Plummer, J.E., Delson, E., Tallman, M., 2017. Evaluating causes of error in landmark-based data collection using scanners. PLoS One 12 (11), e0187452. https://doi.org/10.1371/journal.pone.0187452.

Sholts, S.B., Wärmländer, S.K.T.S., Flores, L.M., Miller, K.W.P., Walker, P.L., 2010. Variation in the measurement of cranial volume and surface area using 3D laser scanning technology. Journal of Forensic Sciences 55 (4), 871–876.

Sholts, S.B., Flores, L., Walker, P., Warmlander, S., 2011. Comparison of coordinate measurement precision of different landmark types on human crania using a 3D laser scanner and a 3D digitiser: implications for applications of digital morphometrics. International Journal of Osteoarchaeology 21 (5), 535–543.

Slice, D.E., 2013. Morpheus et al, Java Edition. Department of Scientific Computing.

Smith, N.E., Strait, S.G., 2008. PaleoView3D: from specimen to online digital model. Palaeontologia Electronica 11 (Issue 2), 11A:17pp. http://palaeo-electronica.org/2008_2/134/index.html.

CHAPTER THREE

Three-dimensional investigations of fragile archaeological human remains

Kengo Ohno[1], Yoshinori Kawakubo[2]

[1]Department of Forensic Medicine, Faculty of Medicine, Saga University, Saga, Japan
[2]Department of Anatomy and Anthropology, Faculty of Medicine, Saga University, Saga, Japan

Introduction

One of the advantages of three-dimensional (3D) data collection in biological anthropology and forensic anthropology is that researchers can capture more morphological information by maintaining the geometrical positional relationship as a set of coordinates in the rectangular coordinate system than they can by using linear measurements with traditional calipers. If, for example, crania are complete or in near-complete form, all coordinate data of desired landmarks can be obtained without missing data. However, the degree of skeletal preservation of archaeological human remains can vary and is influenced by various factors such as acidity of soil, content of calcium or other chemical substances, grain-size of soil, stratum composition, exposure of sites, decomposing action of soil microorganisms, geographic location and climate, and style of burials (Nakahashi and Nagai, 1985). Preservation condition can introduce obstacles and constraints for 3D data collection. In this chapter, we describe a case study of poorly preserved archaeological human remains excavated in Japan. Then, we discuss several difficulties that researchers may encounter during acquisition of landmark coordinate data using a digitizer from poorly preserved crania. For example, (1) how to correctly handle crania to meet the requirements from curators and (2) how to establish a stable setting to anchor crania for capturing 3D coordinate data.

Poorly preserved archaeological human skeletal remains from archaeological sites in Japan

Archaeological human remains excavated in Japan are often in fragile and fragmented condition due to chemical dissolution. Suitable conditions

3D Data Acquisition for Bioarchaeology, Forensic Anthropology, and Archaeology
ISBN: 978-0-12-815309-3
https://doi.org/10.1016/B978-0-12-815309-3.00003-6

for good skeletal preservation require that the soil be alkaline or high in calcium content (Brothwell, 1981; Miwa, 1958), yet the Japanese archipelago has acidic soil in general. Most areas of the Japanese archipelago are characterized by relatively high precipitation throughout the year, and there is good drainage, which results in water soaking into the soil and washing away alkalizing minerals, such as calcium (Ca) and magnesium (Mg), which causes soil acidification. Additionally, many soils in Japan originate from volcanic ash, meaning that even calcium phosphate, an inorganic component of bone that prevents decomposition from bacteria in the soil, is dissolved. As a result, bones buried in the soil in the Japanese archipelago (with the exception of the Nansei Islands) may be destroyed in a span of 100 years or less, and in some cases, destruction can occur in just a few decades. Nakahashi and Nagai (1985) investigated the state of preservation of human skeletal remains from the late Jomon Period to the Medieval Period (1500 BCE–CE 1600) in Japan, and they concluded that human skeletal remains were generally preserved well in soil above pH 7.5 (KCl), pH 8.0 (H_2O), and 10 me/100 g Ca content. However, human skeletal remains cannot be preserved without damage in soil that is under pH 6.0 (KCl) and pH 7.0 (H_2O). Human remains dating to the Yayoi Period that were buried in jar coffins and cist burials were preserved because the remains did not contact the soil directly.

The preservation of human skeletal remains and the environment of the archaeological sites in Japan are as follows. Most of the human skeletal remains of the late Paleolithic (38,000–11,000 BCE) and the Jomon Period (11,000–500 BCE) were recovered from alkaline soils such as those found on the Nansei Islands (the small islands located southeast of the main islands of Japan) and from shell mounds, which consist of soils with calcium-rich limestone. It has been rare to recover remains from the late Paleolithic. However there are human skeletal materials unearthed from the Minatogawa site at Okinawa Island (Baba and Narasaki, 1991; Matsu'ura and Kondo, 2011). And, recently, at least 19 individuals were excavated at the site of Shiraho-Saonetabaru on Ishigaki Island (Nakagawa et al., 2010). Many remains of the Yayoi period (500 BCE–CE 300) have been recovered in the northern part of Kyushu Island. The Yayoi people of northern Kyushu performed a special burial practice in which individuals were buried in jar coffin tombs. The Yayoi remains from northern Kyushu generally have good bone preservation. However, many jars have cracked, allowing soil to leak in, resulting in few skeletal elements left in such jar coffins over time. This type of burial practice is seen in the Kanenokuma site in

Fukuoka Prefecture, the Mitsu-Nagata site in Saga Prefecture, and many other sites in northern Kyushu. In other cases, numerous human bones were excavated from a sandy beach that contained large quantities of shellfish and coral pieces at the Doigahama Yayoi site in Yamaguchi Prefecture and the Koura site in Shimane Prefecture. Additionally, many human bones have been found in the soil low marsh area in a vacuum-packed state in Tottori Prefecture (the Aoya-Kamijichi site).

The Kofun period (CE 300–700) burial practices are characterized by large burial mounds, thought to be a distinct practice of higher social classes. Skeletal remains of the Kofun period exhibit relatively good preservation due to placement in a burial chamber rather than in the soil. However, parts that were in contact with the ground are often degraded and contain very fragile bones (Fig. 3.1).

In the archaeological sites of Kanagawa Prefecture and Yamaguchi Prefecture, a large number of medieval (CE 1100–1600) human skeletal remains have been excavated from locations on the beach and near the coast. Relatively well-preserved human remains from various areas in Japan have also been excavated from graves from the early modern period (CE 1600–1800) and likely display good preservation due to their recent burial date. Although relatively well-preserved human skeletons have been

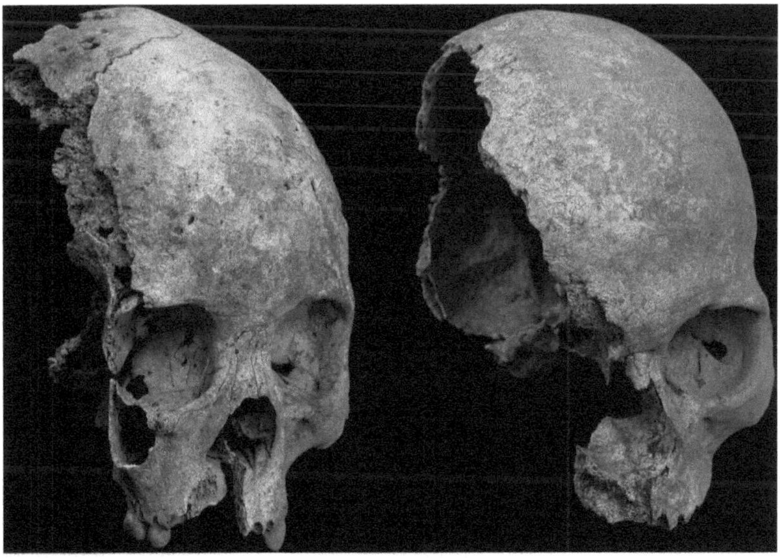

Figure 3.1 Fragile crania of the Kofun period with a defective part. Both crania have lost parts that were in contact with the ground.

excavated in reclaimed land areas which used to be under the sea, or in groundwater-rich areas near rivers in the old Edo city and in coffin jar burials, the skeletal remains from well-drained area are usually poorly preserved.

Devices used in the process of 3D data collection of fragile human crania

As mentioned above, the preservation of archaeological human remains excavated from the Japanese islands is generally poor. If we choose only well-preserved crania to measure in order to analyze variations of cranial morphology using a 3D digitizer, the sample size would be drastically reduced. To maximize the sample size, it is necessary to measure fragile and partially damaged human crania, which requires extreme care and attention. Although computed tomography (CT) and surface shape scanners are ideal for capturing data as they require no direct contact with skeletal material, CT imaging machines are not yet portable and bringing skeletal material to medical facilities for scanning is extremely difficult. Furthermore, a portable-type surface laser scanner with high data quality is still expensive for researchers seeking to acquire a high-accuracy mode of surface data. In addition, it may be difficult to acquire data on a specimen that has been reconstructed using paraffin wax due to laser reflection. On the other hand, a direct contact type of digitizer with a stylus arm is relatively inexpensive, portable, and easy to set up and use. However, to record landmarks on fragile crania with a digitizer, it is necessary to undertake many preparatory steps to avoid damaging the specimen during the measurement/data-capturing process. These include (1) fixing the skull to a stable surface; (2) marking Type III landmarks directly on the bone surface; and (3) bringing the digitizer stylus (probe tip) of the arm to the bone surface.

On marking landmarks on bone

The digitizer requires bringing the digitizer stylus, or probe tip, of the arm directly in contact with the surface of the cranium to acquire coordinates; therefore, it is desirable to mark the anatomical landmarks (homologous landmarks: functional correspondence between morphological features) on the surface of the bone in advance. Type III landmarks such as maximum and minimum breadths, widths, lengths, and heights (Bookstein, 1991; Slice et al., 2008) must be marked in advance, and also Type I landmarks, the intersection of sutures, and Type II landmarks, point of maximum or minimum curvature along boundaries, should be marked as well because it is often difficult to find the exact physical locations of landmarks. Without preliminary marks, the observer may confuse landmarks, as locations may be observed differently from different orientations. From our experiences, museum curators usually grant permission to use a pencil for marking bone surfaces. A hard-core pencil can cause damage to fragile bone surfaces; we therefore use a soft-core pencil, taking care to use very light pressure when indicating locations on a bony surface (Fig. 3.2). Needless to say, it is necessary to follow the instructions of the museum curators when handling fragile bones to carefully protect from further damage, as not all collections will allow pencil markings on skeletal materials. For example, in cases when marking a landmark with a pencil is forbidden, we use peelable small glue dots on the landmarks instead of pencil markings.

It is common on Japanese crania to observe pencil marks made by previous researchers, so it is necessary to confirm with the curators and administrators if the pencil marks can be erased. A kneaded eraser is convenient to erase these pencil marks without friction and pressure on the bone because it is soft and has the plasticity to change its shape (Fig. 3.2). In addition, kneaded erasers can be useful for other tasks. For example, we often encounter situations in which we are not able to obtain permission from curators to repair or reconstruct a cranium using glue, but a cranium can be perfectly measurable if the sutures are connected. In this case, a kneaded

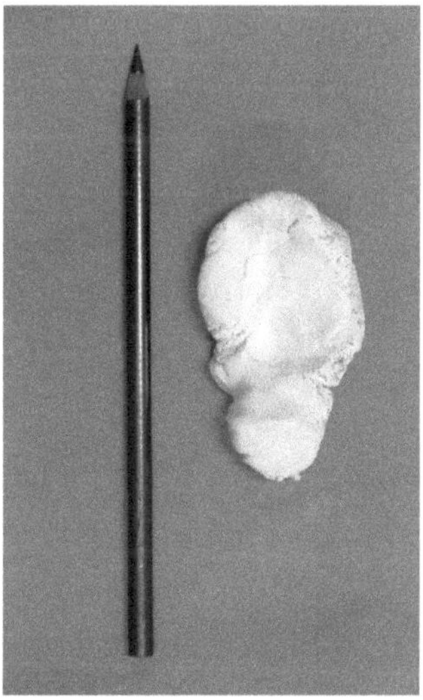

Figure 3.2 Pencil and kneaded eraser for drawing used for marking landmarks.

eraser is useful and can temporally adhere to cranial sutures. When a researcher plans to use an anatomical specimen, in which the calotte has been removed, it is useful to connect the calvaria to the rest of the skull using a kneaded eraser. In some skeletal collections, it is not permissible to repair bondable bone fragments (or cranial bones that have been separated from sutures) with glue. In this case, a kneaded eraser can be used to adhere to bones temporarily. Additionally, when the cranium needs to have the mandible articulated, an eraser can be used as a spacer to reconstruct the temporomandibular joint.

Device for fixing crania

It is extremely important to anchor the cranium securely to a solid, immobile surface when recording 3D data with a digitizer, to ensure no movement during this process. If the cranium or digitizer base moves during the measurement of a specimen, serious errors occur in the positional relationship between the previously acquired coordinate data and subsequently recorded landmarks. In that case, it is necessary to start over from the beginning of the landmark series and rerecord the entire cranium. If recording landmarks that represent an entire cranium, the digitizer arm needs to be able to reach the cranial base, facial skeleton, and neurocranium without moving the specimen or the digitizer. Therefore, it is inappropriate to set a cranium directly on the flat surface of a desk or table, as the stylus will not be able to record landmarks on the portion of the skull that is in contact with the desk.

To solve this problem, many researchers implement a method of setting a cranium on a tripod and use a small mirror to capture landmarks on the cranial base. Three clay towers can also be used in lieu of a metal tripod. The clay should not contain oil, as this can damage bone.

Another technique that is sometimes used involves intentional movement of the skull. First, the cranium is positioned on its base in fine granules of sand, and landmarks of the neurocranium and facial skeleton are recorded, to include a set of three positioning landmarks that will be used to orient coordinate data once the skull is flipped. The cranium is then positioned in the sand so that the cranial base is turned upward, and the same three-point coordinates previously taken in the beginning must be recaptured so that they can be matched in a computer program, and then the landmark data of the cranial base should be collected.

As described previously, most techniques require zero movement of the specimen after the first landmark has been recorded. Therefore, it is

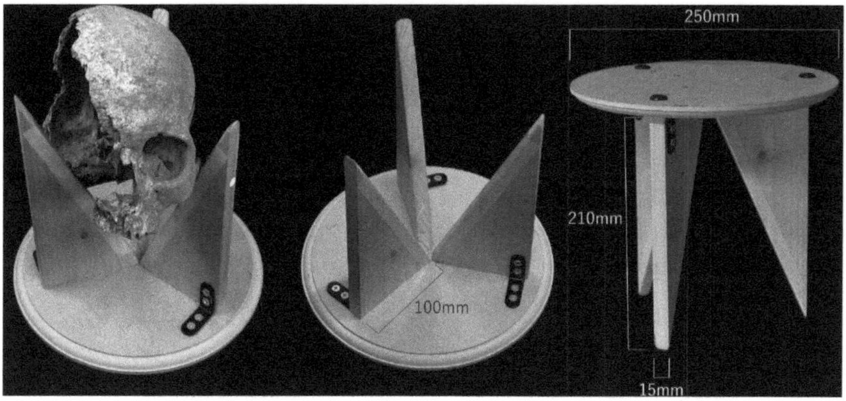

Figure 3.3 Wooden table to be used for fixation of the skull.

important to set or mount a cranium on a stable surface and to ensure that the arm of the digitizer can reach all desired landmarks. We designed a wooden device that can support the cranium using three points of contact. The detail of this wooden device can be seen in Fig. 3.3. The cranium is placed between the slope sides of the three right triangle–shaped walls standing on a round table, which firmly mounts the cranium. This upper portion of the opening is wider than the lower portion to allow for a cranium-sized object to be snugly held by the upper portion of the triangles. Smaller objects, such as bone fragments or the mandible, can be supported by the lower portion of the triangles. This device uses vinyl tape to cover the edges of the triangles where the cranium is in direct contact, which protects the cranial surface from abrasion and also provides gentle friction to prevent any slippage. Moreover, three buttons are placed on the backside of the round base. The buttons on the backside are in direct contact with the table (ground plane) and prevent any wobbling during landmark recording.

All of the techniques described in this section require consultation and permission granted by the skeletal collection curator. It is important to describe data collection techniques in detail when applying to visit a research collection and writing a research proposal.

Detecting abnormal value during measurements

Although an experienced researcher is able to recognize measurement errors during acquisition of linear measurements, it is difficult to catch errors during the recording process of coordinate data. If a researcher does not notice that the bone has moved during recording, or records a landmark in the wrong location, these errors will not be identified until the data are uploaded into a computer program for processing and will influence any future analyses significantly. To prevent this, researchers should record every skull twice or more if time permits or researchers should carry out an intra-observer error study on a subset of skulls. However, most researchers will not have time to measure each bone several times if the collection contains hundreds or even thousands of crania and depends on what research agenda the researchers have.

Process of mirror reversing of defective data acquired from broken crania

The 3D landmark data acquisition process requires sequential data collection, that is, landmarks recorded in the same order on all crania that are to be used in an analysis. Typically, only the well-preserved crania tend to be selected for data collection. However, when working with archaeological human remains, many crania may be fragmentary or poorly preserved. As a cranium is a symmetrical object, unilateral landmarks exist in the midsagittal plane, and bilateral points exist everywhere else. When one side of a skull is lost due to damage or poor preservation and coordinate data cannot be captured, the partners of bilateral landmarks can be mirrored and computed by inverting the mirror point on the normal (undamaged) side with respect to the midsagittal plane. The complemented landmarks can be used for analysis, although not for analyses of bilateral asymmetry. Such processing may be useful for analyses using fragile Japanese crania (Ohno et al., 2016). The procedures that compute missing coordinate data and create bilaterally symmetric coordinate data of a cranium are shown in the following. The concept of mirror image reversal is referred to by Ogihara et al. (2006).

1. The centroids of existing bilateral points are used in conjunction with any preserved midsagittal points to establish a midsagittal plane. The centroids of $(x1, y1, z1)$ and $(x2, y2, z2)$ on the 3D space are obtained by the following formula: $\{(x1+x2)/2, (y1+y2)/2, (z1+z2)/2\}$
2. These midpoints and the points on the midsagittal plane do not necessarily all ride on the same plane because the cranium is not perfectly symmetrical in nature. Therefore, a plane that minimizes the sum of squares of distances from all these midpoints is calculated by the method of least squares, and this plane is defined as a midsagittal plane. The

distance from a certain point *(x0, y0, z0)* to the plane $ax + by + cz + 1 = 0$ can be defined from the formula of the distance between the point and the plane as follows:

$$\frac{|ax_0 + by_0 + cz_0 + 1|}{\sqrt{a^2 + b^2 + c^2}}$$

The sum of squares of the distances from the *n* points can be expressed as "*S*" as follows:

$$S = \sum_{i=1}^{n} \frac{|axi + byi + czi + 1|^2}{a^2 + b^2 + c^2}$$

Then, find *a, b, c* that minimizes the "*S*." Here, since *xi, yi, zi* are constants, *S* can be regarded as a function of *a, b, c* and can be shown as follows:

$$S(a, b, c) = \sum_{i=1}^{n} \frac{|axi + byi + czi + 1|^2}{a^2 + b^2 + c^2}$$

If *b* and *c* are fixed, *S* becomes a quadratic function of *a*. Similarly, if *a* and *c* are constants, *S* becomes a quadratic function of *b*, and if *a* and *b* are constants, *S* is a quadratic function of *c*, so partial derivatives with *a, b, c* of 0, then finds the extremum. Since *xi, yi, zi* are constants, the following three simultaneous equations are solved.

$$\frac{\partial s}{\partial a} = 2x_i^2 a + 2x_i y_i b + 2z_i x_i c + 2x_i = 0$$

$$\frac{\partial s}{\partial b} = 2x_i^2 b + 2x_i y_i a + 2y_i z_i c + 2y_i = 0$$

$$\frac{\partial s}{\partial c} = 2z_i^2 c + 2z_i x_i a + 2y_i z_i b + 2z_i = 0$$

3. The coordinate of one of the bilateral landmarks is inverted with respect to the midsagittal plane determined in **2**.
4. If the corresponding landmark is ahead of the reversed point, then the centroid between that point and the inverted coordinate is determined. If the corresponding marker point is absent, then use the inverted coordinate as it is.
5. The landmark coordinates calculated in **4** are inverted again with respect to the midsagittal plane.

According to Makishima and Ogihara (2009), the data reconstructed landmark coordinates extracted from the cranium, which are strictly asymmetric, and symmetrically reconstructed landmarks are the results of multivariate analysis based on the cranial measurement value of the conventional scalar quantity.

Conclusion

In this chapter, we summarize what researchers need to be cautious of in 3D data acquisition and interlandmark measurements of crania with poor preservation. Archaeological human bones in Japan are generally not well preserved due to the acidic soil. Therefore, various devices are required for 3D measurements in using the contact type of digitizer. The soft-core pencil and the kneaded eraser are useful for marking landmarks to handle specimens carefully, and in some cases, peelable seals can be substituted. Because the research of archaeological skeletal remains will keep contributing to human knowledge in the future, it is also one of the responsibilities of the museum to care for the materials for posterity and to prevent further deterioration of them. It is natural that careful handling be requested from the curator; therefore, negotiation is important. At the same time, it is important for researchers to stick to the accuracy of data and the sample size among various constraints. In this chapter, we also introduced a table to fix crania to prevent measurement errors. The table can support the bone in various orientations, and it is also effective for partial bones and weak bones. We also encouraged multiple measurements per individual to check for errors if time permits.

It is challenging to increase the sample size in research using fragmentary archaeological human bones. In addition to the mirror image inversion described above, there are some cases where one wants to perform analyses of certain parts of the morphology (e.g., parts related to chewing stress). These methods contribute to making available specimens with few residual parts and increasing the sample size, in addition to allowing a focus on more important morphological changes. On the other hand, it is better to set a lot of landmarks that represent the whole cranium at the time of measurement (if time permits) and acquire the data. This may lead to the discovery of a previously unknown covariation between morphological variations. In this chapter, we have addressed some but not all of the issues we have experienced, from creative efforts and methods for 3D data acquisition to working with administrators and curators concerning careful handling of the fragile human skeletal remains. Researchers may encounter further situations, which are not described here. As better methods are developed, they should be shared.

References

Baba, H., Narasaki, S., 1991. Minatogawa Man, the oldest type of modern Homo sapiens in East Asia. The Quaternary Research 30, 221–230.

Bookstein, F.L., 1991. Morphometric Tools for Landmark Data: Geometry and Biology. Cambridge University Press, Cambridge [England]. New York.

Brothwell, D.R., 1981. Digging up Bones. Cornel University Press, Ithaca.

Makishima, H., Ogihara, N., 2009. Three-dimensional geometric morphometric study of craniofacial variations in Jomon populations. Anthropological Science 117, 11–21 in Japanese.

Matsu'ura, S., Kondo, M., 2011. Relative chronology of the Minatogawa and the Upper Minatogawa series of human remains from Okinawa Island, Japan. Anthropological Science 119, 173–182.

Miwa, F., 1958. Agronomical tests of the strata producing human skeletons. Journal of the Anthropological Society of Nippon 66, 197–201 in Japanese with English summary.

Nakagawa, R., Doi, N., Nishioka, Y., Nunami, S., Yamauchi, H., Fujita, M., Yamazaki, S., Yamamoto, M., Katagiri, C., Mukai, H., Matsuzaki, H., Gakuhari, T., Takigami, M., Yoneda, M., 2010. Pleistocene human remains from shiraho-saonetabaru cave on Ishigaki island, Okinawa, Japan, and their radiocarbon dating. Anthropological Science 118 (3), 173–183.

Nakahashi, T., Nagai, M., 1989. Preservation of human bone in prehistoric and historic sites of Western Japan. Asian Perspectives 27, 15–27.

Ogihara, N., Nakatsukasa, M., Nakano, Y., Ishida, H., 2006. Computerized restoration of nonhomogeneous deformation of a fossil cranium based on bilateral symmetry. American Journal of Physical Anthropology 130, 1–9.

Ohno, K., Kawakubo, Y., Kuraoka, A., 2016. Re-evaluation of temporal changes in alveolar protrusion in Japan according to two newly introduced craniometric angles. Anthropological Science 124, 63–72.

Slice, D.E., Bookstein, F.L., Rolfe, F.J., 2008. A Glossary for Geometric Morphometrics Web Site. http://life.bio.sunysb.edu/morph.

CHAPTER FOUR

Landmark and semilandmark data collection using digitizers and data processing

Beatrix Dudzik
Department of Anatomy, DeBusk College of Osteopathic Medicine, Lincoln Memorial University, Harrogate, TN, The United States of America

Introduction

The utility of geometric morphometric (GM) approaches is significant compared with traditional morphometric analyses using two-dimensional metric data. The analysis of landmark data in three dimensions allows for visualization of similarities and/or differences of the entire specimen that has been recorded, rather than just isolated dimensions of metric differences, and thus variation can be assessed in various dimensions (Marcus and Corti, 1996). Geometric morphometric analyses have become increasingly useful for studies of skeletal anatomy, including craniofacial shape, description of muscle attachments, sexual dimorphism, etc. Recently, researchers have incorporated coordinate data and GM approaches to investigate craniofacial morphology in an effort to ascertain shape differences among groups to examine population history and to improve ancestry estimation techniques for practitioners (Humphries et al., 2015; Kimmerle et al., 2008; Urbanová and Ross, 2016).

This chapter is devoted to describing data collection protocol to include commonly used approaches for coordinate data collection of physical specimens between single and multiple observers.

- This chapter will describe how data acquisition is carried out on physical models using direct digitizers (e.g., Microscribe) and how data can be stored for later analysis.
- It will summarize some of the approaches and software used to preprocess direct digitizer landmark data to allow for statistical analysis.
- Additionally, statistical analyses available that can perform comparisons and predictions will be described.

3D Data Acquisition for Bioarchaeology, Forensic Anthropology, and Archaeology
ISBN: 978-0-12-815309-3
https://doi.org/10.1016/B978-0-12-815309-3.00004-8

- This section discusses choosing the best alignment method for the collected data based on various circumstances.

Data collection procedures

Manual collection of three-dimensional data can be carried out using digitizing equipment. Digitizers are small machines that are connected to a computer, which provide a convenient approach that is portable, affordable, and user-friendly. A moveable stylus and point collection button are used to collect Cartesian coordinates (the x, y, and z position) at each designated landmark (Fig. 4.1). The user decides which landmarks are to be collected. Free software programs are available, such as 3Skull, which has preprogrammed landmark prompts and can automatically export recorded x, y, and z values to an Excel or .txt file (Ousley, 2004). If the user does not use data collection software with landmark prompts, any combination or creation of new landmarks can be used. Brand-specific software is typically provided with digitizer models that allow the user to populate an Excel file with Cartesian coordinates, resulting in an x, y, and z column, with each row representing the order of landmarks recorded. If the user desires to

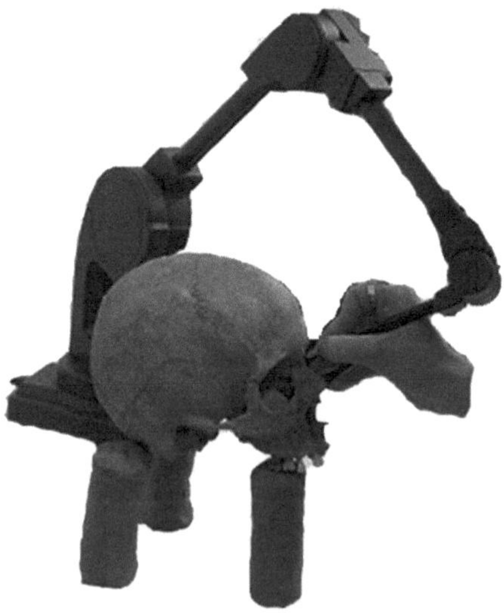

Figure 4.1 Mechanical collection of landmark data, using a digitizer, which is connected to a computer to record positional information electronically. *From Dudzik, Beatrix, "Investigating Cranial Variation in Japanese Populations Using Geometric Morphometrics." PhD diss., University of Tennessee, 2015. https://trace.tennessee.edu/utk_graddiss/3576.*

implement a landmark of his or her own creation, or a specific combination of variables, care must be used to record the landmarks in the exact order on each specimen, as the output coordinate data will not have an associated landmark name, just a designated value for all three dimensions. Commonly, users will use a combination of cranial landmarks defined by W.W. Howells, generally referred to as "Howells' definitions." These landmarks are a revised definition set based on Martin's (1914) publication, which built on the work of Morton and Broca (Martin, 1914), and commonly taken cranial landmarks are summarized in Table 4.1.

The positional values that are recorded can then be used in a three-dimensional analysis or be converted into interlandmark distances, or the distance between the averages in position of the x, y, and z value between two landmarks indicated by the user.

Data preprocessing

Before comparison or any statistical analyses can be carried out on a coordinate data set, the landmarks must be converted into a standardized plane, so that homologous points of different observations can be compared with one another. Typically, this preprocessing involves superimposition and translation of all recorded landmarks onto a common coordinate system.

Procrustes superimposition is a least squares method that estimates the parameters for location and orientation that minimize the sum of squared distances between corresponding points on two configurations (Rohlf and Slice, 1990; Slice, 2007). Generalized Procrustes analysis (GPA) is a widely used method that is typically the first step in coordinate data preprocessing. GPA is also commonly referred to as a Procrustes fit, least squares fitting, and/or Procrustes superimposition. A GPA differs only slightly from other Procrustes fit approaches in that after translation, scaling, and rotation, an iterative average is taken to calculate the mean of each specimen and is continued until there is no significant change from iteration to iteration. The free software package MorphoJ uses a full Procrustes fit, which uses orthogonal projection and is a slightly more robust approach that puts less weight on outlier landmarks when performing the fit (Dryden and Mardia, 1998).

This approach combines homologous landmarks of all recorded specimens to translate and rotate configurations so that the sum of squared distances across all landmarks is minimized, and each configuration is scaled to a common size (Fig. 4.2). Centroid size (center of a form) is calculated

Table 4.1 Commonly used cranial landmarks.

Landmark	Definition	Abbreviation
Alare (bilateral)	Instrumentally determined as the most lateral points on the nasal aperture in a transverse plane.	AL
Asterion (bilateral)	Intersection of the temporal, parietal and occipital bone.	AST
Basion (unilateral)	Intersection of the midsagittal plane with the most anterior portion of the foramen magnum.	BAS
Bregma (unilateral)	The ectocranial midline point where the coronal and sagittal sutures intersect.	BRG
Dacryon (bilateral)	The apex of the lacrimal fossa.	DAC
Ectoconchion (bilateral)	The most anterior point on the lateral border and its intersection with a bisection line of the orbit on the long axis.	ECT
Euryon (bilateral)	Instrumentally determined ectocranial points on opposite sides of the skull that form the termini of the line of greatest cranial breadth.	EUR
Frontomalare anterior (bilateral)	The most anterior point on the frontomalar suture.	FM:A
Frontomalare (bilateral) temporale	The most laterally positioned point on the frontomalar suture.	FMT
Frontotemporale (bilateral)	The point where the temporal line reaches its most anteromedial position on the frontal.	F
Glabella (unilateral)	Midline protrusion in the supraorbital region.	GLB
Inferior point, nasal aperture (bilateral)	Lowest point on border of nasal aperture.	NIL
Lambda (unilateral)	Intersection of the sagittal and lambdoidal sutures, at the apex of occipital bone.	LAM
Nasion (unilateral)	The point of intersection between the nasofrontal suture on the frontal.	NAS
Opisthion (unilateral)	The inferior edge of the posterior border of the foramen magnum in the midline.	OS

Table 4.1 Commonly used cranial landmarks.—cont'd

Landmark	Definition	Abbreviation
Opisthocranion (unilateral)	Instrumentally determined most posterior point of the skull not on the external occipital protuberance.	O
Prosthion (unilateral)	The most anterior point on the midline on the alveolar process.	PRS
Radiculare (bilateral)	The point on the lateral aspect of the root of the zygomatic process at the deepest incurvature.	RA
Subspinale (unilateral)	Deepest point from lateral view below anterior nasal spine.	SSP
Zygion (bilateral)	The most laterally positioned point on the zygomatic arches. The position of zygion is defined from the measurement of bizygomatic breadth.	ZY
Zygoorbitale (bilateral)	Intersection of the orbital margin and the zygomaxillary suture.	ZO

Adapted from Martin and Knussmann (1988), Howells, (1973), Langley et al., (2016).

by summing all the squared distances and then taking the square root of that sum (Zelditch et al., 2004). Centroid size will then be set to one, which will remove isometric size. Centroid size can also be calculated based on inter-landmark distances. Centroid size is the one measure of size that is

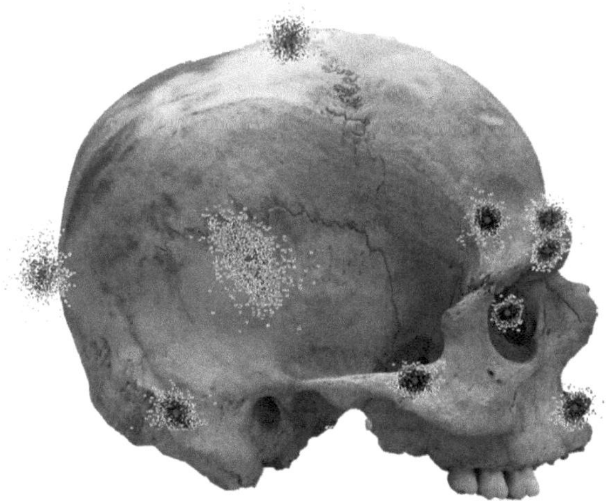

Figure 4.2 Example of a Procrustes fit, showing the cluster of landmarks of each digitized observation, distributed around a centroid.

independent of shape as it is orthogonal. However, independence of size by calculation of group centroids is only valid if scaling (changes in size) does not affect the shape. If size is not isometric and proportions within a form change when size variables are disrupted, then size cannot be considered orthogonal and/or independent of shape.

Following a Procrustes superimposition, the coordinates are representative of shape coordinates, which can be analyzed using statistical methods. However, these coordinates do not function in Euclidean space, which can be thought of as a two-dimensional plane. Thus, the new coordinates need to be projected onto a curved space that is more akin to a hemisphere. Statistical analyses are available that can approximate the curved space represented by the Procrustes shape coordinates.

Discrete landmark statistical analysis

Statistical analysis of Cartesian coordinates of cranial landmarks has been shown to be a viable means of investigating biological relationships and distances between human populations. Mckeown and Jantz (2005) evaluated the use of craniometric versus coordinate data. These methods showed high distances among the Sully site of the Arikara, where previous craniometric analysis did not show the same divergence. It is shown that the coordinate data analysis encompasses more phenotypic variation not present in the craniometric data. Geometric morphometric software packages allows for projection of these coordinates into a curved space that approximates a Euclidean space so that multivariate (linear) statistical analysis can be performed.

To analyze three-dimensional data using linear distance-based methods, such as Euclidean distance-matrix analysis, comparison of the linear distances that connect landmarks in one form to the interlandmark distances of another form is performed. Linear distances are written as a form matrix, rather than a matrix of coordinate data, and thus contain the distances between landmarks of a form (Richtsmeier et al., 2005). Each linear distance of different forms can be compared as a ratio or an absolute difference.

Principal component analysis and analysis of variance

After performing a Procrustes fit, a new data set of Procrustes coordinates will be produced, which transfers the raw coordinates onto a common coordinate system among samples and allows for statistical analysis of the shape variables contained within the data.

Generally, most analyses start with an exploratory step that involves principal component analysis (PCA) using the Procrustes coordinates. PCA is a multivariate statistical method that rotates and groups data by variable expression along axes, referred to as principal components. PCA will maximize the within sample variance of a linear combination of variables, which is effectively the opposite of discriminant function analysis. As there is no prior group assignment, variance representative of the entire sample is used.

Results of PCA will result in axes (dimensions) that can be visualized to assess biological variation. The first two axes will typically express the majority of variation observed among groups of observations in a sample. PCA is performed on the fitted coordinates, which produces principal component scores that can be statistically analyzed to assess patterns of group variation.

Unlike PCA on linear variables, which rotates the data using a correlation matrix, PCA in geometric morphometrics uses the variance-covariance matrix to build the principal components.

Analysis of variance can additionally be performed on Procrustes data sets to assess patterns of asymmetry. Procrustes ANOVA also can be used to evaluate inter- and/or intraobserver error of coordinate data sets (Klingenberg and McIntyre, 1998 and by Klingenberg et al., 2002).

Regression approaches

Traditional multivariate regression approaches can be used to assess influencing factors on shape, where shape is the dependent variable. Regression is often used to look at measures of allometry or factors influencing shape and size during growth and can be applied to three-dimensional coordinate data (Bookstein, 1991; Mitteroecker and Gunz, 2009).

Discriminant function and canonical variate analysis

GPA will produce a new data set made up of Procrustes coordinates that are representative of an average shape that is scaled to a common size. Therefore, the Procrustes coordinates can be thought of as a shape-only representation of the x, y, and z dimension for each of the landmarks included. The new shape coordinate data set can be used in discriminant function analysis (DFA) or canonical variate analysis (CVA) to assess group structure in three or more subsets.

Discriminant function analysis or linear discriminant analysis is a multivariate statistical approach, which uses a linear combination of the variables included in an analysis to reach maximum separation between included groups in a study (Pietrusewsky, 2000; Tatsuoka, 1970). A combination of variables can be selected with a stepwise algorithm, which will in turn provide a discriminant function between each combination of samples. If an analysis examines more than two groups, this approach is referred to as canonical variate analysis, as the functions are now called canonical variates. Observations in a sample are allotted a discriminant function score that can be plotted along axes for visual representation of single observations, group centroids, and the relationship between samples.

Unlike PCA, DFA and CVA assume group or subset relationship is a priori known, which allows the user to assess biological shape relationships among the defined groups. If using CVA for group membership prediction purposes, it is important to note that even cases that do not belong to the reference groups included will be allocated, even if the fit is poor.

Semilandmark analysis

In addition to recording singular landmarks, semilandmarks can also be recorded. Semilandmarks are representative of curves and outlines, where the stylus is gently dragged across a surface and records a coordinate value at set intervals (such as recording a point every 0.5 mm). Semilandmark coordinate data analysis is arguably more complex than discrete landmarks, as there are not defined, homologous landmark locations between specimens, but rather a defined start and stop point, and the number of semi- or sliding landmarks in between these points will depend on the size and shape of the curve or outline being recorded (Mitteroecker et al., 2012). Bookstein (1982, 1991) defines semi- or sliding landmarks as based on thin-plate spline, an interpolation technique that can help visualize shape differences across a transformation grid. Superimposition of semilandmarks of a homologous structure of specimens allows for the exportation of coordinate data, which can be analyzed using standard approaches as described with discrete landmarks (Mitteroecker et al., 2012).

Semilandmark algorithms identify coordinates located perpendicular to the outline or curvature being recorded and allow the equidistant points to slide along the curved trajectory until differences between observations are minimized and an average shape variable can be identified. Mitteroecker and Gunz (2009) describe two versions of the semilandmark algorithm, which differ in the iterative processes used to arrive at comparable outlines of homologous outlines. The two approaches will either iteratively reduce shape differences among observations or smooth out the range of deformations among the various outlines observed (Sheets et al., 2004; Webster and Sheets, 2010).

Fourier analysis is also often used to analyze shape outlines and uses a combination of sine and cosine functions, or harmonics, to mathematically describe the shape of the recorded object. Fourier coefficients represent the variables, or shape, of the outline that are responsible for the most variation among samples (Kaesler, 1997).

Outliers

Detection of outliers can also be performed in software packages, such as MorphoJ, which allows for a visual display of variation exhibited at each landmark for each specimen. This approach allows for the detection of landmarks that could have been recorded incorrectly (such as swapping landmarks) and allows for removal from the dataset if necessary. Observation of principal component plots of observations is also a common way to identify extreme outliers.

Alignment

Two commonly used methods of alignment include alignment by principal axes and alignment by landmark. The principal axes method is used when the digitized object exhibits symmetry and will align along a plane of symmetry. Alignment by landmark allows selection of specific landmarks so that the angle of object axis can be adjusted by the researcher by selecting which landmark to align with.

Geometric morphometric analysis caveats

von Cramon-Taubadel et al. (2007) outlines the problems of inter/intra-observer error in geometric morphometrics and state that when raw configurations are superimposed using a least squares criterion (generalized Procrustes, etc.), the variance of individual landmarks is smeared out over all landmarks, which can be detrimental to studies that assess error or asymmetry, as the variance of essential landmarks can be distributed/allocated to other landmarks, referred to as "the Pinnochio effect." Despite these caveats, research has shown that using GM approaches can provide more insight into biological variability among samples. For example, Ross et al. (1999) were able to better describe where morphological variability exists among comparisons of American White and Black cranial samples.

Conclusions

The analysis of landmark data in three dimensions allows for visualization of similarities and/or differences of the specimen in question, rather than just isolated dimensions of metric differences, and thus variation can be assessed in several dimensions simultaneously. Interlandmark distances have additionally been shown to more accurately estimate population affinity than standard cranial measurements (Spradley and Jantz, 2016). As geometric morphometric software, new statistical approaches, and public databases such as 3D-ID (Slice and Ross, 2009) become more readily available, undoubtedly interesting patterns of morphology and the predictive power of shape analysis will continue to be revealed through the collection and analysis of coordinate data.

References

Bookstein, F.L., 1982. Foundations of morphometrics. Annual Review of Ecology and Systematics 13 (1), 451–470.
Bookstein, F.L., 1991. Morphological Tools for Landmark Data; Geometry and Biology. Cambridge University Press.
Dryden, I.L., Mardia, K.V., 1998. Statistical Analysis of Shape. Wiley.
Howells, W.W., 1973. Cranial variation in man: a study by multivariate analysis of patterns of difference among recent human populations. Peabody Museum of Archaeology and Ethnology, Harvard University.
Humphries, A.L., et al., 2015. A geometric morphometric study of regional craniofacial variation in Mexico. International Journal of Osteoarchaeology 25 (6), 795–804.
Kaesler, Roger L., 1997. Phase angles, harmonic distance, and the analysis of form. Fourier descriptors and their applications in biology 106, 125.
Kimmerle, E.H., Ross, A., Slice, D., 2008. Sexual dimorphism in America: geometric morphometric analysis of the craniofacial region. Journal of Forensic Sciences 53 (1), 54–57.
Klingenberg, C.P., Barluenga, M., Meyer, A., 2002. Shape analysis of symmetric structures: quantifying variation among individuals and asymmetry. Evolution 56 (10), 1909–1920.
Klingenberg, C.P., McIntyre, G.S., 1998. Geometric morphometrics of developmental instability: analyzing patterns of fluctuating asymmetry with Procrustes methods. Evolution 52 (5), 1363–1375.
Langley, N.R., Jantz, L.M., Ousley, S.D., Jantz, R.L., Milner, G., 2016. Data collection procedures for forensic skeletal material 2.0. University of Tennessee and Lincoln Memorial University.
Marcus, L.F., Corti, M., 1996. Overview of the new, or geometric morphometrics. In: Advances in Morphometrics. Springer, pp. 1–13.
Martin, R., Knussman, R., 1988. Anthropologie. Handbuch der vergleichenden Biologie des Menschen. Band I, Wesen und Methoden der Anthropologie. Gustav Fischer Verlag: Stuttgart.
Martin, R., 1914. Lehrbuch der Anthropologie in systematischer Darstellung mit besonderer Berücksichtigung der anthropologischen Methoden. Gustav Fischer, Jena.

McKeown, A.H., Jantz, R.L., 2005. Comparison of coordinate and craniometric data for biological distance studies. In: Modern Morphometrics in Physical Anthropology. Springer, pp. 215–230.
Mitteroecker, P., Gunz, P., 2009. Advances in geometric morphometrics. Evolutionary Biology 36 (2), 235–247.
Mitteroecker, P., et al., 2012. How to explore morphological integration in human evolution and development? Evolutionary Biology 39 (4), 536–553.
Ousley, S.D., 2004. 3Skull Computer Program. Version 2.
Pietrusewsky, M., 2000. Metric Analysis of Skeletal Remains: Methods and Applications. Biological Anthropology of the Human Skeleton. Wiley-Liss, New York, pp. 375–415.
Richtsmeier, J.T., Lele, S.R., Cole III, T.M., 2005. Landmark morphometrics and the analysis of variation. Variations: A central concept in biology 49–69.
Rohlf, F.J., Slice, D., 1990. Extensions of the Procrustes method for the optimal superimposition of landmarks. Systematic Biology 39 (1), 40–59.
Ross, A.H., McKeown, A.H., Konigsberg, L.W., 1999. Allocation of crania to groups via the "new morphometry". Journal of Forensic Sciences 44, 584–587.
Sheets, H.D., Kim, K., Mitchell, C.E., 2004. A combined landmark and outline-based approach to ontogenetic shape change in the Ordovician trilobite Triarthrus becki. In: Morphometrics. Springer, pp. 67–82.
Slice, D.E., 2007. Geometric morphometrics. Annual Review of Anthropology 36, 261–281.
Slice, D.E., Ross, A.H., 2009. 3D-ID: Geometric Morphometric Classification of Crania for Forensic Scientists: Version.
Spradley, K.M., Jantz, R.L., 2016. Ancestry estimation in forensic anthropology: geometric morphometric versus standard and nonstandard interlandmark distances. Journal of Forensic Sciences 61 (4), 892–897.
Tatsuoka, M.M., 1970. Discriminant Analysis: The Study of Group Differences: Inst. For Personality and Ability Testing.
Urbanová, P., Ross, A.H., 2016. Advanced methods in 3-D craniofacial morphological analysis. In: Biological Distance Analysis. Elsevier, pp. 61–90.
von Cramon-Taubadel, N., Frazier, B.C., Lahr, M.M., 2007. The problem of assessing landmark error in geometric morphometrics: theory, methods, and modifications. American Journal of Physical Anthropology 134 (1), 24.
Webster, M.A.R.K., Sheets, H.D., 2010. A practical introduction to landmark-based geometric morphometrics. Paleontological Society Papers 16, 163–188.
Zelditch, M.L., Lundrigan, B.L., Garland, T., 2004. Developmental regulation of skull morphology. I. Ontogenetic dynamics of variance. Evolution and Development 6 (3), 194–206.

CHAPTER FIVE

Landmark and semilandmark data collection using 3D virtual model and data processing

Mary-Margaret Murphy
Department of Anthropology, The University of Montana, Missoula, MT, The United States of America

Introduction

Three-dimensional (3D) landmark data collected with a digitizer has been covered in the previous chapter. This type of data collection requires physical access to materials. Both materials and access can be in very short supply and neither can be considered permanent. Materials can degrade under storage conditions, which might add further insult to whatever level of taphonomic preservation might have existed for biological materials or artifacts. Access depends on the goodwill of property owners, governments at all levels, and institutions—and even after careful cultivation, time may degrade these as well.

W.W. Howells developed a large collection of human cranial measurements, which are still referenced today. The Howell's data collections are measurements of populations from specific moments in time. The populations measured have undergone in situ changes that reflect health and environment. Although the data are rich with metrics, measuring this way still reduces the individual to a few measurements. Comparatively, digitized data are dimensionally advanced over two-dimensional (2D) metrics; however, it is still a reductive method of data collection, simplifying the sample unit into a series of homologous landmarks and/or curves. Areas lacking in homologous landmarks are poorly represented by this simplification (Howells, 1973, 1996; Klingenberg, 2010).

Human observation and landmark recording of digital models has a variable margin of error that can be influenced by differences in visual presentation that could vary with hardware, software, and experience. These potential sources of variability contribute to the differences between handling actual skeletal material and remote study. Thus far, the accepted

3D Data Acquisition for Bioarchaeology, Forensic Anthropology, and Archaeology
ISBN: 978-0-12-815309-3
https://doi.org/10.1016/B978-0-12-815309-3.00005-X

assumption is that the error from digital capture methods is mathematically small, but differences could increase in magnitude at every stage between capture and final model (Ross and Williams, 2008; Smith and Strait, 2008; Sholts et al., 2010).

Landmark-type considerations—example

Landmark type—based on the *location or definition* of an individual landmark point—is expected to correspond to degrees of variation between observations, sample units, or whole samples. The type can be determined by the characteristics of the landmark location. A landmark based on a suture intersection or on a structure would be classified as Type I, with the exception of extremal structures. A landmark on the most projecting point of a bone would be considered an extremal landmark and would be a Type II landmark. Type III landmarks are defined in terms of a structural or geometric dependency. Variation in the dependency—such as working orientation—would result in variations in the terminal definition of the landmark location. Between individuals and between observations would result in coordinate values with higher variation and lower congruence in a sample. For an Euclidean distance matrix analysis (EDMA), such as interlandmark distance (ILD), a highly variable landmark is a terminal point of an ILD, will have an influence on the ILD variation for all distances that include the Type III landmark (Ross and Williams, 2008). This can be significant but is more likely to create noise in the data. At the same landmark, an experienced observer would be expected to show consistency in selection of a landmark even in the case of a highly variable landmark. If that consistency prevents the conclusion of statistically significant differences, then such a variable landmark would not contribute to a rejection of the null hypothesis (Shearer et al., 2017).

The subject of alignment has been discussed in previous chapters and will be further highlighted in this chapter with regard to the 3D models and 3D landmark sample data from both sources. Should alignment to a defined coordinate space be ignored or applied inconsistently, the results would fall under the argument by Lele and Richtsmeier (2001) as discussed in Ch. 2. As spatial dimensionality increases, so does the likelihood of spatial error. The methods of Ross and Williams (2008) and Ercan et al. (2008) were influenced by the concerns of this type of error and are clear about the importance of careful consideration of alignment. Without a system to maintain consistency, spatial error can become a noise signal through analytical data that risk spurious conclusions.

If a landmark coordinate cannot be placed because it cannot connect to the observed surface, it will impact the overall accuracy of the landmark sample or the sample size if it results in a false missing point. During landmark selection, several nonmanifold models for both processing resolutions were found to have defects that had a slight impact on the observation and selection of landmarks. The defects were found to be nonincident faces that created defective geometry and caused the selected coordinate of a point to appear to exist below the surface to the crania. To solve this kind of data problem, it may be necessary to revisit the mesh processing steps.

Often, a nonmanifold model is larger in computational size than the manifold counterpart. This can be caused by mesh density or redundant data. The observable results could be irregular face or vertex normals, or non-incident faces (Hoppe et al., 1993). This bears repeating at this stage due to the effect it can have during the landmark coordinate selection process.

Landmark selection

Data quality and availability

Selecting the landmarks that will be used in an analysis is important at the point of data planning as well as for data processing. It is the process of determination of desired or necessary landmarks for a robust analysis. Consider not only the research questions you have but also the preservation and quality of the sample. For example, the tiny and thin bones of the nasal area would be a poor choice for a historic sample unless preservation is exceptional.

Stability must also be considered. In this context, *stability* refers to structures being present in high frequency and exhibiting low frequency of damage. Taphonomic damage is an important factor for the application of 3D research methods using historical specimens. These samples may be small and due to damage or deterioration have a very small number of stable structures. However, historical samples are the record of the moments and the eras of human history, and the study of such samples is important. One advantage to the use of 3D models is the ability to virtually reconstruct damage and deformation (Jantz et al., 2013; Schlager, 2017; Weinberg and Kolar, 2005).

The process of elimination based on the requirements determined above aids in choosing a final list of landmarks for the 3D digital data collection that well represent your sample. The landmarks that best represent the sample should be present on most individuals within the collection and remain after the application of processing to the mesh model. The selected landmarks characterize the primary global structures of the original objects.

Collecting landmark coordinates

Placement and recording of landmark points can be accomplished in a digital environment by any one of several available methods. Software designed for manipulation and rendering of 3D models includes functions for placing a reference point on a model and logging the location of that point relative to the 3D environment. For the purposes of the examples in this chapter, Stratovan Checkpoint software (Stratovan Corporation, Davis, CA) was selected. This software has advantages beyond the basic capabilities of placing landmarks and outputting to various formats. It was selected for having advanced viewing options (Fig. 5.1)—having simultaneous global 3D and transected views of the axial (anterior-posterior and lateral), coronal (superior-inferior and lateral), and sagittal (superior-inferior and anterior-posterior), and for being user-friendly.

Stratovan Checkpoint is commercial software that allows selection and placement of points, connected semilandmarks, patches, and landmark labels. Export of the collected landmark points is available in several file formats. For general versatility, the *.CSV (comma-separated values) have been used to export the landmark point coordinates from Stratovan Checkpoint software (Stratovan Corporation, Davis, CA).

Noncommercial software packages are also available to accomplish 3D landmark collection from mesh models. Cloudcompare (Girardeau-Montaut, 2014), Meshlab (Cignoni et al. 2008), and various packages of R (R Core

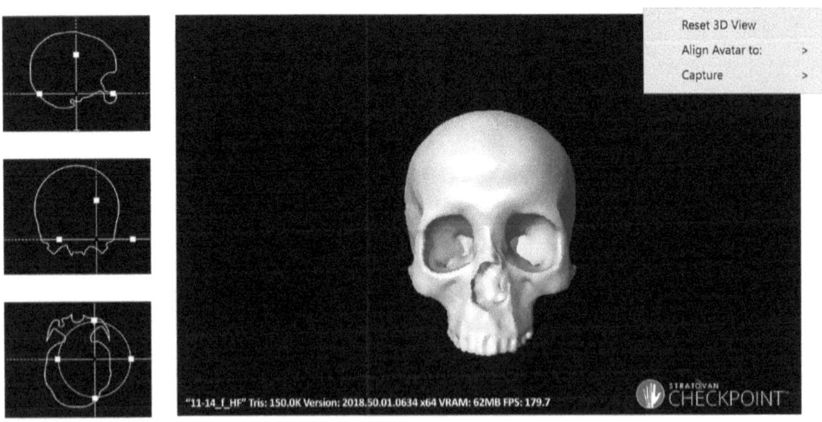

Figure 5.1 Stratovan checkpoint © surface tab. *From Stratovan Corporation. Stratovan Checkpoint [Software]. Version 2018.08.07. Aug 07, 2018. URL: https://www.stratovan.com/products/checkpoint. Used with permission from Stratovan Corporation.*

Team 2018) have this capability and are worth consideration. Stratovan Checkpoint is also based on an earlier software package - Landmark. That early version is still available, however the project has not been updated since 2007.

Landmark data processing

After coordinate landmark data have been collected, there are still treatments that can be applied to the data to improve layout such as the registration to a common origin and orienting coordinates to a particular direction in the virtual space. The coordinate data found in the chapter example were registered and oriented to put all data on common origin and orientation. Changes in scale can also be applied when the analytical interest justify it.

Missing data

Determine from the coordinate data the kind and frequency of missing data. If the specific coordinates are missing, define what overall proportion is that coordinate missing across the sample. It is also important to determine if the missing coordinates are the result of a sample factor such as damage, or a poor visualization of the landmark on the scan model.

Treatment of missing data

Missing data can be treated in a few different ways. This step should not be skipped over due to the necessity of complete data for several types of 3D analysis. Often the simplest method for the researcher is to allow software to replace the missing data by an imputation implementation that is provided internally. In this case, the method should be described in the software manual, which should be taken note of. In most cases, it would also be acceptable to replace missing coordinates with a sample average.

If a large proportion of a specific landmark is missing from a sample, then it should be considered for removal from further analysis. The point at which the proportion becomes large enough to practically remove for the data set has a lot to do with the number of landmarks and the size of the sample. A sample with a large number of landmarks per sample unit, as well as a sample with a small number of overall units, would be justified in most instances to remove a landmark that exhibits a significant proportion of missing data.

Alignment

Box 5.1 Sample data translation

Translation

Translation is the term applied to directional movement of data in a 3D space. The procedure is the same as described in Chapter 2; only the list of points is less dense. Translation can be accomplished in any direction by breaking down the Euclidean distance between the starting and ending point.

Rotation

Rotation of 3D landmark coordinates is complicated. Although the angle of rotation along any plan is the same for all coordinates, the distance that a coordinate moves during rotation is directly related to the distance from the origin of rotation. Just as two points on a record travel different distances in the same number or degrees of rotation. Following the record example, the x and y coordinates change as a result of the rotation. Rotation of 3D coordinates adds another rotational plane, and completion of the rotation will change the z coordinates and change either the x or y coordinates from the position determined by the first rotational plane.

Scale

Scaling of 3D objects can be thought of as analogous to a z-score of single-factored data. If shape is of greater interest than size between sample units, then the application of scale is justified (Fig. 5.2).

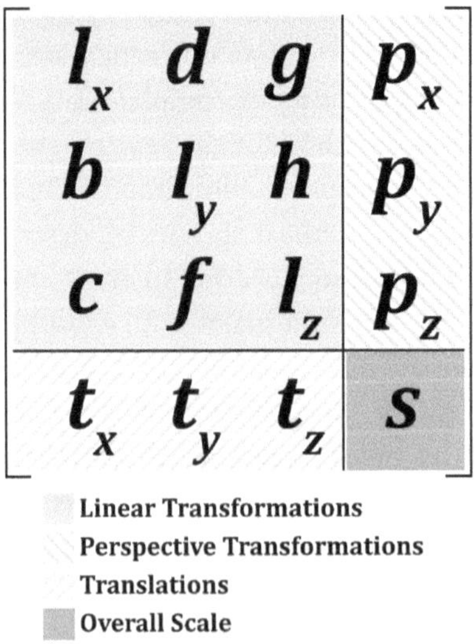

Figure 5.2 Translation matrix.

Box 5.2 Bookstein alignment

(Fig. 5.3) Bookstein alignment bases the origin, orientation, and unit scale on the landmarks of the sample. In the situation of the example data, Bookstein alignment was a functional solution because it was known that the only difference between the samples was the processing and the collection—a modified repeated collection sample. The greatest difficulty in using the Bookstein alignment is the limited number of software applications. It is available in Morpheus et al. (Slice, 2013).

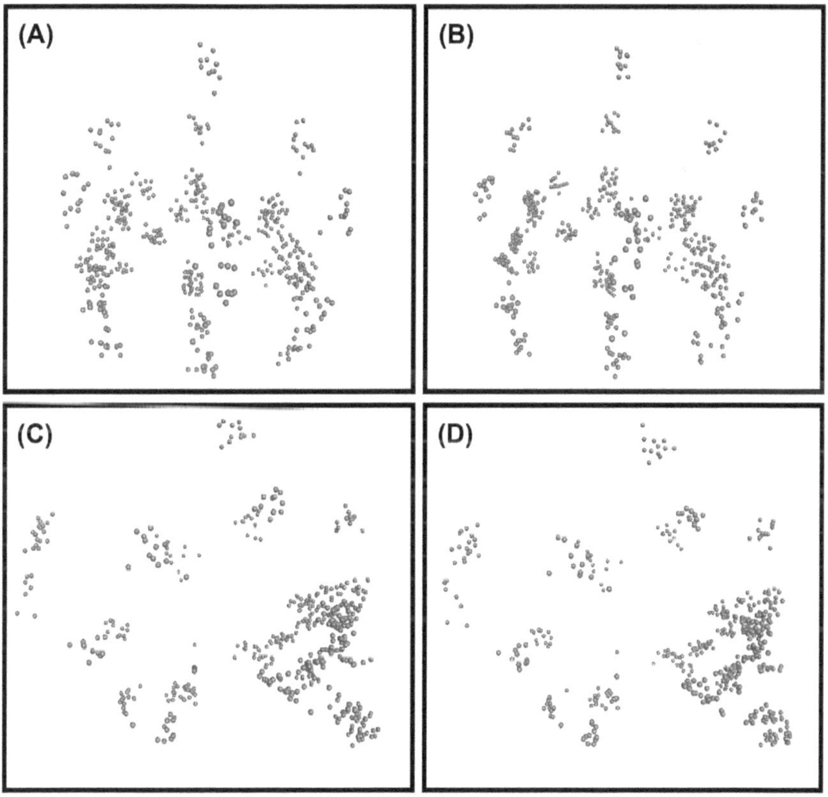

Figure 5.3 Stages of Bookstein alignment. (A) "raw" landmark point data. (B) scaled against the distance between two specified landmarks (left and right porion). (C) rotated to minimize the variation of the third specified landmark (zygoorbitale left). (D) translated to uniform alignment on Frankfurt Horizontal plane (y, & z of porions have a value of 0, y of zygoorbitale has a value of 0 for this arrangement - see Fig. 5.13 for the corrections applied to the sample data to conform to this particular coordinate system).

Box 5.3 Procrustes alignment

(Fig. 5.4) The Procrustes distance calculates a number that describes the minimal differences between two sets of coordinates. This can be between two real sample units or between sample units and a derived average of all samples. GPA and partial GPA (calculated without the scale factor) are used frequently.

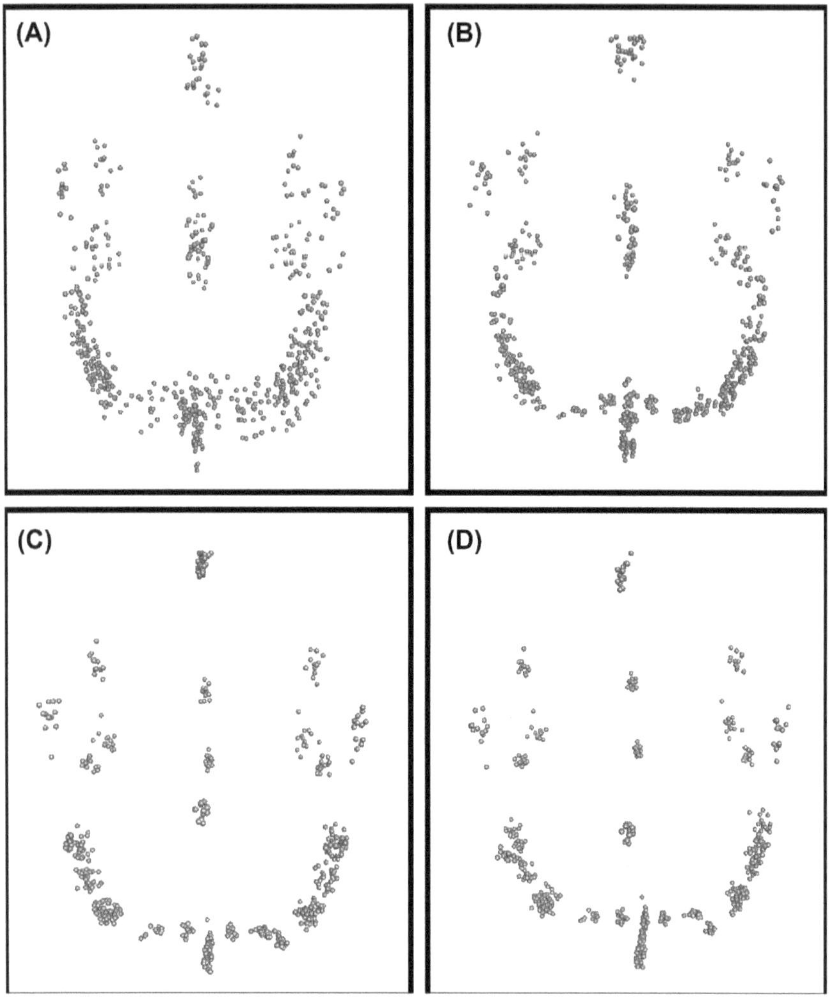

Figure 5.4 The stages of Procrustes aligment. (A) the "raw" landmark point data. (B) scaled landmark point data. (C) rotated landmark point data. (D) translated (linear movement) landmark point data. This method aligns the landmarks by an overall generalization.

In practice—landmark coordinate collection

Preparation for landmark coordinate data collection

Review the following items to evaluate the readiness of your sample mesh models for landmark coordinate collection.

Box 5.4 Landmark coordinate software

As the user, are you familiar with the software you want to use? For publication purposes, the software manual will become part of your bibliography, but typically these manuals are circumspect and may not contain the workflow and solutions your particular situation calls for. Having resources for troubleshooting beyond just the manual is always good. If you find yourself isolated from persons who can help you directly, find remote contacts, perhaps even chat groups of other users. It saves time to find these beforehand.

Box 5.5 Codebook

Before collecting landmark coordinate data, list and describe the sample in the codebook. To begin the process of collecting landmark coordinate data, prepare the following:

1. **Landmarks**—definitions and descriptions

   For cranial data, Table 5.1 and Fig. 5.10 indicate the listed and defined landmarks and show the landmark placement used in the Chapter

Table 5.1 Landmarks for 3D comparison.

	Abbreviation	Landmark	Type	Definition
1	prosH	Prosthion-Howells	II	Most anterior point of the midline interdental, between central incisors.
2	Ssp	Subspinale	II	Deepest point directly inferior to the projection of the nasal spine.
3	prosM	Prosthion-Martin	II	Most inferior point of the maxilla on the midline, between the central incisors.
4	Nas	Nasion	I	The intersection determined by the sutures between the frontal and nasal bones.
5	Glb	Glabella	III	Anterior projecting extrema of the midline of the frontal bone proximal to the orbital torus.

(Continued)

Table 5.1 Landmarks for 3D comparison.—cont'd

	Abbreviation	Landmark	Type	Definition
6	Spglb	Supraglabellare	III	Convex midline point superior to glabella on the midline of the frontal bone.
7	Brg	Bregma	I	Intersection of the coronal and sagittal sutures between the frontal and parietal bones.
8	Lam	Lambda	I	Intersection of the sagittal and lambdoidal sutures between the parietal and occipital bones.
9	opg	Opisthocranion (GOL)	III	Posterior extrema of the crania on the midline.
10	ops	Opisthion	II	Most posterior point of the foramen magnum on the midline.
11	bas	Basion	II	Most anterior point of the foramen magnum on the midline.
12	zygomr	Zygomaxilare R	III	Inferior extrema of the suture between the zygomatic and maxillary bones
13	jugr	Jugale R	II	Deepest point (anterior) of the transition between the frontal and zygomatic processes.
14	fmtr	Frontomalare temporale R	III	Posterior extrema of the suture between the frontal and maxillary bones.
15	fmar	Frontomalare anterior R	III	Anterior extrema of the suture between the frontal and maxillary bones.
16	ectr	Ectoconchion R	III	Most lateral point of the margin of the ocular orbit.
17	Zygoor	Zygoorbitale R	II	Location of the zygomaxillare suture crossing the margin of the ocular orbit and the inferior orbital plate.
18	dacr	Dacryon R	II	Alternate definitions place at the sutural intersection of the lacrimal, maxillary, and frontal bones or the apex of the lacrimal fossa. The definitions may be concurrent, or indeterminate depending on the individual.
19	dacl	Dacryon L	II	

Table 5.1 Landmarks for 3D comparison.—cont'd

	Abbreviation	Landmark	Type	Definition
20	Obhi	Lower orbital border L	III	The most inferior point of the margin of the ocular orbit.
21	Obhs	Upper orbital border L	III	The most superior point of the margin of the ocular orbit.
22	ectl	Ectoconchion L	III	Most lateral point of the margin of the ocular orbit.
23	Zygool	Zygoorbitale L	II	Location of the zygomaxillare suture crossing the margin of the ocular orbit and the inferior orbital plate.
24	fmal	Frontomalare anterior L	III	Anterior extrema of the suture between the frontal and maxillary bones.
25	fmtl	Frontomalare temporale L	III	Posterior extrema of the suture between the frontal and maxillary bones.
26	jugl	Jugale L	II	Deepest point (anterior) of the transition between the frontal and zygomatic processes.
27	zygoml	Zygomaxilare L	III	Inferior extrema of the suture between the zygomatic and maxillary bones
28	zygl	Zygion L	III	The lateral extrema of the
29	zygr	Zygion R	III	zygomatic arches.
30	eurr	Eurion R	III	The lateral extrema of the
31	eurl	Eurion L	III	greatest cranial breadth.
32	stpl	Stephanion L	I	Intersection of the coronal
33	stpr	Stephanion R	I	suture and the superior temporal line (ridge caused by the temporal fascia attachment).
34	Porr	Porion R	III	Point superior to the external
35	Porl	Porion L	III	auditory meatus, also may be determined by the posterior root of the zygomatic arch.
36	mastr	Mastoideale R	II	Inferior extrema of the mastoid
37	mastl	Mastoideale L	II	process.

See Fig. 5.10*: Landmark map* for locations. Colors are used as visual cues to group the lateral landmarks for data collection and maintain the collection index for the codebook workflow. (Bookstein, 1997; Howells 1973, 1996; White and Folkens, 2000).

example. If your research is not craniometric in nature, then this will be something to carefully research and consider from the current literature of the discipline.

2. **Previous works**—publications on the sample

   Unless a sample is new and unique, the work of any other persons involved in the collection, processing, or a project or publication including this sample should be noted. It is important to know if the data have any issues. This extends to the next question and includes conversations with trusted resources during the course of preparation for data collection. Take notes and ask if there are terminal references to the information.

   If this is an entirely new data set, previous works that use the same or similar data, analysis, or hypothesis would serve as well.

3. **Previous works**—Landmark collection software

   Assuming taking place in an institutional setting, such an entity would be the best place to start collecting this type of reference. Understanding that this suggests a lab setting, consult with the instructors, technicians, and curators who deal with the lab equipment and the materials. If any previous publication or experimentation that has taken place can inform decisions regarding data collection, it can help avoid pitfalls and save time.

Box 5.6 Sample data preparation

Regardless of the origin of a sample—original data or from another individual or institution—take some time to evaluate the quality of the start landmark coordinate. This is also a good time to make sure that the sample mesh models are in a format that is compatible with the software to be used. The following are also helpful to consider if you are new to the digital environment or if you are not familiar with your sample.

1. **Processed mesh files**—models of the sample

   Mesh models of the sample refined from the original scanned data. Processed files having a balanced data density (high enough number of points to accurately represent the surface, but not so dense as to cause computational problems due to file size) and smooth surface (no nonincident faces and water-tight manifold state).

2. **Alignment and registration**—coordinate system and space

   Models are aligned in a coordinate system (registration). When this registration is done before collecting landmark coordinate data, it maintains the highest possible consistency in the identification of landmarks by definitions. It is the same consideration applied to the process of taking physical landmarks (such as with a Microscribe). This reduces the estimate of interobserver margin of error (Ross and Williams, 2008).

   The subject of alignment has been discussed in previous chapters and will be further highlighted in this chapter with regard to the 3D models and 3D landmark sample data from both sources. Should alignment to a defined coordinate system be ignored or applied inconsistently, the results could fall into the problems argument by Lele and Richtsmeier (2001) spatial dimensionality increases, so does the likelihood of spatial error. The methods of Ross and Williams (2008) and Ercan et al. (2008) were influenced by the concerns of this type of error and are clear about the importance of careful consideration of alignment. Without a system to maintain consistency, spatial error can become a noise signal through analytical data that risks spurious conclusions.

Box 5.7 Data collection protocol

1. Import and align—Import processed meshes into landmarking software. If necessary, align samples to common coordinate system.
2. Primary coordinate collection—Collect landmark points in order as indexed in Codebook, or using automatic method.

Manual placement	Automatic placement*:
• Codebook based on midline, structural, and paired lateral landmarks, as described in Table 5.1 and shown on Fig. 5.1. • *note: For automated landmark placement, one sample must be manually collected to use as the basis for the template. • Make sure to follow codebook, then label each landmark in the list, to use manual landmarking for a full sample, labels must be repeated for each unit of the sample	• Anchor template based on alignment landmarks, a subset from the codebook list. • Autoplace template based on a set of manually placed from the codebook list. • Expect automatic placement to require refinement; however, the labels and general placement can be helpful. It is NOT recommended to apply automated landmark template without postapplication position refinement.

3. Apply data management—Save the initial landmark coordinate data in data management archive. Continue to the next sample unit.
4. Secondary coordinate collection/refinement—Import sample unit with initial landmark coordinate data; inspect the sample units to review the landmark placement for adherence to description and definition.
5. Apply data management—Save the refined landmark coordinate data in data management archive. Continue to the next sample unit.

Completed data set can be prepared for statistical analysis. The method will depend on the saved output format and the input format requirements of the analysis software.

Box 5.8 Stratovan checkpoint—cranium

1. Alignment—Set transect views to Frankfurt horizontal and sagittal planes.
   a. Import the specimen(s) (Fig. 5.5).
   b. In the 3D view, select an estimated location for porion L. Note the axis that appears in the 3D window. It should intersect the cranium near the defined location of porion L, and if the superior/inferior orientation is good, porion R will also be close to the place the axis intersects the cranium (Fig. 5.6). If the scan data have been aligned before loading into Checkpoint, the default orientation should be upright and forward facing. To go back to the initial orientation, right click on the view and select the Reset menu item.
   c. Use the transect views to align the Sagittal plane. The sliders on the right side of the transect views can be used to scroll through the transect as slices.
2. Landmarks—To place landmarks, select Landmark icon. (Fig. 5.7)
   a. Align cursor over the location corresponding to the landmark.
   b. Hold Shift key and left click the cursor.
3. Semilandmarks—To place semilandmarks (Fig. 5.8).
   a. Place landmarks for the start and end of the semilandmark curve.
   b. Place a curve between the two landmark points by following these steps:
      i. Select the Curve primitive from the menu Edit | Add Curve.
      ii. Place the start and endpoint of your curve near the two landmarks you want to join with.
      iii. Select the Hand tool from the menu Edit | Edit Landmarks.
      iv. Hit the spacebar to clear the selection (if any).
      v. Click on one of your originally placed landmark points. This should color the landmark red. (It will be colored yellow while you hover over it.)
      vi. Click on the nearest endpoint of your curve. This should color the endpoint white. (It will be colored yellow while you hover over it.)
      vii. Join the two points by selecting Edit | Combine Landmarks. This will join the curve endpoint to the preexisting landmark point. The joined points will take the position of the red-colored point.
      viii. Repeat this process for the second endpoint of the curve.

   Note: Placement of patches is not addressed in this text; however, the process is similar to the placement of semilandmark curves as above.
4. Export landmark and semilandmark data (Fig. 5.9).
   a. Click Export tab.
   b. Export format: CSV, Using these units: Millimeters
   c. Under From Surface: choose All. Select Export Landmarks

Box 5.9 Stratovan checkpoint—cranium figures

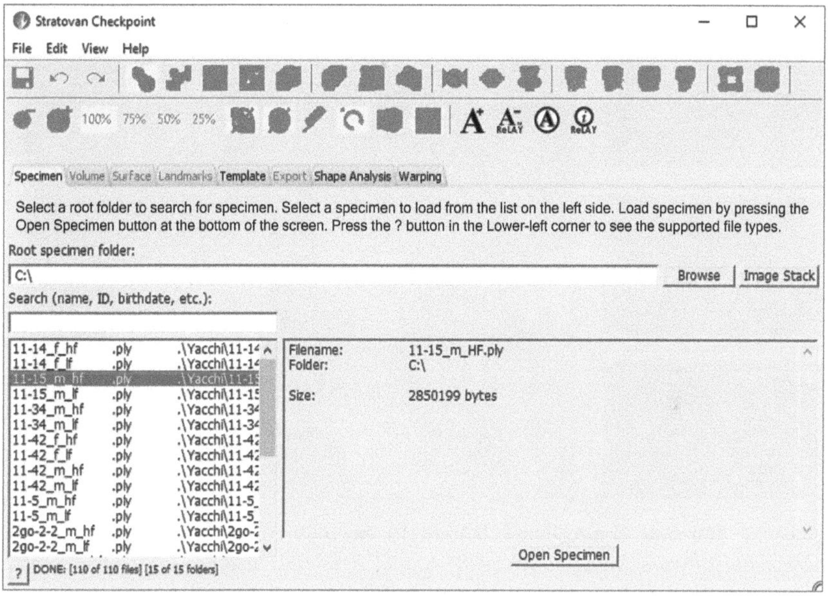

Figure 5.5 Stratovan checkpoint © import. *From Stratovan Corporation. Stratovan Checkpoint [Software]. Version 2018.08.07. Aug 07, 2018. URL: https://www.stratovan.com/products/checkpoint. Used with permission from Stratovan Corporation.*

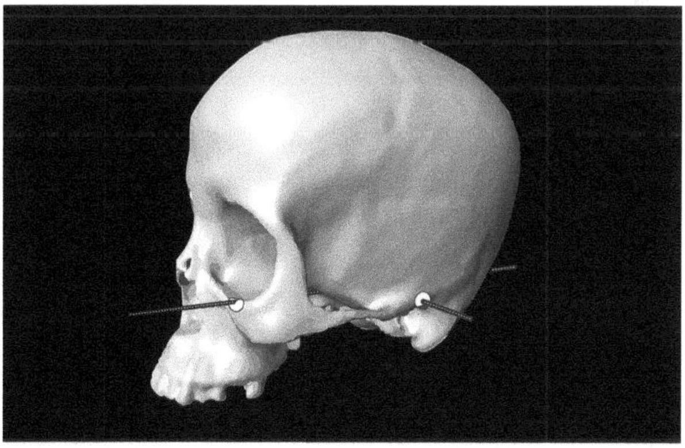

Figure 5.6 Stratovan checkpoint © porion L and zygoobitale. *From Stratovan Corporation. Stratovan Checkpoint [Software]. Version 2018.08.07. Aug 07, 2018. URL: https://www.stratovan.com/products/checkpoint. Used with permission from Stratovan Corporation.*

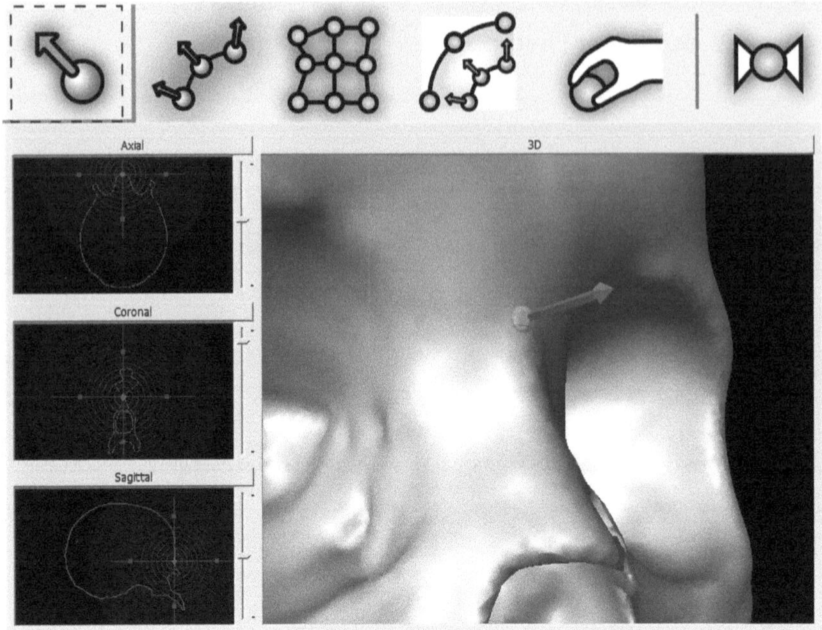

Figure 5.7 Stratovan checkpoint © landmarks. *From Stratovan Corporation. Stratovan Checkpoint [Software]. Version 2018.08.07. Aug 07, 2018. URL: https://www.stratovan.com/products/checkpoint. Used with permission from Stratovan Corporation.*

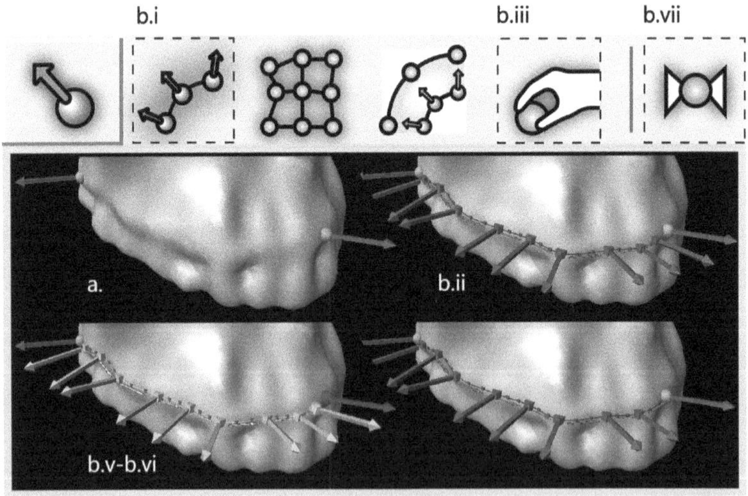

Figure 5.8 Stratovan checkpoint © semilandmarks. *From Stratovan Corporation. Stratovan Checkpoint [Software]. Version 2018.08.07. Aug 07, 2018. URL: https://www.stratovan.com/products/checkpoint. Used with permission from Stratovan Corporation.*

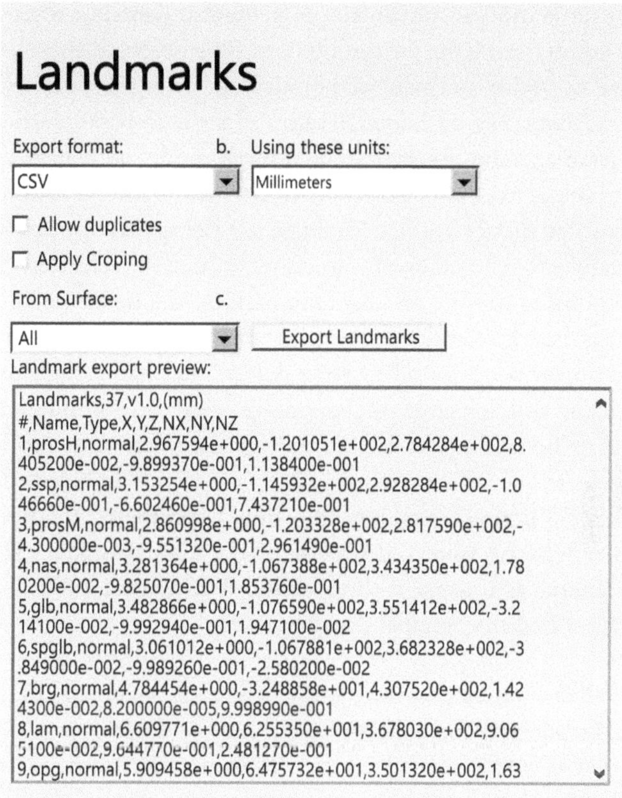

Figure 5.9 Stratovan checkpoint © export. *From Stratovan Corporation. Stratovan Checkpoint [Software]. Version 2018.08.07. Aug 07, 2018. URL: https://www.stratovan.com/products/checkpoint. Used with permission from Stratovan Corporation.*

Landmark example

This example outlines the applied process of landmark coordinate data collection for the Yacchi cranial samples as used in several chapters (Fukumine et al., 2001). This example uses four models for each original sample unit. The original sample was derived from 13 crania from the Yacchi materials. Landmark coordinates were collected from all 52 models processed from the scan data (Murphy, 2015).

Data quality

Within the sample of mesh models, 9 of the 13 crania have nonmanifold models with larger computational size than the manifold counterpart. This suggests that some models contain components that were not removed at the higher-face count during the processing steps. The observable results could be irregular face or vertex normals, or nonincident faces (Hoppe et al., 1993). The problems that could be caused in terms of the landmark selection process for the software and the observer using a mesh model with such defects are both real and subjective. The real problems arise when a point cannot connect with the observed surface at the coordinate it is being placed on. The subjective consequence for the observer is to either change the selection coordinate or note the point as missing for that landmark on the defective sample.

During landmark selection, several nonmanifold models for both processing resolutions were found to have defects that had a slight impact on the observation and selection of landmarks. For this sample, the defects were found to be nonincident faces that created defective geometry and caused the selected coordinate of a point to appear to exist below the surface to the crania. Wherever possible, selection coordinates for points were adjusted to reflect the observed surface of the cranial model. This means leaving landmarks as missing if the location is damaged, even if the mesh processing has filled the original damage.

Landmark list

Landmarks selected for collection and analysis for this test (Table 5.1) were required to meet several criteria (Ross and Williams, 2008; Sholts et al., 2010; Saitou et al., 2011). First, it was necessary to select landmarks that had been part of the Microscribe/ThreeSkull (Ousley, 2010) data collection. The list of landmarks was reduced from this first list to satisfy several further requirements: (1) each landmark must exist on most or all crania in the sample; (2) each landmark must be visible either directly or accurate to estimate based on the 3D mesh models with the highest resolution (high-face count models). In the case of these models, due to the particular scanner used, some landmarks could not be visualized. Landmarks that could not be visualized were removed from the final list.

Table 5.1*: **Landmarks for 3D comparison:*** Examples of landmarks that could not be accurately estimated without direct visualization are asterion and superior and inferior zygotemporale. The mesh models under study here were captured without texture, which prevents the visualization of these areas for selection of landmark locations. Asterion is an intersection that is found within an area of convoluted sutures between the temporal and occipital bones. The zygotemporale landmarks are not only dependent on visualization of the suture between the zygomatic arch and the temporal arch but also dependent on accurate capture of the small, fragile structure.

The process of elimination resulted in the final 37 landmarks present on most crania in the sample and remaining after the application of processing parameters for all models. These landmarks characterize the global structures of the crania and structures of the craniofacial area that are stable (Table 5.1).

The comparison of two samples used in this chapter example allows the consideration of the influence that the landmark type—the *location or definition* of an individual landmark point—might have on the variation between multiple observations. The same comparison further considers that the influence variation between observations could have on the measure of the linear relationship between landmark points singularly and throughout the coordinate system.

Data collection

1. Imported processed meshes into Stratovan Checkpoint.
2. Collected landmark points in order as indexed in Codebook.
   a. Table 5.1: Landmarks for 3D comparison
   b. Fig. 5.10: Landmark map

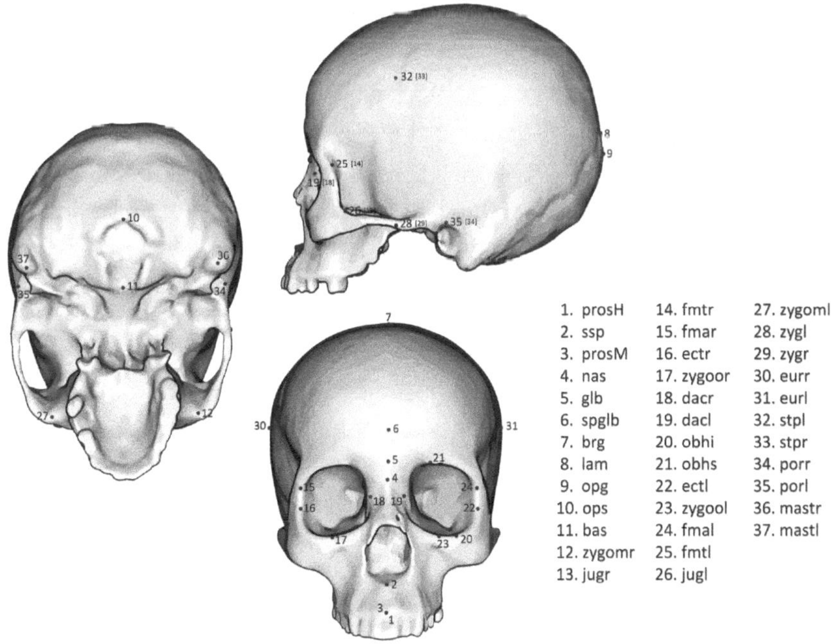

Figure 5.10 Landmark map.

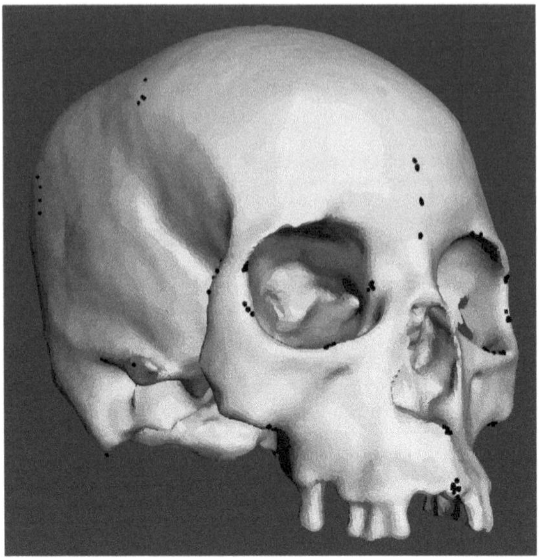

Figure 5.11 Example of landmark point sample.

   c. Fig. 5.11: Example of landmark point sample
   d. Data management
2. Exported landmark point coordinates as comma-separated value (*.CSV) files.

Landmark coordinate data

The landmarks for craniometric analysis are long established, and beyond a few specific debates, the definitions are invariant. The landmarks applied in this chapter example are an abbreviated list and were selected specifically for the sample and scan quality.

Porion (porr, porl) is used as an alignment landmark; therefore, variation between the process models and the digitizer landmarks is reduced strictly to the difference along one vector. This follows a standard for craniometric analysis of the application of the Frankfurt horizontal plane. The plots of the values for the distances between processes for the porion landmark points (left and right) indicate very low variation.

Supraglabellare (spglb) landmark points have significantly different coordinate locations between the process samples collected from the 3D models from the Microscribe (Revware, Raleigh, NC, USA) digitizer observation. This is because of both the significantly different definitions applied by the observers and the difference in the observation of the landmark in cross section. Supraglabellare is significant in defining anterior projection of the frontal and nasal bones along the midline (Howells, 1973). Variations are inherent to measures based off supraglabellare due to difficulties selecting directly by lateral observation, or on a lateral cephalograph (X-ray). Strictly defined as a midline structure, the point should be most accurately collected from a properly aligned cranium in cross section. If the cranium is not perfectly aligned, or the observer is collecting point from a 2D image, the points will be much less likely to closely match between different observations, observers, or selection methods.

Prosthion *(Howells)* (prosH), subspinale (ssp), and prosthion *(Martin)* (prosM) are midline and all Type II (Ousley, 2010). Howells (1973) discusses the deferential definitions that have been historically applied to prosthion. The prosthion selections for both the Howells and Martin definition are included in the ThreeSkull software (Ousley, 2010) and apply slightly different definitions of the location of prosthion. Points 4–11 are midline and can reflect differences in overall size. Three are Type III; glabella (glb), supraglabellare (spglb), and opisthicranion (ops)—having measurements that are dependent on the orientation of the crania during sample. Three are Type I, nasion (nas), bregma (brg), and lambda (lam), and are dependent on the visual evaluation of the intersection of cranial sutures (Bookstein, 1997; Ousley and McKeown, 2001).

Right and left craniofacial landmark points are each collected for all crania, with the exception of the orbital height landmarks (obhi, obhs). When the right and left landmarks are considered separately, the left craniofacial landmarks are slightly more correlated to the digitizer landmarks than the right or all processes, which agrees with the findings of several previous studies (McKeown and Jantz 2005; Jantz et al., 2013).

Missing data

Table 5.2 lists the landmark points with missing coordinates.

Coordinate points were missing from the process model sample data from eight landmark points. Missing points were the result of insufficient scan capture problems or file corruption occurring between scanning and the refinement, alignment, and processing steps. This number is low because before the landmark coordinate data were collected, it was determined what landmarks were and were not identifiable for the majority of the sample crania. For an example, asterion was collected by Microscribe on the physical

Table 5.2 Missing data.

	1. prosH	10. ops	11. Bas	13. jugr	28. zygl	29. zygr	36. mastr	37. mastl
Total	4	16	8	4	8	8	20	8
hf	1	4	2	1	2	2	5	2
hfnm	1	4	2	1	2	2	5	2
lf	1	4	2	1	2	2	5	2
lfnm	1	4	2	1	2	2	5	2
dd	0	0	0	0	0	0	0	0

Missing values influence rank order correlation methods. If not removed, average values are substituted with a central tendency value, resulting in an artificially high or low correlation depending on the central tendency of the sample subset.

sample. The scans collected were collected without any surface texture (color) data. Without the visualization of the color variation of the sutures between the posterior parietal and superior occipital, asterion cannot be correctly identified.

Landmark coordinate data processing

Alignment of landmarks—example

The Frankfurt horizontal (Fig. 5.12) is operationally defined as the plane intersecting the right and left porion landmark points and the left zygoorbitale in accordance with the standard accepted definition. For registration to a common origin, standard coordinate system, and to the coronal

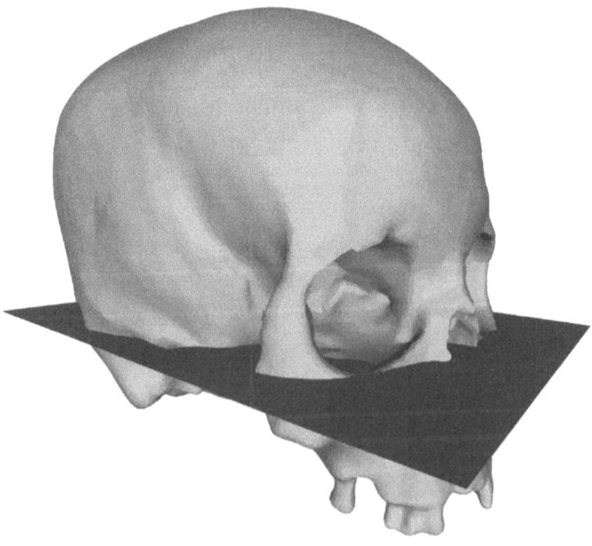

Figure 5.12 Frankfurt horizontal.

and sagittal planes, which define the Y and Z planes respectively, the points must be translated and rotated to orient the left and right porion landmark points to Y and Z values of zero (0) and X values that equilaterally split the Euclidean distance between the two points.

To bring the points back to the correct orientation in the XYZ coordinate plane for the Frankfurt horizontal standard, the sign (±) of the X coordinates is reversed, and the Y and Z coordinates are reversed. (Eqs. 5.1–5.4) (Fig. 5.13) (NOTE: When saving a file in Morpheus et al. (Slice, 2013), it is not unusual to have a file with no extension. Remedy this by renaming the file and adding *.mdt* at the end of the filename.)

Bookstein superimposition transformation—unit—scale (Lele and Richtsmeier, 2001).

Obs = observation, the set of collected landmarks (n = 37) from a crania in the sample.

Prc = processing, the type and level of processing applied to the crania before landmarks are collected.

n = the landmarks collected on each observation, also indicated by abbreviations of the location name.

Scale factor is the interlandmark (Euclidean) distance value calculated between the first (porl) and second (porl) landmarks selected from an observation for Bookstein superimposition. This process is reversed postsuperimposition to preserve the original scale of the sample units.

$$Obs_{Prc} = \begin{bmatrix} X_{bas} & Y_{bas} & Z_{bas} \\ X_{brg} & Y_{brg} & Z_{brg} \\ \vdots & \vdots & \vdots \\ X_n & Y_n & Z_n \end{bmatrix}$$

$$Scale\ Factor: v_{(x,y,z)} = v_x = v_y = v_z$$

$$= \sqrt{(X_{porl} - X_{porr})^2 + (Y_{porl} - Y_{porr})^2 + (Z_{porl} - Z_{porr})^2}$$

$$nas = \begin{bmatrix} X_{nas} \\ Y_{nas} \\ Z_{nas} \\ 1 \end{bmatrix} \quad Scale\ nas = \begin{bmatrix} v_X & 0 & 0 & 0 \\ 0 & v_Y & 0 & 0 \\ 0 & 0 & v_Z & 0 \\ 0 & 0 & 0 & 1 \end{bmatrix} * \begin{bmatrix} X_{nas} \\ Y_{nas} \\ Z_{nas} \\ 1 \end{bmatrix} = \begin{bmatrix} X_{nas(v_X)} \\ Y_{nas(v_Y)} \\ Z_{nas(v_Z)} \\ 1 \end{bmatrix} \tag{5.1}$$

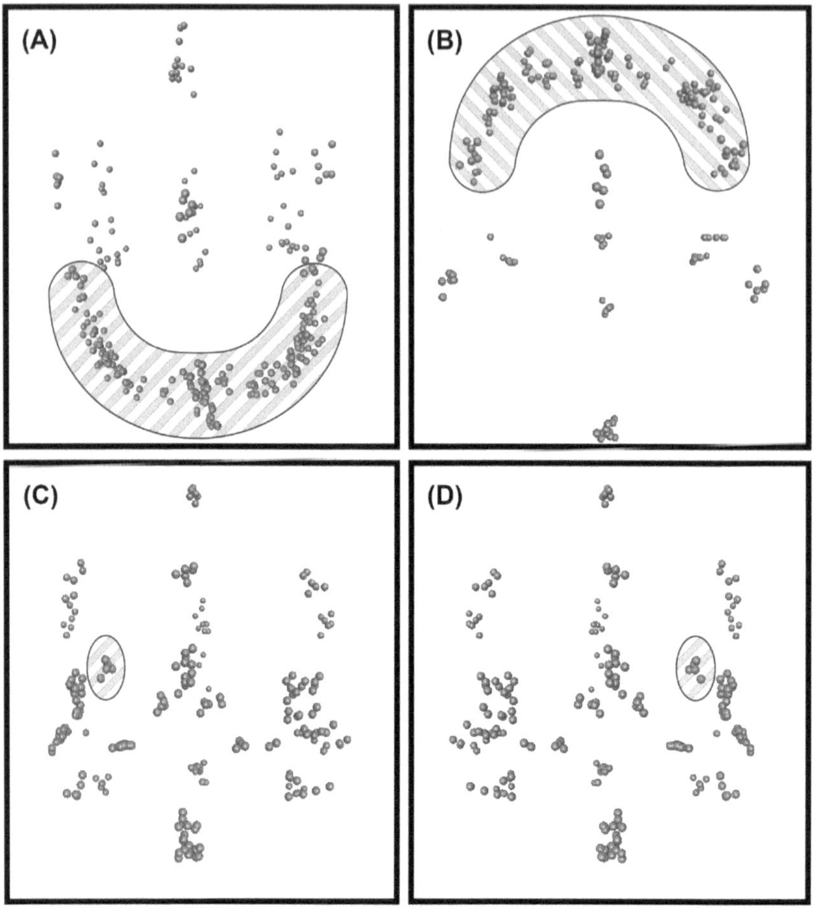

Figure 5.13 Correction of Bookstein alignment. Bookstein alignment of landmark point data allows for a set of points to be aligned to a specific subset of points, rather than a derived data centroid as with GPA. (A) The original orientation of the landmark point data imported into Morpheus et al. (Slice, 2013). Facial landmarks are circled. (B) The orientation after the application of the Bookstein alignment. The scatter of the points has been reduced, but the data are not aligned to the correct axes. Facial landmarks are circled. (C) Transposition of the data of the Y and Z axes corrects the alignment to the default 3D orientation but results in a mirroring effect on the data of the X axis. Left porion landmark point cluster is circled. (D) Inversion of the sign (±) of the data corrects for the mirroring effect and completes the process. Left porion landmark point cluster is circled.

Bookstein superimposition transformation—plane—rotation (Lele and Richtsmeier, 2001).

Rotation factor is the degrees of rotation around the origin necessary on the x, y, and z coordinate system planes to bring the second landmark (*porl*) into coincidence with the first landmark (*porl*) on the x plane and reduce difference of the y and z values between the first and second landmarks to zero.

$$porr = \begin{bmatrix} X_{porr} \\ Y_{porr} \\ Z_{porr} \\ 1 \end{bmatrix}$$

$$Rotate\ porr = \begin{bmatrix} \cos(\alpha)\sin(\varnothing) & \sin(\alpha)\cos(\varnothing) & \sin(\varnothing) & 0 \\ -\sin(\alpha) & \cos(\alpha) & 0 & 0 \\ -\cos(\alpha)\sin(\varnothing) & -\sin(\alpha)\sin(\varnothing) & \cos(\varnothing) & 0 \\ 0 & 0 & 0 & 1 \end{bmatrix} * \begin{bmatrix} X_{porr} \\ 0_{porr} \\ 0_{porr} \\ 1 \end{bmatrix} \quad (5.2)$$

Bookstein superimposition transformation—root—translation (Lele and Richtsmeier, 2001).

Translation factor is the linear shift required to root the first landmark (*porl*) to the origin of the coordinate system, which results in x, y, and z values of zero.

$$porl = \begin{bmatrix} X_{porl} \\ Y_{porl} \\ Z_{porl} \\ 1 \end{bmatrix} \quad Translate\ porl = \begin{bmatrix} X_{porl} \\ Y_{porl} \\ Z_{porl} \\ 1 \end{bmatrix} - \begin{bmatrix} X_{porl} \\ Y_{porl} \\ Z_{porl} \\ 0 \end{bmatrix} = \begin{bmatrix} 0_{porl} \\ 0_{porl} \\ 0_{porl} \\ 1 \end{bmatrix} \quad (5.3)$$

Bookstein superimposition transformation—correction for standard coordinate system.

Reverse scale, swap Y and X, inverse sign for X

$$BSC(Obs_{Prc}) = \begin{bmatrix} X_{bas} & Y_{bas} & Z_{bas} \\ X_{brg} & Y_{brg} & Z_{brg} \\ \vdots & \vdots & \vdots \\ X_n & Y_n & Z_n \end{bmatrix}$$

$$Correct\ BSC(Obs_{Prc}) = \begin{bmatrix} (X_{bas}) & Z_{bas} & Y_{bas} \\ -(X_{brg}) & Z_{brg} & Y_{brg} \\ \vdots & \vdots & \vdots \\ -(X_n) & Z_n & Y_n \end{bmatrix} \quad (5.4)$$

There is an important consequence of this registration on the landmark points used to define the orientation. The multidimensional variation of the three is reduced such that left and right porion points only vary in X values, and zygoorbitale only varies in X and Z values. This does not reduce the analytical validity of the global, as the changes to the vector matrix of the points do not lose orientation relative to each other. This alignment at this stage is important for the sake of the internal consistency it maintains for the landmark data. Alignment steps taken at the 3D surface scanning stage are applied to maintain as high a degree of collection consistency across the scanning sample. Alignment of 3D models for the collection of landmark and semilandmark data is done to adhere to as strict a landmark definition as is possible, most significantly with regard to Type II and Type III landmark definitions.

Treatment of missing data

Missing data were imputed by column substitution by the EDMA process for the ILD sample in PAST v1.93 (Hammer et al., 2001). This is only one of the ways to substitute missing data. The concept to keep in mind is that all ILDs for the substituted point on those sample units will be slightly affected. A smaller sample or a larger number of missing values would have each increased the impact of the imputed values. The decision to keep or remove missing data needs to be made carefully.

Alignment and registration

Concatenate and align multiple types of landmark coordinate data

Because of the differences in the technologies used to collect the experimental and criterion data, the sets of points representing each cranium have different orientations in the coordinate system (the y or the z as the superior/inferior axes). Aligned models are set up the same in a coordinate system. This is done before collecting landmark coordinate data, most importantly because it maintains the highest possible consistency in the identification of landmarks by definitions. It is the same consideration applied to the process of taking physical landmarks (such as with a Microscribe). This reduces the estimate of interobserver margin of error.

The aligned orientation between the landmark points collected in each of the technologies needs to be applied to minimize potential spatial error and allow for comparison. Each sample set of landmark points, Stratovan Checkpoint software (Stratovan Corporation, Davis, CA) and those collected using the Microscribe (Revware, Raleigh, NC, USA) were entered into a text file. This file is formatted for use with Morpheus et al. (Slice, 2013) software with each point matched for serial position in the list of landmarks for each example.

Within Morpheus et al. (Slice, 2013) software, the sets of coordinate data are processed with a 3D Bookstein alignment as described in the example, setting an origin [*i*] (porion left), translating and rotating a secondary point [*j*](porion right) to zero for each the Y and Z directions, then lastly rotating the third point [*k*] (zygoorbitale) around the X vector to zero for the Z direction. These alignment procedures also apply a scaling factor. In this instance, the distance between the [*i*] and [*j*] coordinates becomes the unit scale (1.0) for all other coordinates. For the purposes of maintaining the data interoperability, reverse the scale factor of the alignment.

Treatment of aligned sample landmark data

Interlandmark distance

ILD is a part of EDMA. This treatment of 3D coordinates is useful as it reduces 3D landmark coordinates to a single factor relative to the rest of the coordinates of the sample unit (Eq. 5.5).

Table 5.3 Example of factor reduction when applying Euclidean distance matrix analysis (EDMA) to coordinate data.

	Coordinate			
Landmark	**X**	**Y**	**Z**	
A	20.4068	224.9265	129.2542	Interlandmark distance
B	12.4943	331.5903	119.3491	from EDMA
Δ	7.9125	106.6638	9.9051	107.4145

Table 5.4 Euclidean distance matrix analysis.

	1	2	3	4	5	6	7	8	9	10	11	12	13	14	15
1															
2															
3															
4															
5															
6															
7															
8															
9															
10															
11															
12															
13															
14															
15															

15 landmarks = 45 data points for each sample unit (15*3 for X Y Z values)

ILD of 15 landmarks results in 113 unique values,

105 if zero values are discarded.

Keeping the data in coordinate format triples the number of factors to be analyzed.

EDMA formula (Lele and Richtsmeier 2001)

$$\textit{Euclidean Distance}: ILD = \sqrt{(X_{porl} - X_{porr})^2 + (Y_{porl} - Y_{porr})^2 + (Z_{porl} - Z_{porr})^2} \quad (5.5)$$

To create the matrix of ILD, PAST v2.17 (Hammer et al., 2001) EDMA functions are used to output the Euclidean distances to tables of each unique pair of points for analysis of the distance between points as a single factor rather than as two points each with three factors. EDMA disassociates *xyz* coordinate data from the 3D environment down to 2D data as a unit of the distance between two coordinates. This results in a loss of spatial sensitivity, which can be thought of as the variation in the coordinates of a specific landmark across a sample. However, when a sample has a low *n*, fewer factors improve the robustness of statistical analysis. It may not be the final data used to examine the similarities and differences of units in a sample, but it can be very helpful as an exploratory statistic when applied to sample data as dense as 3D data.

The correlation of the ILDs is insensitive to the orientation within the coordinate system of each sample unit relative to the whole sample. EDMA data convey linear distances, and by reducing the 3D data to a single value, EDMA does not retain the multidimensional orientation of the original sample (Tables 5.3 and 5.4). However, error is easily introduced as variations in landmark selection. Because orientation and alignment can have an impact on the selection of a landmark, by definition, alignment still serves to control for potential error under this analytical framework.

Conclusion

These descriptions and examples have been presented to supply a functional understanding from which to proceed with digital 3D landmark coordinate collection. In the next chapter, this type of data is applied to a test of validity.

References

Bookstein, F.L., 1997. Morphometric tools for landmark data: geometry and biology. Cambridge University Press, Cambridge [England], New York.

Cignoni, P., Callieri, M., Corsini, M., Dellepiane, M., Ganovelli, F., Ranzuglia, G., 2008. MeshLab: an Open-Source Mesh Processing Tool.

Ercan, I., Guney, I., Ocakoglu, G., Yazici, B., 2008. Adaptation of Generalizability Theory for Inter-rater Reliability for Landmark Localization.

Fukumine, T., Doi, N., Ishida, H., Zukeran, C., Sensui, S., Saso, A., Higa, T., 2001. Human skeletal remains from the Yacchi-no-Gama and Kanjinbaru grave sites. In: Okinawa Prefectural Archaeological Center (Ed.), Yacchi-no-Gama, Kanjinnbaru Grave Sites. Prefectural Archaeological Center Research Report, No. 6, Okinawa, pp. 345–385 (in Japanese).

Girardeau-Montaut, D., 2014. Cloud compare - Open Source Project. http://www.cloudcompare.org: CloudCompare - Open Source Project.

Hammer, Ø., Harper, D.A.T., Ryan, P.D., 2001. Paleontological statistics software package for education and data analysis. Palaeontologia Electronica 4 (1), 9.

Hoppe, H., DeRose, T., Duchamp, T., McDonald, J., Stuetzle, W., 1993. Mesh optimization. In: Proceedings of the 20th Annual Conference on Computer Graphics and Interactive Techniques. ACM, Anaheim, CA, pp. 19–26.

Howells, W.W., 1973. Cranial variation in man: a study by multivariate analysis of patterns of difference among recent human population. Papers of the Peabody Museum of Archaeology and Ethnology 67, 1–259.

Howells, W.W., 1996. Howells' craniometric data on the internet. American Journal of Physical Anthropology 101, 441–442.

Jantz, R., Mahfouz, M., Shirley, N.R., Abdel Fatah, E., 2013. Improving Sex Estimation from Crania Using 3-dimensional CT Scans. U.S. Department of Justice. https://www.ncjrs.gov/pdffiles1/nij/grants/240688.pdf.

Klingenberg, C.P., 2010. Evolution and development of shape: integrating quantitative approaches. Nature Reviews Genetics 11, 623–635.

Lele, S., Richtsmeier, J.T., 2001. An Invariant Approach to Statistical Analysis of Shapes. Chapman & Hall/CRC, Boca Raton, Fla.: Boca Raton, Fla.

McKeown, A.H., Jantz, R.L., 2005. Comparison of Coordinate and Craniometric Data for Biological Distance Studies. In: Slice, D.E. (Ed.), Modern Morphometrics in Physical Anthropology. Developments in Primatology: Progress and Prospects. Springer, Boston, MA.

Murphy, M.-M., 2015. Validity of Landmark Selection Given Different 3D Scan Processing Parameters: Landmark Location on 3D Models of Yacchi Crania. Thesis. University of Montana, p. 4565. Theses, Dissertations, Professional Papers.

Ousley, S., McKeown, A., 2001. Human remains: conservation, retrieval and analysis: proceedings of a conference held in Williamsburg, VA, Nov. 7–11th 1999. In: Williams, E. (Ed.), BAR International Series: Archaeopress, pp. 173–184.

Ousley, S.D., 2010. Threeskull. Version 2.0.

R Core Team, R., 2018. A Language and Environment for Statistical Computing. R Foundation for Statistical Computing, Vienna, Austria. https://www.R-project.org.

Ross, A.H., Williams, S., 2008. Testing Repeatability and Error of Coordinate Landmark Data Acquired from Crania. Journal of Forensic Sciences 53 (4), 782–785.

Saitou, N., Kimura, R., Fukase, H., Yogi, A., Murayama, S., Ishida, H., 2011. Advanced CT images reveal nonmetric cranial variations in living humans. Anthropological Science 119 (3), 231–237.

Schlager, S., 2017. Morpho and rvcg – shape analysis in R: R-packages for geometric morphometrics, shape analysis and surface manipulations. In: Zheng, G., Li, S., Szekely, G. (Eds.), Statistical Shape and Deformation Analysis: Methods, Implementation and Applications, pp. 217–255.

Shearer, B.M., Cooke, S.B., Halenar, L.B., Reber, S.L., Plummer, J.E., Delson, E., Tallman, M., 2017. Evaluating causes of error in landmark-based data collection using scanners. PLoS One 12 (11), e0187452. https://doi.org/10.1371/journal.pone.0187452.

Sholts, S.B., Wärmländer, S.K.T.S., Flores, L.M., Miller, K.W.P., Walker, P.L., 2010. Variation in the measurement of cranial volume and surface area using 3D laser scanning technology. Journal of Forensic Sciences 55 (4), 871–876.

Slice, D.E., 2013. Morpheus et al, Java Edition. Department of Scientific Computing. Florida State University.

Smith, N.E., Strait, S.G., 2008. PaleoView3D: from specimen to online digital model. Palaeontologia Electronica 11 (2), 1.00.

Weinberg, S.M., Kolar, J., 2005. Three-dimensional surface imaging: limitations and considerations from the anthropometric perspective. Journal of Craniofacial Surgery 16 (5), 847–851.

White, T.D., Folkens, P.A., 2000. Human osteology. Academic Press, San Diego: San Diego.

Wiley, D., 2006. Landmark Editor 3.0. Institute for Data Analysis and Visualization. University of California, Davis. http://graphics.idav.ucdavis.edu/research/EvoMorph.

CHAPTER SIX

Validity assessment: validity testing of mixed data by multiple devices, methods, and observers

Noriko Seguchi[1,2] Mary-Margaret Murphy[2], Shiori Yonemoto[3]
[1]Faculty of Social and Cultural Studies, Kyushu University, Fukuoka, Japan
[2]Department of Anthropology, The University of Montana, Missoula, MT, The United States of America
[3]The Kyushu University Museum, Kyushu University, Fukuoka, Japan

Introduction

Recent advancements in three-dimensional (3D) technology have impacted the field of biological anthropology and the use of geometric morphometrics. 3D digitizers such as Microscribe (Revware, Raleigh, NC, USA) serve as excellent tools for collecting landmark and semilandmark data. However, Microscribe requires direct access to skeletal materials, which is a problem on several levels. For example, access to archaeological skeletal collections can often be limited and access can be further impeded by restrictions mandated by the curation authority. Additionally, recording semilandmark data over curved areas of bone with a physical probe can compromise poorly preserved specimens. By collecting only the landmarks and distances directly from skeletal remains with a 3D digitizer, a researcher cannot return to the data and ask questions about shapes and features that are not represented by the collected points. Taking the time to collect 3D models of samples from which to collect simple and complex data for analysis affords greater flexibility and an ongoing advantage to the researcher. Considering these issues, this chapter examines an assessment of the validity of landmark data acquired by Microscribe versus Checkpoint software (Stratovan Corporation, Davis, CA, USA) from the perspective of the difficulties and challenges found with bioarchaeological materials.

The structure of this chapter is to compare landmarks and semilandmarks collected with a digitizer against data from laser scans using multiple individuals and different laboratory conditions. We separate this chapter into

3D Data Acquisition for Bioarchaeology, Forensic Anthropology, and Archaeology
ISBN: 978-0-12-815309-3
https://doi.org/10.1016/B978-0-12-815309-3.00006-1

two sections: (1) validity assessment of landmark data taken by 3D digitizer vs. 3D laser surface scans and (2) validity assessment of semilandmark data taken by 3D digitizer versus 3D laser surface scans.

Validity of three-dimensional models for cranial landmark data under variable processing parameters

Both caliper-based two-dimensional (2D) craniofacial metric data and digitized 3D point data have proven validity in the field of bio-anthropological study (McKeown and Jantz, 2005; Olszewski et al., 2010). However, it is worth considering that the nature of the information conveyed is limited by the reductive nature of landmark data. The measurement construct of craniometrics derived from 3D landmarks directly collected represents an established criterion method. Craniometric Cartesian landmarks derived from multidimensional models in a digital environment are a method for which validity is to be established. Criterion validity tests assess the validity of a method based on the level of correlation with a criterion. Assessing the correlation of the landmark variation under the processing levels proposed here establishes the presence or absence of concurrent validity of the data collected and processed in the digital environment to the data collected directly from a physical specimen.

Validity analysis is useful to assess whether the variability between different processing methods introduces systematic error, resulting in significantly different metric data. Microscribe (Revware, Raleigh, NC, USA) digitizer landmarks have been used as the "gold-standard" metric for geometric morphometric study for much of the last two decades. To evaluate landmark data collected from virtual models in three dimensions for use alongside Microscribe-type data, a criterion validity experiment serves to evaluate the agreement between the samples under the differing processing conditions with the criterion method (Carmines and Zeller, 1979).

Validity testing on landmark data

The following example will consider five points to determine the validity of the metric samples from four variant processing methods applied to crania models.

1. Overall correlation of the sample values from each of the four processing methods.

2. Correlation of the overall sample values between the two types of processing methods; between points and within points.
3. Examination of the correlation coefficients of the sample data for patterns and determining if any patterns are likely the result of the characteristics of the sample, or a result of the processing method(s).
4. Examination of the coefficient of determination (covariance, R^2) for patterns of correlation due to random error.
5. Examination of the validity coefficients and the findings of validity as described by Carmines and Zeller (1979) for systematic error, which would confound the findings of validity (Nance and Ball, 1986)

Carmines and Zeller (1979) informs the levels of validity coefficients that are considered to reflect validity. For this study, the levels of correlation necessary are set to a moderate level—conservative to avoid validating data that is too variable to be useful and moderate to account for the variability in terms of observation bias and individual cranial variations (size, sex, etc.), which represent variability in the resulting measurements under all landmark sample conditions. In cases of testing the validity of a new metric, the level of correlation need not be set at a highly conservative level. This reflects the instance that even moderate correlations suggest a probable improvement with the use of the new metric or method (Carmines and Zeller, 1979).

The choice of criterion-related validity test also divides the collected samples for comparison between the Microscribe (Revware, Raleigh, NC, USA) digitizer sample (criterion) and the samples collected from the 3D mesh models. For a criterion-related test of validity, the rejection of validity is influenced by the presence of systematic error—which does not necessarily reflect on the reliability of the test method.

Reliability is often tested concurrently with validity when this type of testing is undertaken. This is not applied to the current experimental design of this chapter. The justification for not applying reliability testing stems from the impact of multiple observers and the testing of combinations of multiple process parameters. When multiple observers are involved in the collection of a sample of any type of observed metric, error and bias are increased and may not always be simple to pinpoint and account for in research design. For the research design presented in this chapter, it was necessary to consider this and apply a test of validity that could inform the results for trends that could be related to the differences in the measurements derived from the process models.

Repeated data collection by a single trained observer would have overcome the concerns created by the multiple original observers. However, for the purposes of testing multiple processing methods as applied here, it was not practical for a single observer to collect the landmark samples from each of the four process models for each of the 13 crania in the sample more than once.

The validity of the model under study in this chapter is based on the theory that positive correlation can be determined between the criterion measurement and the measurements under examination if they are both measuring the same thing. This concept is applied to a sample of the Yacchi-no-gama crania (Fukumine et al., 2001) that have been subjected to 3D data collection using 3D surface scans and Microscribe (Revware, Raleigh, NC, USA) landmark point digitizing. Landmarks derived from digital models having each undergone one of two levels of processing parameters to result in four models were analyzed for correlation to the set of landmarks collected using the direct digitizing method using two analytical schemes.

There is an expectation based on Bookstein's landmark definitions that Type I landmarks will have the most conservative variability between samples of the same point. Type II landmarks are slightly less conservative, and Type III landmarks are expected to show the most variation between point samples (Bookstein 1991). If the correlations of the sampled landmark points and the Microscribe (Revware, Raleigh, NC, USA) digitizer landmark points indicate any separation within the definitions of Type I, II, and III landmarks, such a pattern should not be classified as a type of random error because it is caused by the documented effect of the definition of the landmark point.

For the examples of landmark validity testing discussed here, the scans and landmarks have been collected by two separate contributors offering very limited feedback and sample descriptions of the crania of the original direct samples. This results in a comparative data sample that is in many ways a blind sample—the two researchers were not attempting to collect the sample data for the purposes of testing one against the other. This speaks to the importance of consistent training and application of research data collection methods, as was found in Shearer et al. (2017).

Two processing parameters are used crosswise to produce four models; two designated with "HF (high face)" with a large number of vertices and faces distributed over the whole model and two contrasting models designated with "LF (low face)" with fewer vertices distributed to concentrate

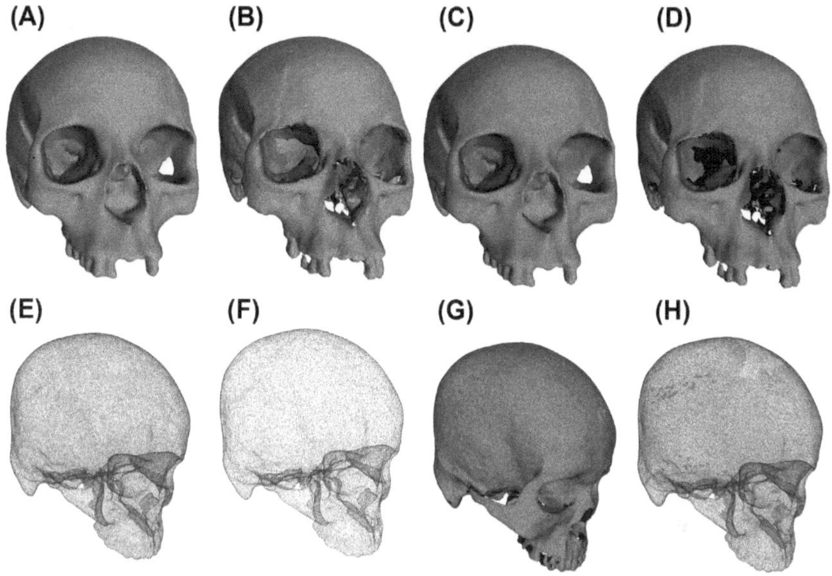

Figure 6.1 ***Examples of processed models and process stages.*** Examples of the mesh models at each of the levels of the processing parameters: (A) low-face count manifold; (B) low-face count nonmanifold; (C) high-face count manifold; and (D) high-face count nonmanifold. Differences between the manifold and nonmanifold process models can be observed in the orbital and nasal cavities and in the dental elements. Examples of mesh models emphasizing the vertices are as follows: (E) high-face count mesh; (F) low-face count mesh; (G) aligned, unprocessed superior and inferior mesh including the faces; and (H) aligned, unprocessed superior and inferior mesh. The examples c and d indicated the areas of overlap and excessive point density resulting from the scanning procedure.

points and faces to areas of greater complexity, each pair differing by manifold state, an open or closed geometric state of a mesh model (Abdel Fatah et al., 2014; Cignoni and Scopigno, 2008; Jantz et al., 2013) (Fig 6.1).

These data were not collected strictly for the testing of methodology. Methodological testing best practices would have dictated replication of the initial collection of the sample data. The number of available samples in the collection was also low, which is very common in samples from bioarchaeological contexts. For these reasons, testing of the convergence of the data could not be accomplished with the same direct statistical methods used by the most common methodological testing. On the other hand, those very qualities of the data—being collected by individual researchers or by groups seeking to ask specific questions of the data—creates common problems with a real need to be solved.

3D data are also a representation that can be presented with variable parameters. Chapter 2 discusses aspects of these parameters, but here we will specifically concentrate on the mesh density, analogous to image resolution, and manifold state, a condition of whether a mesh is a continuous surface. Given the possibilities of those parameters, it became an important practical consideration to determine that the variability between parameters did not introduce significant error.

Development and testing of *robust statistical methods* as defined by Huber (1981) to apply to analysis of 3D surface data has been undertaken by a significant number of researchers (Abdel Fatah et al., 2014; Jantz et al., 2013; Mahfouz et al., 2007). These methods are enjoying acceptance as the successor of 2D metric statistics traditionally applied to 2D data. However, for now, an imposing challenge still exists in the consideration of the source and the consistency with which 3D surface data are collected, processed, and applied. Myriad variables of sample size and quality, digital data collection technology, and available software of highly variable accessibility to the researcher confound the ability to treat all 3D data and research as commensurate. Inconsistency creates problems for reproducing results. Reproducible results are an integral part of the scientific method. Expanding qualitative-to-quantitative morphometric theories from the initial test samples (typically either forensic or academic collections) to the medicolegal fields and historical and archaeological samples is inherently challenging. Samples from these fields are rarely complete and often suffer small sample size and high variability. This can result in analytical problems of no clear correlation or a high proportion of outliers. A forensic or academic collection—hand-picked for use in the types of studies referred to above—typically rejects individuals from the sample for having some kind of preservation defect. But a sample drawn from a burial context or contemporary forensic context would have a strong chance of suffering defects that could compromise application of certain methods.

Materials and methods

The data set for these two tests of validity consists of digitized cranial landmarks collected via Microscribe (Revware, Raleigh, NC, USA) and 3Skull software (Ousley, 2010) by Beatrix Dudzik and 3D surface scans collected via Z-Scanner 800 (3DSystems, Rock Hill, SC, USA) by Noriko Seguchi. The collected crania represent 18th century burials found in the Yacchi-no-gama (Yacchi cave) site on Kumejima (Kume Island) in Okinawa

Prefecture and housed at the Okinawa Prefectural Archaeology Center, Okinawa, Japan (Fukumie et al., 2001). This sample has not had any selection criteria applied to eliminate individuals based on preservation, age, or sex. The inhabitants of the Okinawa Island chain have been attributed as belonging to a distinct population group from those of the surrounding regions of the Japanese Archipelago and the East China Sea—the Central China Coast, the Southern Korean Peninsula, and Taiwan (Consortium J.A.H.P.G et al., 2012; Fukase et al., 2012; Fukumine et al., 2006; Moiseyev, 2009). These population theories propose that the particular characteristics of the Okinawa Island populations—and the Ryukyu Kingdom that was the recorded historical culture of the southern Okinawa Islands—were attributes connecting the populations to the pre-Yayoi Jomon hunter-gatherer Culture. The Jomon link as a theory has been researched by various investigators seeking either to bolster or refute the suggestion of a Jomon ancestry in biological data from the Okinawa Islands (Fukumine et al., 2006; Koganebuchi et al., 2012). Studies of craniofacial and dental characteristics relied heavily on qualitative analysis of scarce samples.

Paired interlandmark distance

To compare the congruence of the coordinate data as it describes the sample unit as a "global" object, Euclidean distance matrix analysis is applied to output a linear translation of the 3D data. This analysis is referred to as paired interlandmark distance (ILD). The paired ILDs are equivalent to the conventional 2D linear distances. This puts this research in line with previous craniofacial metric studies in both two and three dimensions.

Validity of a linear distance method for paired ILD of coordinates for multiple processing methods can evaluate how closely the linear distances between landmarks selected from 3D surface scans indicate statistical correlation with the linear distances of the digitized point data for the distance between all unique pairs of landmarks (Fig. 6.2).

Landmark point variation

The use of landmark point variation (LPV) is applied here to evaluate the spatial relationship of individual point selection given the multiple processing methods. This portion of the analysis relies on the 3D relationship among the observer-selected coordinates of each point for each processing method.

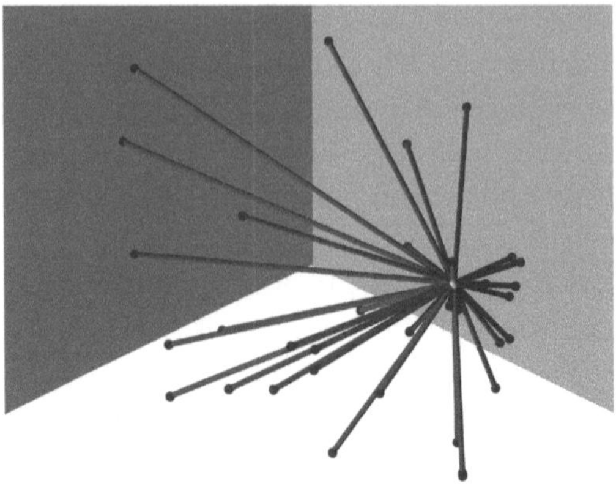

Figure 6.2 Sample from paired interlandmark distances.

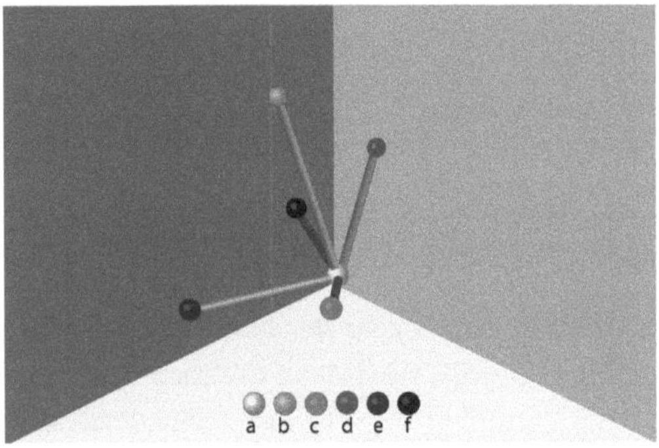

Figure 6.3 ***Sample from landmark point variation.*** (a) Microscribe coordinate; (b) high-face count coordinate; (c) low-face count coordinate; (d) high-face count nonmanifold coordinate; (e) low-face count nonmanifold coordinate; and (f) mean coordinate.

Validity of a 3D coordinate method for LPV: the landmark variation for each of the multiple processing methods can be assessed as the degree of correlation between the criterion landmark point coordinates and the corresponding selected landmark point coordinates of each of the processing models for which parameters are defined and data landmark data have been collected (Fig. 6.3). The permutation method applied with the Mantel test (Mantel, 1967) —using PAST three programs (Hammer, Ø. & Harper, D.A.T. 2006, version 3.11, 2015)—was an advantage as the available data to be collected from bioarchaeological materials is necessarily low.

Landmark point variation is typically the focus of medical and surgical research, whereas anthropological studies tend to examine regions, or modules of interest in the skull. This is especially significant to the forensic aspects of biological anthropology and considers the importance of high-dimension imaging technology applied to medical and surgical studies, with both referring to individual outcomes rather than population outcomes. Within anthropology, the subject of interest is more often the study of group morphology and distances. Although care is taken to study morphology, it is taken as a relative or global type of data, such as a group of landmarks that can be used to describe the relationship of the nasal and facial width, or the parameters of a principal component. Medical studies have a greater need to understand individual morphological differences. To study whether different imaging or observer training has an effect on landmark selection could have a direct impact on a patient outcome. For that, the variation of a single landmark is a significant data point.

Olszewski et al. (2010) investigated the accuracy and reproducibility of landmarks, given various methods of collection. This article forms the basis for the landmark point variation analysis in this chapter. The authors investigate landmark collection in terms of the scatter introduced by repeated landmark selection by observers and using selection models that differ. The metrics derived from this method evaluate the landmark coordinate variation for each landmark against the criterion, without the influence of other points.

Results

Results of validity testing for paired interlandmark distance

For the crania of the Kumejima sample under the experimental processing methods applied, the average distance between the direct digitizer ILDs and the process ILD was less than 2 mm over all landmarks over all processes for all types. This is within the margin of the differences between the mean of direct measurements and model measurements determined by Abdel Fatah et al. (2014).

For the results of this analysis, validity is determined by the calculation of several correlation coefficients. With the agreement of the data for the two types of analysis—interlandmark and landmark variation—with the findings of previous research, so long as our correlation is good and positive, we can consider it sufficient to validate the data collected for the process models. As we find our overall correlation of the ILDs to be $\sim r = 0.83$ or better for all processes, it is reasonable to accept the validity of the landmark points derived from all process models and consider all combinations of the processing parameters to be representative of the original physical materials they represent.

There are landmarks with characteristics that result in a higher variability even when selected by the same observer in the same or different sessions (Table 6.1). These landmarks have a very loosely bound definition and often are difficult to locate by definition using the Microscribe (Revware, Raleigh, NC, USA) (Ross and Williams, 2008; Sholts et al., 2011). ANOVA Generalized Linear Model (GLM) applied to the ILD sample with R software (Team, 2014) suggests the relative distance differences from the paired ILD-sampled landmarks have a higher relative variability for 8 landmarks out of 37.

The eight landmarks that have this higher variability are defined by Bookstein (1991) as Type II or Type III, and represent all the landmarks for any process correlation coefficient less than 0.8 for the ILD analysis. This refutes a conclusion of random error for the measurement of these landmarks due to the noted definitional variation acting on the point samples of these landmarks.

Higher variability of the eight landmarks under ANOVA GLM could not be attributed to missing values. None were among the eight landmarks with missing values. Landmarks with missing values were assessed (Table 6.2) and generally indicated high correlation. Removal of the imputed values used to replace missing values and reanalysis of the correlation of ILD did not indicate a strong influence on correlation caused by the imputation of missing values.

Applying a general linear model of an analysis of variance test to the ILD sample values allows for the consideration of whether the values of the ILD are likely given the criterion values of the direct digital sample or if they could have occurred randomly. Given the resulting high values of the F-statistic and very low *P*-value, it is reasonable to conclude that the values of the ILD sample are not due to chance.

Results of validity assessment for landmark point variation

When examining the preliminary plot of distance data for correlation, the values for the Microscribe (Revware, Raleigh, NC, USA) distance are higher than the values of the distances between processes for each process coordinate point for all but one landmark. This indicates that the distance between a process point and all other process points is less than the distance between the process point and the digitizer point for that landmark.

Table 6.1 ILD Correlation by Point (hf & hfnm).

			Correlation coefficient (Pearson's r/Spearman's rs)									
	Type	**Point**	**Process**	**Coef.**	**COD**	**Min**	**Max**	**Process**	**Coef.**	**COD**	**Min**	**Max**
1	**2**	**prosH**	hf	**0.8671**	0.7519	0.3960	0.9874	hfnm	**0.8310**	0.6906	0.3031	0.9848
2	**2**	**ssp**	hf	**0.8950**	0.8010	0.3486	0.9924	hfnm	0.7728	0.5972	0.4432	0.9655
3	**2**	**prosM**	hf	**0.8003**	0.6405	0.3960	0.9474	hfnm	0.7210	0.5198	0.2765	0.9202
4	**1**	**nas**	hf	**0.8564**	0.7334	−0.0166	0.9944	hfnm	**0.8496**	0.7218	0.3120	0.9940
5	**3**	**glb**	hf	**0.8242**	0.6793	0.1671	0.9917	hfnm	0.7974	0.6358	0.2234	0.9917
6	**3**	**spglb**	hf	0.6467	0.4182	0.1671	0.9803	hfnm	0.7936	0.6298	0.0464	0.9752
7	**1**	**brg**	hf	**0.8969**	0.8044	0.2201	0.9883	hfnm	**0.8673**	0.7522	0.0464	0.9876
8	**1**	**lam**	hf	**0.9099**	0.8279	0.3731	0.9946	hfnm	**0.8715**	0.7595	0.2290	0.9961
9	**3**	**opg**	hf	**0.8948**	0.8007	0.3731	0.9965	hfnm	**0.8640**	0.7465	0.3425	0.9987
10	**2**	**ops**	hf	**0.9100**	0.8281	0.2757	0.9917	hfnm	**0.8866**	0.7861	0.4160	0.9940
11	**2**	**bas**	hf	**0.8710**	0.7586	0.4564	0.9806	hfnm	**0.8653**	0.7487	0.5661	0.9939
12	**3**	**zygomr**	hf	**0.8906**	0.7932	0.2782	0.9874	hfnm	**0.8485**	0.7200	0.3923	0.9825
13	**2**	**jugr**	hf	**0.8659**	0.7498	0.2467	0.9967	hfnm	**0.8689**	0.7550	0.3923	0.9981
14	**3**	**fmtr**	hf	**0.8565**	0.7336	0.4398	0.9733	hfnm	**0.8630**	0.7448	0.3847	0.9908
15	**3**	**fmar**	hf	**0.9079**	0.8243	0.5975	0.9840	hfnm	**0.9049**	0.8188	0.1311	0.9914
16	**3**	**ectr**	hf	**0.8774**	0.7698	0.6071	0.9839	hfnm	**0.8864**	0.7857	0.5380	0.9821
17	**2**	**zygoor**	hf	0.7965	0.6344	0.3944	0.9777	hfnm	**0.8182**	0.6695	0.3878	0.9908
18	**2**	**dacr**	hf	**0.8580**	0.7362	0.4914	0.9942	hfnm	**0.8003**	0.6405	0.0995	0.9988
19	**2**	**dacl**	hf	**0.8410**	0.7073	0.2467	0.9934	hfnm	**0.8386**	0.7032	0.4994	0.9936
20	**3**	**obhi**	hf	**0.8682**	0.7538	0.4622	0.9976	hfnm	**0.8503**	0.7230	0.5300	0.9988
21	**3**	**obhs**	hf	**0.8114**	0.6584	−0.0166	0.9918	hfnm	**0.8021**	0.6434	0.2234	0.9967
22	**3**	**ectl**	hf	**0.8992**	0.8086	0.5252	0.9976	hfnm	**0.8997**	0.8095	0.5387	0.9988
23	**2**	**zygool**	hf	**0.8617**	0.7425	0.5524	0.9796	hfnm	0.7152	0.5115	0.1190	0.9904

(Continued)

Table 6.1 ILD Correlation by Point (hf & hfnm).—cont'd

			Correlation coefficient (Pearson's r/Spearman's rs)									
	Type	**Point**	**Process**	**Coef.**	**COD**	**Min**	**Max**	**Process**	**Coef.**	**COD**	**Min**	**Max**
24	**3**	**fmal**	hf	**0.8608**	0.7410	0.4648	0.9836	hfnm	**0.8411**	0.7074	0.1190	0.9914
25	**3**	**fmtl**	hf	**0.8658**	0.7496	0.5914	0.9699	hfnm	**0.8072**	0.6516	0.3738	0.9932
26	**2**	**jugl**	hf	**0.8705**	0.7578	0.1410	0.9731	hfnm	**0.8493**	0.7213	0.2202	0.9922
27	**3**	**zygoml**	hf	**0.8643**	0.7470	0.3486	0.9897	hfnm	**0.8301**	0.6891	0.1033	0.9925
28	**3**	**zygl**	hf	**0.8070**	0.6512	0.3944	0.9936	hfnm	0.7618	0.5803	0.2202	0.9970
29	**3**	**zygr**	hf	**0.8200**	0.6724	0.1410	0.9902	hfnm	**0.8124**	0.6600	0.1033	0.9962
30	**3**	**eurr**	hf	**0.8461**	0.7159	0.5252	0.9922	hfnm	**0.8074**	0.6519	0.4705	0.9970
31	**3**	**eurl**	hf	**0.8587**	0.7374	0.4971	0.9951	hfnm	**0.8023**	0.6437	0.0995	0.9821
32	**1**	**stpl**	hf	**0.8481**	0.7193	0.4670	0.9946	hfnm	**0.8470**	0.7174	0.5028	0.9961
33	**1**	**stpr**	hf	**0.8361**	0.6991	0.2658	0.9967	hfnm	**0.8362**	0.6992	0.5085	0.9987
34	**3**	**porr**	hf	**0.9047**	0.8185	0.2782	0.9992	hfnm	**0.8357**	0.6984	0.1311	0.9991
35	**3**	**porl**	hf	**0.9169**	0.8407	0.4734	0.9967	hfnm	**0.8705**	0.7578	0.3847	0.9981
36	**2**	**mastr**	hf	**0.9236**	0.8530	0.7186	0.9992	hfnm	**0.9035**	0.8163	0.6078	0.9991
37	**2**	**mastl**	hf	**0.9173**	0.8414	0.6731	0.9967	hfnm	**0.8966**	0.8039	0.5984	0.9945
1	**2**	**prosH**	lf	**0.8767**	0.7686	0.2203	0.9903	lfnm	**0.8806**	0.7755	0.4688	0.9853
2	**2**	**ssp**	lf	**0.8792**	0.7730	0.5930	0.9927	lfnm	**0.8853**	0.7838	0.5823	0.9868
3	**2**	**prosM**	lf	0.7954	0.6327	0.2203	0.9544	lfnm	0.7998	0.6397	0.4688	0.9694
4	**1**	**nas**	lf	**0.8598**	0.7393	−0.0379	0.9930	lfnm	**0.8562**	0.7331	0.0920	0.9875
5	**3**	**glb**	lf	0.7994	0.6390	0.1981	0.9942	lfnm	**0.8039**	0.6463	0.1195	0.9895
6	**3**	**spglb**	lf	0.7640	0.5837	−0.1818	0.9790	lfnm	0.6284	0.3949	−0.0105	0.9775
7	**1**	**brg**	lf	**0.8483**	0.7196	−0.1818	0.9891	lfnm	**0.9036**	0.8165	−0.0105	0.9828
8	**1**	**lam**	lf	**0.9155**	0.8381	0.4108	0.9940	lfnm	**0.8989**	0.8080	0.0987	0.9962
9	**3**	**opg**	lf	**0.8998**	0.8096	0.4108	0.9983	lfnm	**0.9005**	0.8109	0.0987	0.9987
10	**2**	**ops**	lf	**0.9295**	0.8640	0.5601	0.9955	lfnm	**0.9334**	0.8712	0.7245	0.9924

11	**2**	**bas**	lf	**0.8994**	0.8089	0.5008	0.9946	lfnm	**0.8855**	0.7841	0.6501	0.9910
12	**3**	**zygomr**	lf	**0.8894**	0.7910	0.3960	0.9885	lfnm	**0.8685**	0.7543	0.4285	0.9828
13	**2**	**jugr**	lf	**0.8986**	0.8075	0.5028	0.9981	lfnm	**0.8915**	0.7948	0.1955	0.9969
14	**3**	**fmtr**	lf	**0.8829**	0.7795	0.6037	0.9931	lfnm	**0.8802**	0.7748	0.5357	0.9839
15	**3**	**fmar**	lf	**0.9319**	0.8684	0.7628	0.9923	lfnm	**0.9177**	0.8422	0.3222	0.9833
16	**3**	**Ectr**	lf	**0.8862**	0.7854	0.5965	0.9895	lfnm	**0.8789**	0.7725	0.4764	0.9847
17	**2**	**zygoor**	lf	**0.8213**	0.6745	0.3455	0.9855	lfnm	**0.8076**	0.6522	−0.1833	0.9876
18	**2**	**dacr**	lf	**0.8800**	0.7744	0.6586	0.9966	lfnm	**0.8731**	0.7623	0.5310	0.9976
19	**2**	**dacl**	lf	**0.8570**	0.7344	0.5028	0.9927	lfnm	**0.8709**	0.7585	0.3228	0.9924
20	**3**	**obhi**	lf	**0.8945**	0.8001	0.4082	0.9962	lfnm	**0.8826**	0.7790	0.4398	0.9959
21	**3**	**obhs**	lf	**0.8377**	0.7017	−0.0379	0.9938	lfnm	**0.8176**	0.6685	0.0097	0.9941
22	**3**	**ectl**	lf	**0.8965**	0.8037	0.4370	0.9966	lfnm	**0.9062**	0.8212	0.4092	0.9976
23	**2**	**zygool**	lf	**0.8240**	0.6790	0.2128	0.9927	lfnm	**0.8199**	0.6722	0.1776	0.9849
24	**3**	**fmal**	lf	**0.8693**	0.7557	0.1999	0.9860	lfnm	**0.8637**	0.7460	0.5108	0.9822
25	**3**	**fmtl**	lf	**0.8424**	0.7096	0.4521	0.9802	lfnm	0.7993	0.6389	0.1148	0.9872
26	**2**	**jugl**	lf	**0.8557**	0.7322	0.0309	0.9831	lfnm	**0.8728**	0.7618	0.1322	0.9875
27	**3**	**zygoml**	lf	**0.8451**	0.7142	0.0234	0.9923	lfnm	**0.8289**	0.6871	−0.0925	0.9908
28	**3**	**zygl**	lf	0.7954	0.6327	0.0309	0.9969	lfnm	0.7783	0.6058	−0.1833	0.9940
29	**3**	**zygr**	lf	**0.8301**	0.6891	0.0234	0.9943	lfnm	**0.8174**	0.6681	−0.0925	0.9908
30	**3**	**eurr**	lf	**0.8411**	0.7074	0.1999	0.9973	lfnm	**0.8406**	0.7066	0.4092	0.9923
31	**3**	**eurl**	lf	**0.8711**	0.7588	0.3178	0.9916	lfnm	**0.8646**	0.7475	0.3284	0.9815
32	**1**	**stpl**	lf	**0.8629**	0.7446	0.5561	0.9981	lfnm	**0.8772**	0.7695	0.5481	0.9962
33	**1**	**stpr**	lf	**0.8691**	0.7553	0.5114	0.9983	lfnm	**0.8318**	0.6919	0.2109	0.9987
34	**3**	**porr**	lf	**0.9036**	0.8165	0.3960	0.9990	lfnm	**0.9039**	0.8170	0.4285	0.9984
35	**3**	**porl**	lf	**0.9162**	0.8394	0.4906	0.9979	lfnm	**0.9190**	0.8446	0.6173	0.9969
36	**2**	**mastr**	lf	**0.9245**	0.8547	0.6586	0.9990	lfnm	**0.9241**	0.8540	0.5854	0.9984
37	**2**	**mastl**	lf	**0.9269**	0.8591	0.6992	0.9962	lfnm	**0.9136**	0.8347	0.6485	0.9969

Highlight indicates points with lowest correlations acrcss all process methods.

Table 6.2 Missing coordinates summary.

	1. prosH	10. ops	11. bas	13. jugr	28. zygl	29. zygr	36. mastr	37. mastl
Total	4	16	8	4	8	8	20	8
hf	1	4	2	1	2	2	5	2
hfnm	1	4	2	1	2	2	5	2
lf	1	4	2	1	2	2	5	2
lfnm	1	4	2	1	2	2	5	2
dd	0	0	0	0	0	0	0	0

Missing values influence rank order correlation methods. If not removed, average values are substituted with a central tendency value, resulting in an artificially high or low correlation depending on the central tendency of the sample subset.

This means that the collection of the landmark data from the process models is internally consistent.

The results of the Mantel's test of correlation were strong enough to find in favor of validity by correlation for most landmarks of the LPV sample. It was notable, however, that for this analysis of the scatter of selected landmarks, the manifold processes had a higher correlation value than for the nonmanifold processes (Table 6.3). This would suggest that the processes that applied manifold adjustments did result in some calculable improvement to the observable quality of the surfaces of the manifold models and resulted in landmark point selection that was slightly more correlated to the landmark point selection of the direct digitizer landmarks.

Given that the collection of landmark points for all process models was randomized and the selected points on the models could be reviewed in the digital selection software, it is reasonable to conclude that the landmark point selection from the manifold processes or the nonmanifold models was not the result of significant systematic bias or error.

Conclusions: validity of paired interlandmark distance and landmark point variation

The results of the LPV and ILD tests on the processing parameters of mesh face count and manifold state and correlation to the Microscribe criterion are positive in indicating the overall correspondence by correlation of the landmark points selected from all tested mesh models with those of the criterion direct digitizer landmark point selections.

The extension of this conclusion is to suggest that the parameters of high- and low-face count and manifold state applied to the 3D models were not the source of any systematic error in the selection of landmarks

Table 6.3 Landmark point variation mantel test by point by process.

		R	*P*-value	R^2	R	*P*-value	R^3	R	*P*-value	R^4	R	*P*-value	R^5
Point	**Type**	**HF**	**HF**	**HF**	**HFNM**	**HFNM**	**HFNM**	**LF**	**LF**	**LF**	**LFNM**	**LFNM**	**LFNM**
nas	1	0.9470	0.0001	0.8968	0.9425	0.0001	0.8883	0.9093	0.0001	0.8268	0.8659	0.0001	0.7498
brg	1	0.7965	0.0001	0.6344	0.6873	0.0003	0.4724	0.7853	0.0001	0.6167	0.8820	0.0001	0.7779
lam	1	0.6582	0.0001	0.4332	0.8020	0.0001	0.6432	0.6933	0.0001	0.4807	0.5671	0.0001	0.3216
stpl	1	0.5975	0.0010	0.3570	0.7581	0.0001	0.5747	0.7383	0.0001	0.5451	0.6861	0.0001	0.4707
stpr	1	0.5691	0.0002	0.3239	0.7787	0.0001	0.6064	0.8157	0.0001	0.6654	0.6221	0.0001	0.3870
prosH	2	0.9186	0.0001	0.8438	0.8016	0.0001	0.6426	0.8947	0.0001	0.8005	0.8800	0.0001	0.7744
ssp	2	0.9106	0.0001	0.8292	0.2418	*0.0469*	0.0585	0.9155	0.0001	0.8381	0.9095	0.0001	0.8272
prosM	2	0.9279	0.0001	0.8610	0.8492	0.0001	0.7211	0.9144	0.0001	0.8361	0.8778	0.0001	0.7705
ops	2	0.8007	0.0001	0.6411	0.8837	0.0001	0.7809	0.8372	0.0001	0.7009	0.8732	0.0001	0.7625
bas	2	0.6453	0.0005	0.4164	0.6344	0.0004	0.4025	0.6645	0.0001	0.4416	0.6516	0.0001	0.4246
jugr	2	0.4564	0.0045	0.2083	0.7359	0.0001	0.5415	0.7188	0.0001	0.5167	0.5428	0.0003	0.2946
zygoor	2	0.8266	0.0001	0.6833	0.8859	0.0001	0.7848	0.8808	0.0001	0.7758	0.8913	0.0001	0.7944
dacr	2	0.8820	0.0001	0.7779	0.3944	0.0007	0.1556	0.7895	0.0001	0.6233	0.7762	0.0001	0.6025
dacl	2	0.8794	0.0001	0.7733	0.7954	0.0001	0.6327	0.7773	0.0001	0.6042	0.7538	0.0001	0.5682
zygool	2	0.8816	0.0001	0.7772	0.7472	0.0001	0.5583	0.8441	0.0001	0.7125	0.8910	0.0001	0.7939
jugl	2	0.8754	0.0001	0.7663	0.8324	0.0001	0.6929	0.8857	0.0001	0.7845	0.8847	0.0001	0.7827
mastr	2	0.9439	0.0001	0.8909	0.9520	0.0001	0.9063	0.9363	0.0001	0.8767	0.9407	0.0001	0.8849
mastl	2	0.9718	0.0001	0.9444	0.9497	0.0001	0.9019	0.9363	0.0001	0.8767	0.9055	0.0001	0.8199

Highlighting indicates an R2 value below 0.5. *Italics indicate a P-value greater than 0.005.*

from which to test the characteristics of the population. By extension, the scanning technology used to collect the cranial surfaces and create the mesh models is accurate.

Validity testing on semilandmark data collection

This section evaluates the accuracy of semilandmarks under the special case of semilandmark data collection using both archaeological human remains and forensic human remains, which are housed in Japan. Semilandmarks refer to a series of points located along a curve or surface that are absent in "traditional anatomical" landmarks (Bookstein, 1997). For anyone who has attempted to collect semilandmark data directly on dry crania using the sensor probe (the stylus point) of Microscribe, the difficulties in acquiring semilandmark data by tracing over the surface are apparent. To follow a curve or structure, and hope to intersect defining landmarks on a complicated surface, is challenging even if the sample units are in an excellent state of preservation. Therefore, good study design should be planned ahead of time before going to the data collection. Are measurement errors, both interobserver and intraobserver, insignificant? Anthropologists often collect data repeating several times and average out the values.

There are great amounts in the human skeletal collections in several institutions in Japan spanning from the Neolithic Jomon Period to modern times. However, archaeological human remains in Japan are preserved poorly and usually fragile as described in chapter 3. A researcher may encounter some problems in the acquisition of 3D digitizing data using the probe point of Microscribe. The possible difficulties are (1) it is simply difficult to capture semilandmark data on complex-shaped human remains (i.e., crania) and (2) the curators of Japanese institutions may hesitate to give permission for the use of Microscribe for data collection because the probe of Microscribe looks pointed and sharp. (A round-shaped probe is also available.)

Fragility of human remains and complex-shaped bone itself can be major obstacles for collecting semilandmarks by 3D digitizer. Although many institutions in Japan used chemical treatments or adhesive coatings on human remains in the past, the newly recovered human skeletal remains are not treated chemically. This change in practice means it is now possible to perform radiocarbon dating, isotope, and amino acid by extraction of the bone collagen from the untreated remains. Moreover, many crania were reconstructed some decades ago using wooden picks and plasticine fillers for connecting each bone. Those reconstructed crania are structurally unstable and fragile. The stylus point probe of the Microscribe could scratch bone surfaces and destroy the poorly reconstructed crania. Consequently, researchers may be prohibited from capturing landmark and semilandmark data directly from human remains in Japanese institutions due to poor preservation and poor reconstruction. In fact, one Japanese institution requested that a researcher use a plastic cover on the fragile crania. It means that the data collection environment can vary significantly between institutions if a researcher is not able to get permission to capture 3D data directly from the crania by Microscribe.

Here, we explore the possibility for integrating semilandmark data captured by 1) multiple observers and 2) multiple methods: using 3D digitizer, Microscribe (Revware, Raleigh, NC, USA) and 3D laser surface scans. To evaluate the possibility, the compatibility by correlation of semilandmarks captured from virtual digital models with the directly captured semilandmarks must be tested. This section investigates compatibility between data acquisition using a digitizer and laser scan approach. It incorporates an assessment of the validity of data acquired by Microscribe versus Checkpoint landmark software (Murphy, 2015) from the perspective of the difficulties and challenges found with bioarcheological materials.

Therefore, we investigate 1) the amount of intraobserver error of semilandmark data on the "difficult" curvatures by Microscribe and 2) the amount of interobserver error between semilandmark data on frontal arcs using Microscribe (Revware, Raleigh, NC, USA) and semilandmark data using Stratovan Checkpoint program (Stratovan Corporation, Davis, CA, USA) on 3D mesh models. For this validity assessment, we chose the frontal arc, which represents an "easy" curve and the maxillary alveolar process as a "difficult" curve.

At last, we also describe how we can slide the "difficult curve" of the alveolar process using Stratovan Checkpoint. This demonstrates the utility of virtual data collection of data for such complex curves.

Materials and methods: data collection and preparation

Materials

The crania are the same samples used in the previous section in this chapter, and they represent 18th century burials found in the Yacchi-nogama (Yacchi cave) site on Kumejima (Kume Island) in Okinawa Prefecture and housed at the Okinawa Prefectural Archaeology Center, Okinawa,

Japan (Fukumine et al., 2001). In addition, samples of 20th century adult Japanese dry crania were used. These crania are in the modern medical collections housed in the Kyushu University Museum, Fukuoka, Japan.

The digitized semilandmarks

Easy curve samples: yacchi-no-gama data

The data set for digitized cranial landmarks and semilandmarks (frontal arc from nasion to bregma [nasion-glabella-supraglabella-bregma]) were collected directly from the crania via Microscribe (Revware, Raleigh, NC, USA) and 3Skull software (Ousley, 2010) by Beatrix Dudzik (Fig 6.4 and 6.5A, B). Then, frontal curves (the nasion-glabella-supraglabella-bregma chord) were collected on 3D virtual mesh models via Stratovan Checkpoint program by Mary-Margaret Murphy (Fig. 6.4 and 6.5).

Difficult curve samples: Modern Japanese data

The samples of 20th century adult Japanese dry crania were selected from the medical collections housed in the Kyushu University Museum, Fukuoka, Japan. For this data acquisition process, the Museum collection manager requested the use of a thin sheet of plastic between the sample surface and the Microscribe probe. In addition, the observer was not allowed to set a cranium directly on dental wax or clay, although the stable setting of a cranium is crucial for 3D data acquisition. Therefore, each cranium was

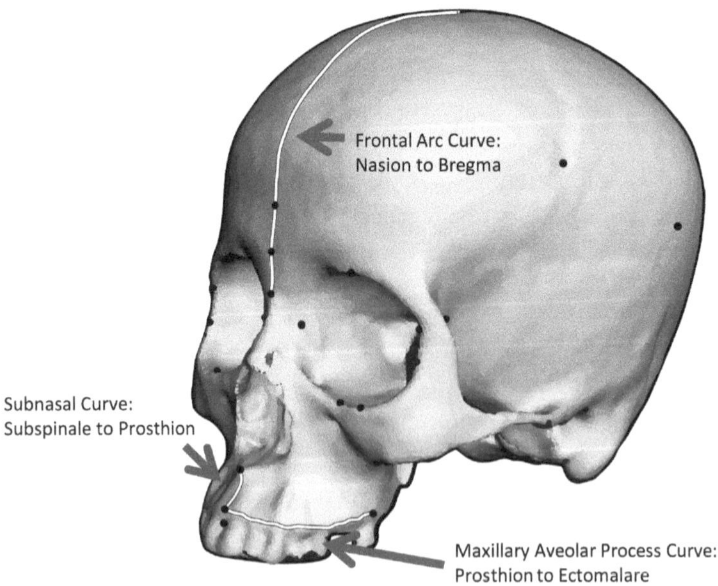

Figure 6.4 Digitized semilandmarks—PEL, per, SSP. Frontal Arc Curve: Nasion to Bregma.

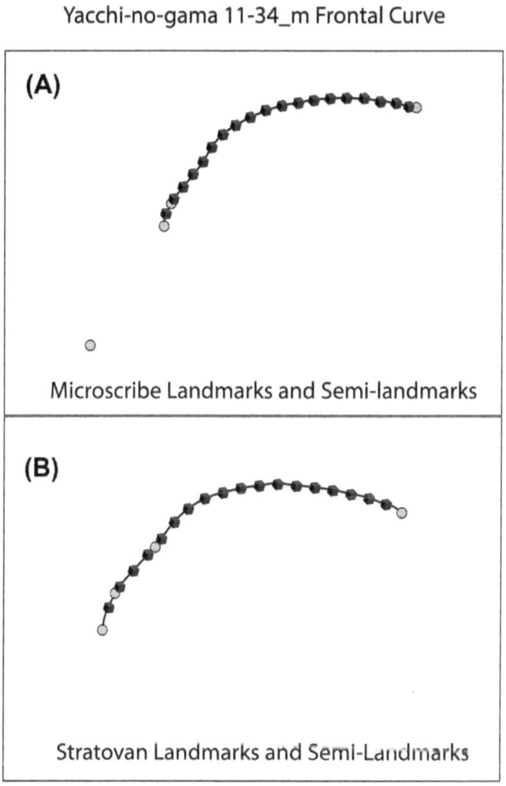

Figure 6.5 Frontal curves with Microscribe and Stratovan. *Visualization from Morpheus et al. From Stratovan Corporation. Stratovan Checkpoint [Software]. Version 2018.08.07. Aug 07, 2018. URL: https://www.stratovan.com/products/checkpoint. Used with permission from Stratovan Corporation.*

affixed on a thin plastic sheet between dental wax and enclosed by blocks of clay before digitization to assure stability as much as possible.

Three arcs of the maxillary alveolar process (PEL-prosthion to left ectomalare; PER-prosthion to right ectomalare; and SSP-subspinale to prosthion) were customized in the 3Skull program by Stephen Ousley for this project. 3D semilandmarks (x, y, z) were collected every 0.5 mm and saved in the 3Skull program. We also set the upper limit on the number we would allow to be taken for the arc from subspinale to prosthion as 80 points. The upper limit on the number for bilateral arcs from prosthion to ectomalare was set to 300 points.

These maxillary alveolar process curvature data (PEL-prosthion to left ectomalare, PER-prosthion to right ectomalare) and subspinale to prosthion (SSP) were captured in the form of a 3D stream of data directly from the crania via Microscribe and 3Skull program (Ousley, 2010; Williams and

Slice, 2010) by Shiori Yonemoto (See Fig. 6.4). Each curve was digitized three times from a cranium.

The semilandmarks collected on virtual mesh models

The 3D mesh models were produced from 3D laser surface scan data. The virtual digital models were produced as high-face manifold models by Mary-Margaret Murphy. We used high-face manifold models, which are the closed geometric state of a mesh model because the use of the manifold model showed slightly higher accuracy than the use of the nonmanifold model (Murphy 2015). In addition, the manifold models do not contain holes or surface damage to interfere with the collection of landmarks. The semilandmarks were captured from the virtual digital models using Stratovan Checkpoint (Stratovan Corporation, Davis CA USA). Then, frontal arc data (the nasion-glabella-supraglabella-bregma chord) were collected on 3D virtual mesh models via Stratovan Checkpoint program by Mary-Margaret Murphy (See Fig. 6.4). The horizontal and the vertical view windows of Stratovan Checkpoint program can show the cross-sectional view of a cranium. The midline and highest cross-sectional portion of the cranium was sliced from nasion to glabella, from glabella to supraglabella, from supraglabella to bregma.

Each set of landmark and semilandmark points for each cranium was entered into Morpheus et al. software (Slice, 2013) to affect the aligned orientation between the landmark endpoints and semilandmarks collected in Stratovan Checkpoint software and those collected by Microscribe. The 3D Bookstein alignment was used, setting an origin (bregma), translating, and rotating a secondary point (nasion) to zero for each Y and Z directions, then rotating the third point (glabella) around X vector to zero for Y direction. This sets all curves into an alignment with a common origin regardless of the "weighted centroid." Morpheus et al. (Slice, 2013) allows the scale factor applied within the alignment process to be reversed, which is done to retain the actual scale of the curves to the scale of the original materials. Using Morpheus et al (Slice, 2013), 20 points are extracted from each frontal arc that was captured by both Microscribe and Stratovan Checkpoint, 10 points are extracted from SSP (subspinale-prosthion) semilandmarks, and 20 points are extracted from PEL (prosthion-left ectomalare) and PER (prosthion-right ectomalare) semilandmarks that were captured by Microscribe.

Statistics method: correlation assessment

These extracted points (x, y, z) originally collected by Microscribe and Stratovan Checkpoint were compared for correspondence correlations.

For the purposes of assessing this statistical relationship, this project used the permutation method of the Mantel test (Mantel, 1967) with the use of Euclidean distances.

Results

Curve data of maxillary alveolar process

Fig. 6.6 displays the visualization of semilandmarks of the maxillary alveolar processes, from prosthion to ectomalare left and prosthion to ectomalare right. The inconsistency of the three trials can be observed in the figure. The point landmark of Prosthion (Pr) was repeatedly collected when three arcs (SSP: Ssp to Pr, PEL:Pr to left ectomalare, and PER: Pr to right Ectomalare) were sliced. The repeated landmarks Pr were visually inconsistent. The 3D coordinates of Pr were inconsistent. The point landmark of Pr often separated and had a gap between PEL (Pr to left ectomalare) and PER (Pr to right ectomalare). This means that the set crania had moved toward the X-axis direction when the landmark Pr was collected and sliced toward ectomalare left or right. This visualization shows that the semilandmarks from prosthion to ectomalare often moved in the Y-axis direction. Repeatability of curve data of maxillary alveolar processes from the modern Japanese crania captured by Microscribe was also compared for correspondence correlations using the Mantel test. Data collection method differed from the case of Yacchi crania. As mentioned before, the modern skull surfaces had to be covered by transparent plastic because the curator of the museum and the observer were concerned that the stylus point probe of Microscribe might hurt the surface of the thin

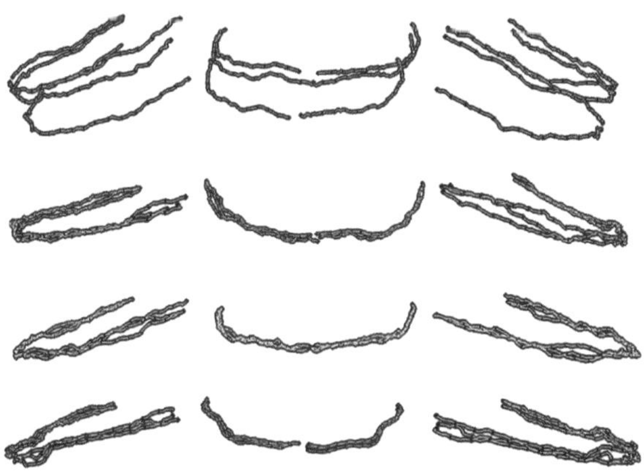

Figure 6.6 Maxillary alveolar curves captured with Microscribe. (visualization from Morpheus et al.)— Modern Japan crania three trials.

alveolar process of the maxilla. However, the observer acknowledged that the plastic cover might disturb accuracy of semilandmark data. In addition, the surface of the maxillary alveolar processes is bumpy and ridged and exhibits a more complex curvature than is found on other surfaces of the cranium. Thus, the semilandmark arcs, especially prosthion to ectomalare, are considered a "difficult to capture" curve, although the curve from subspinale to prosthion is somewhat less complex and considered an "easy to capture" curve.

Fig. 6.7 shows the results of Mantel tests of three trials of digitizing of semilandmarks of curvatures of maxillary alveolar process captured directly from the crania by Microscribe. Table 6.4 shows correlation coefficients of SSP, PEL, and PER of three trials. Intraobserver errors on the repeatability of curves on SSP (Ssp-Pr) are subtly smaller than those of the

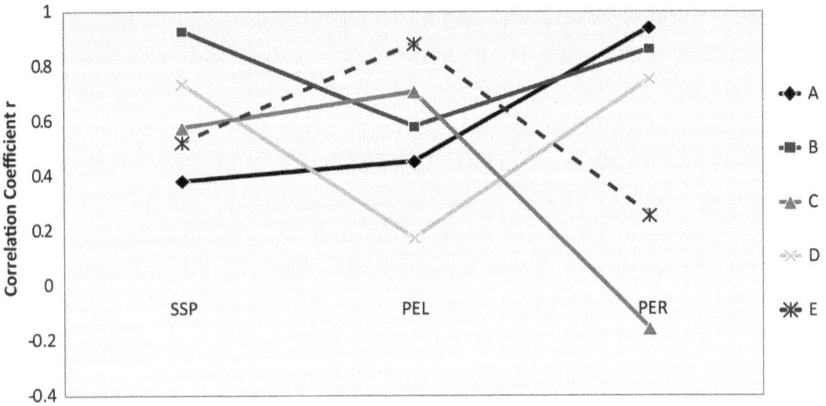

Figure 6.7 The results of Mantel tests of three trials of the digitizing of semilandmarks of curvatures of maxillary alveolar processes captured directly from the crania by Microscribe.

Table 6.4 Results of Mantel tests.

	Correlation coefficient r					
ID	**SSP**	***P*-value**	**PEL**	***P*-value**	**Per**	***P*-value**
A	0.3839	0.004	0.4553	0.0001	0.9427	0.0001
B	0.93	0.0001	0.5828	0.0001	0.8664	0.0001
C	0.5782	0.0001	0.7118	0.0001	−0.1537	0.9504
D	0.7385	0.0001	0.1776	0.0231	0.7576	0.0001
E	0.5237	0.0027	0.8845	0.0001	0.2577	0.0023
Permutation numbers = 9999				*P*-value: One tailed		

Correlation coefficient r for three trials of *SSP* (subspinale to Prosthion), *PEL* (Prosthion to left Ectomalare), and *PER* (Prosthion to right ectomalare).

maxillary alveolar process. Correlation coefficients ranged from 0.3839 to 0.93. Intraobserver errors on curves of maxillary alveolar processes (directly captured by Microscribe) are large. Correlation coefficients of PEL (prosthion to left ectomalare) ranged from 0.1776 to 0.8845, and correlation coefficients of PER (prosthion to right ectomalare) ranged from 0.1537 to 0.9427. These low correlations indicate that the average values of several repetitions of semilandmark data do not compromise the accuracy. These results impel caution on combining semilandmark data by different collection technology and by multiple observers.

Frontal arc semilandmark

The curve data of the frontal bone from the Yacchi crania captured by Microscribe and Stratovan Checkpoint were examined for correspondence correlations by the Mantel tests. The frontal arc is an "easy to capture" curve. Interobserver errors on frontal arc (taken by Microscribe on actual crania directly and by Stratovan Checkpoint on virtual models) are not significant. Fig. 6.8 shows that the results of Mantel tests for correlation of Microscribe and Stratovan captured frontal arc. Correlation coefficients ranged from 0.90 to 0.98 except one case by Microscribe in which the nasion was misplaced by ssp, which shows a correlation coefficient of 0.2465. It might be the case that the alignment by Microscribe was disturbed, or that the cranium may have been moved after the start of landmark recording (Also see Fig 6.5A).

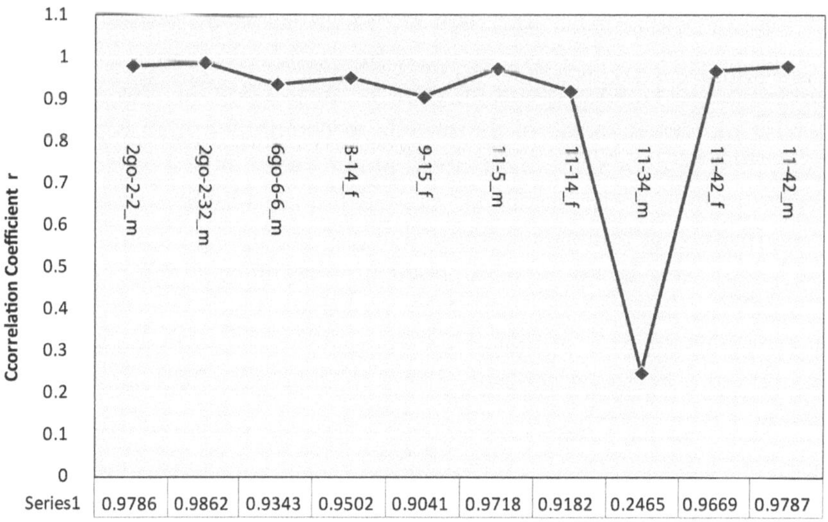

Figure 6.8 The results of Mantel tests for correlation of Microscribe and Stratovan captured frontal arc.

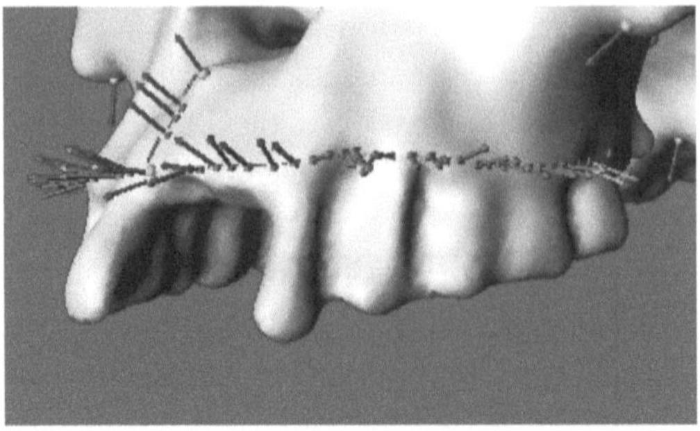

Figure 6.9 The curvatures of maxillary alveolar process (prosthion to left ectomalare—prosthion to right ectomalare) and the curvature of subspinale to prosthion captured on 3D virtual mesh models via Stratovan Checkpoint program. *From Stratovan Corporation. Stratovan Checkpoint [Software]. Version 2018.08.07. Aug 07, 2018. URL: https://www.stratovan.com/products/checkpoint. Used with permission from Stratovan Corporation.*

Lastly, we demonstrate how to slide the curvatures of the maxilla (prosthion to left ectomalare: prosthion to right ectomalare) and the curvature of subspinale to prosthion on 3D virtual mesh models via Stratovan Checkpoint program (Fig. 6.9). At first, ectomalare left and right have to be determined. Ectomalare is defined as the most lateral point on the buccal surface of the alveolar margins of the maxilla, often opposite to the middle of the second molar tooth (Langley et al., 2016; Martin and Knussmann, 1988). When an observer uses Microscribe, she/he has to first use calipers to determine the location of the ectomalare landmark on the maxilla, mark the location with a pencil and then record the marks by Microscribe. By Stratovan (see chapter 5 Box 5.8), the horizontal and the vertical view windows of Stratovan Checkpoint program are used to see the cross-sectional view of the dental arcade of the maxilla to determine paired ectomalare. Using these windows, the most lateral points on the buccal surface of the alveolar margins of the maxilla are easily determined by Stratovan Checkpoint. Identifying landmarks corresponding to maximum/minimum width and length using Stratovan Checkpoint program offers a more consistent approach that improves accuracy. After the landmark prosthion is recorded, the semilandmark from prosthion to ectomalare can be sliced and identified by Stratovan Checkpoint program. The semilandmarks of SSP, subspinale to prosthion are also easily sliced and identified.

Discussion and conclusions

It is true that researchers can save a tremendous amount of data collection time using a digitizer and manually collecting landmark coordinate data. It is faster than using traditional calipers to measure and manually record cranial measurements, which account for the majority of traditional craniometric studies. It can take as little as 15 minutes to record up to 60 cranial measurements and craniofacial coordinate data using Microscribe and 3Skull software (Ousley, 2010). Digitizers are portable and can collect massive amounts of 3D information in very little time.

However, error can easily be introduced when observers often do not realize that they skip over landmarks, the x, y, z position of a landmark had not been recorded by the computer, landmark order becomes mixed up or transposed, or the position of the cranium can move slightly during data collection. During data collection, particularly when involving international travel, time and access to material is often limited, and data processing often occurs once the researcher has returned to their home institution. On data processing, errors in landmark recordings may be discovered, and the observations cannot be easily remeasured after a data collection trip has ended. If the error was endemic to the entire data collection period, it is possible that all the data are unreliable and may have to be discarded entirely. These problems can be circumvented by using visualization tools available in software packages such as Morpheus, which can identify errors that happen during data collection so that they can be corrected or remeasured simultaneously.

Again, curvatures on specific areas of the cranium can be challenging to capture manually using a digitizer. When digitizing and using the 3Skull program to record landmarks, a researcher is not able to identify errors with recorded landmarks or semilandmark arcs until reviewed with software such as Morpheus et al. (Slice, 2013) or MorphoJ (Klingenberg, 2011). If the focus in the field is capturing the 3D scan data, landmark data collection can take place in the virtual environment at a researcher's home institution without conceding to the pressures of limited data collection periods in the field.

Additionally, if a researcher is well-trained, "easily captured" curve data such as frontal arcs collected with a digitizer can be combined with the curve data collected on 3D virtual models. However, it can be computationally difficult, whereas the process of acquiring curve data on virtual cranial models by using Checkpoint software improves data quality and benefits research by 1) improving accuracy when identifying landmarks corresponding to maximum width and length and 2) visualizing curve data, which allows for the determination of data quality and necessary adjustments.

Based on our validity assessment, point landmark data captured by a digitizer and on virtual models by multiple individuals are consistent enough to be used and can be combined in a single dataset if the landmarks protocol and criterion are shared. However, capturing semilandmark data by a digitizer can cause errors: intraobserver error is far greater on "difficult to capture" types of curvatures than "easy to capture" types of curvatures. It is not recommended to use semilandmark data that are manually recorded on complex morphology, such as the outline of the hard palate, due to the difficulties that result in high amounts of intra- and interobserver error. Semilandmark data representing complex morphology should be captured using 3D scan images, although it is acknowledged that this approach is a more time-consuming process. However, once the virtual mesh models are produced, it is easy and quick to capture 3D semilandmark data from the virtual models using programs such as Stratovan Checkpoint. If the stable cranium-setting environment is provided and the surface of its morphology is simple and smooth, it is possible to combine semilandmark data captured both by Microscribe directly from the crania and by Stratovan Checkpoint from the virtual mesh models because the effects of observer errors are smaller, but it requires caution.

Capturing landmarks and semilandmarks on the virtual mesh model using Stratovan is easy and exhibits higher accuracy. Moreover, the use of Stratovan Checkpoint is beneficial because the landmark/semilandmark data collection under the digital environment used by this software can be repeated. This method appears to be the most reliable. Our assessment demonstrates that the difficulty of visualization and landmark/semilandmark collection using Microscribe is markedly higher than that of the virtual data collection method; thus the virtual data collection method results in a more accurate set of data for analysis.

The researchers must take all possible situations (permission, collection time, etc.) into account carefully before data collection field work. In this chapter, our analysis explored the difficulties of 3D data collection on poorly preserved crania of Japan. However, the first author of this chapter experienced similar restrictions during analysis of the Kennewick Man cranium. Permission to capture semilandmark data was denied, even for data collection from the duplicated cast of the Kennewick cranium using the stylus probe of a Microscribe.

Thus, collecting scan data appears to be the most beneficial, least invasive method when working with poorly preserved remains. However, it is necessary to communicate with the curators of institutions to inquire about the data collection environment and what tools researchers can use and what way researchers can collect data before the data collection trip.

References

Abdel Fatah, E.E., Shirley, N.R., Jantz, R.L., Mahfouz, M.R., 2014. Improving sex estimation from crania using a novel three-dimensional quantitative method (Report). Journal of Forensic Sciences 59 (3), 10.

Bookstein, F.L., 1997. Landmark methods for forms without landmarks: morphometrics of group differences in outline shape. Medical Image Analysis 1, 225–243.

Bookstein, F.L., 1991. Morphometric Tools for Landmark Data: Geometry and Biology. Cambridge University Press, Cambridge [England]. New York.

Carmines, E.G., Zeller, R.A., 1979. Reliability and Validity Assessment. Sage Publications, Beverly Hills, CA.

Cignoni, P., Scopigno, R., 2008. Sampled 3D models for CH applications: a viable and enabling new medium or just a technological exercise? Journal on Computing and Cultural Heritage 1 (1), 1–23.

Consortium, J.A.H.P.G., et al., 2012. The history of human populations in the Japanese archipelago inferred from genome-wide SNP data with a special reference to the Ainu and the Ryukyuan populations. Journal of Human Genetics 57 (12), 787.

Fukase, H., Wakebe, T., Tsurumoto, T., Saiki, K., Fujita, M., Ishida, H., 2012. Facial characteristics of the prehistoric and early-modern inhabitants of the Okinawa islands in comparison to the contemporary people of Honshu. Anthropological Science 120 (1), 23–32.

Fukumine, T., Doi, N., Ishida, H., Zukeran, C., Sensui, S., Saso, A., Higa, T., 2001. Human skeletal remains from the Yacchi-no-Gama and Kanjinbaru grave sites. In: Okinawa Prefectural Archaeological Center (Ed.), Yacchi-no-Gama, Kanjinnbaru Grave Sites. Okinawa Prefectural Archaeological Center Research Report, No. 6, Okinawa, pp. 345–385 (in Japanese).

Fukumine, T., Hanihara, T., Nishime, A., Isida, H., 2006. Nonmetric cranial variation of early modern human skeletal remains from Kumejima, Okinawa and the peopling of the Ryukyu Islands. Anthropological Science 114, 141–151.

Hammer, Ø., Harper, D.A.T., 2006. Paleontological Data Analysis. Blackwell.

Huber, P.J., 1981. Robust statistics. Wiley, New York: New York.

Jantz, R., Mahfouz, M., Shirley, N.R., Abdel Fatah, E., 2013. Improving Sex Estimation from Crania Using 3-dimensional CT Scans. U.S. Department of Justice. https://www.ncjrs.gov/pdffiles1/nij/grants/240688.pdf.

Klingenberg, C.P., 2011. MorphoJ: an integrated software package for geometric morphometrics. Molecular Ecology Resources 11, 353–357.

Koganebuchi, K.A.E., Katsumura, T., Nakagome, S., Ishida, H., Kawamura, S., Oota, H., The Asian Archival DNA Repository C, 2012. Autosomal and Y-chromosomal STR markers reveal a close relationship between Hokkaido Ainu and Ryukyu islanders. Anthropological Science 12 (3), 199–208.

Langley, N.R., Meadows Jantz, L., Ousley, S.D., Jantz, R.L., Milner, G., 2016. Data Collection Procedures for Forensic Skeletal Material. The University of Tennessee, Knoxville. https://fac.utk.edu/wp-content/uploads/2016/03/DCP20_webversion.pdf.

Mahfouz, M.R., Merkl, B.C., Abdel Fatah, E.E., Booth, R., Argenson, J.N., 2007. Automatic methods for characterization of sexual dimorphism of adult femora: distal femur. Computer Methods in Biomechanics and Biomedical Engineering 10 (6), 447–456.

Mantel, N.A., 1967. The detection of disease clustering and a generalized regression approach. Cancer Research 27 (2), 209–220.

Martin, R., Knussmann, R., 1988. Anthropologie: Handbuch der vergleichenden Biologie des Menschen. Gustav Fischer, Stuttgart.

McKeown, A.H., Jantz, R.L., 2005. Comparison of Coordinate and Craniometric Data for Biological Distance Studies. In: Slice, D.E. (Ed.), Modern Morphometrics in Physical Anthropology. Springer, Boston, MA, pp. 215–230.

Moiseyev, V.G., 2009. On the origin of the Ryukyu Islanders: the integration of craniometrics and cranial nonmetric data. Archaeology, Ethnology and Anthropology of Eurasia 37 (4), 146–152.

Murphy, M.M., 2015. Validity of landmark selection given different 3D scan processing parameters: Landmark location on 3D models of Yacchi crania. MA Thesis. Department of Anthropology, University of Montana, Missoula.

Nance, J.D., Ball, B.F., 1986. No surprises? The reliability and validity of test pit sampling. American Antiquity 51 (3), 457–483.

Olszewski, R., Tanesy, O., Cosnard, G., Zech, F., Reychler, H., 2010. Reproducibility of osseous landmarks used for computed tomography based three-dimensional cephalometric analyses. Journal of Cranio-Maxillofacial Surgery Scotland 214–221.

Ousley, S.D., 2010. Three Skull Version 2.0.

Ross, A.H., Williams, S., 2008. Testing repeatability and error of coordinate landmark data acquired from crania*. Journal of Forensic Sciences 53 (4), 782–785.

Shearer, B.M., Cooke, S.B., Halenar, L.B., Reber, S., Plummer, J.E., Delson, E., Tallman, M., 2017. Evaluating causes of error in landmark-based data collection using scanners. PLoS One 12 (11), e0187452.

Sholts, S.B., Flores, L., Walker, P., Warmlander, S., 2011. Comparison of coordinate measurement precision of different landmark types on human crania using a 3D laser scanner and a 3D digitizer: implications for applications of digital morphometrics. International Journal of Osteoarchaeology 21 (5), 535–543.

Slice, D.E., 2013. Morpheus et al, Java Edition. Department of Scientific Computing, The Florida State University, Tallahassee, Florida, U.S.A. Available from http:/morphlab.sc.fsu.edu/.

Williams, S.E., Slice, D.E., 2010. Regional shape change in adult facial bone curvature with age. American Journal of Physical Anthropology 143 (3), 437–447.

CHAPTER SEVEN

3D data analysis using R

3D data processing, shape analysis, and surface manipulations in R

Stefan Schlager*
Department of Biological Anthropology, Albert-Ludwigs University Freiburg, Freiburg, Germany

Introduction

The statistical/mathematical platform *R* (R Core Team, 2015) is an open source framework designed for quantitative data processing and analysis. It is relatively easy to use (without previous programming experience), provides a package manager, as well as a build-in documentation system, and allows analyzing the data with a vast number of extensions (called *packages*), allowing sophisticated state-of-the art statistical analyses. The fact that many scientists working with biological data are already familiar with R is also beneficial for sharing code and making it available to researchers with no or only little proficiency in software programming.

Compared with software programs using a graphical user interface (GUI) that are limited to the features implemented by the developers, using R is a more flexible approach. With some knowledge of the R language, users can design their own workflow routines that can be run subsequently. The benefits are obvious: infinite possibilities to combine and extend the existing functionality, sharing code with fellow researchers or publishing together with a manuscript, making the analyses reproducible for interested readers. The greatest benefit, however, is the fact that all data loaded into the R workspace can be analyzed with other R-packages, thus drastically increasing the possibilities for quantitative analyses of these data. Rather than providing a single processing pipeline, R can be viewed as the playing field on which this pipeline can be designed and used. To give the reader a better understanding, this chapter introduces statistical analysis of 3D data by presenting some necessary tools and applying those tools to example data. The reader is encouraged to reproduce these examples by using the provided code.

* Stefan Schlager retains copyright for the original software programming codes appearing in his contribution.

3D Data Acquisition for Bioarchaeology, Forensic Anthropology, and Archaeology
ISBN: 978-0-12-815309-3
https://doi.org/10.1016/B978-0-12-815309-3.00007-3

This chapter will mainly rely on two packages created by the author: *Morpho*[1] for landmark-based shape analysis and *Rvcg*[2] for computations involving 3D triangular meshes, that is, surfaces represented by a concatenation of triangular cells. Both packages are multiplatform and available via the CRAN[3] repository (Section 2). Readers unfamiliar with R will find introductory literature on https://cran.r-project.org/manuals.html. This chapter will introduce both packages and provide workflow examples and code snippets allowing readers to readily reproduce the analyses. For documentation on using R, please refer to https://cran.r-project.org/ where a large amount of documentation for all proficiency levels is provided. The reader is further assumed to have a basic understanding of geometric morphometrics and statistical shape analysis and to be familiar with triangular surface meshes (Schneider and Eberly, 2002). Although data processing and handling in R allows the use of a wide variety of statistical procedures, this chapter will mainly concentrate on those that are shipped with the packages written by the author.

Preliminaries and installation

Installation is, thanks to the CRAN repository, quite easy. To install the packages presented in this chapter, issue the following command from your R-command line:

```
> install.packages('Morpho')
```

This will also take care of the dependencies, one of which is the second package presented here: *Rvcg*.

For installing a development snapshot, the R-package *devtools* provides the functionality to install and build a package from git repositories such as github.[4] As both packages contain code that needs compilation, appropriate compilers and toolchain need to be installed. Although this will be already the case on most Linux systems, OS X users will need to install XCODE[5] and Windows users can use *Rtools*.[6] To install the latest development snapshot, using *devtools*, run.

[1] https://cran.r-project.org/package=Morpho.
[2] https://cran.r-project.org/package=Rvcg.
[3] https://cran.r-project.org/.
[4] https://github.com.
[5] https://developer.apple.com/xcode/.
[6] https://cran.r-project.org/bin/windows/Rtools/.

```
> devtools::install_github('zarquon42b/Morpho') ## or
> devtools::install_github('zarquon42b/Rvcg') ## respectively
```

As required by all packages distributed via CRAN, all public functions are documented and include self-contained working example code and data. The example landmark set provided by *Morpho* via the data set *boneData* was placed in 3D image data according to the definitions in (Schlager, 2013). It consists of 10 manually placed landmarks on the bone surface of 80 human noses. The digitization was performed on surfaces with a much higher resolution than the one also included in the example data (belonging to the first specimen), which is strongly decimated and some structures, such as sutures, are close to invisible. In all examples provided below, it is assumed that the packages *Morpho*, *Rvcg*, and *rgl* are already loaded into the current workspace (e.g., by issuing `require(packagename)`).

About the example data used in this chapter

The data used in this chapter will be the surface scans from the Yacchi sample (Okinawa Prefectural Archaeology Center, 2001). Landmarks were placed both on the surface scans using the Stratovan Checkpoint software as well as recorded on the original skulls using a Microscribe TX device. For the examples in this chapter, it is assumed that the R working directory contains a folder called "*Data*" with a subfolder named "Yacchi-HF" containing the high-resolution surface scans and landmark files. Below is the code to download and unzip the file in R. This will automatically obtain the data and set up the correct folder structure to run all examples in this chapter.

```
> download.file(url="http://bit.ly/2L2174p","Yacchi-Example-
                Data.zip")
> unzip("Yacchi-Example-Data.zip")
```

Data import/export

The convention for storing and processing landmarks using *Morpho* is to store single landmark configurations of k landmarks in m dimensions as $k \times m$ matrices and a sample of size n as arrays of dimensionality $k \times m \times n$. That way, the landmark data can also be processed by other packages dealing with landmark configurations, such as *shapes*[7] or *geomorph.*[8] R provides the functionality to parse all kinds of text (and binary) files, which means that the user is not restricted by any given file format the data are stored in. However, writing a function to import such data might be constrained by the user's capabilities in using R. For that reason, *Morpho* provides a variety of import functions dealing with common file formats used to store landmark data (Table 7.1). The IDAV-landmark editor[9] is still quite a popular choice for digitizing landmarks and its commercial successor Checkpoint[10], that has been used for digitizing some of the landmarks serving as example data, supports the same formats. To accommodate for this fact, there are the functions `read.pts` to read single landmark configurations and `read.lmdta` for entire samples exported by landmark editor with the *dta* option enabled. As the type of landmark (standard landmark, semi-landmark on curves or surfaces) are encoded in the landmark name, the function `cExtract` allows for obtaining this information conveniently from data imported with the functions above.

For importing and exporting digital surface data, *Morpho* provides the functions `ply2mesh`, `mesh2ply`, `obj2mesh`, `mesh2obj`, that allow import and export of surface data stored in ascii-based.ply/.obj file format. Additionally, `file2mesh`, a wrapper for the function `vcgImport` from the package *Rvcg*, allows importing *obj*, *ply* and *stl* files both in ASCII and binary format. Section 5 provides an example on how to convert data stored in a spreadsheet table into an array to be processed in R.

Note on triangular meshes

Surface structures in 3D can be represented via discretized approximations by (oriented) triangular surface meshes. This means that a set of 3D coordinates (vertices) are interconnected to form a mesh consisting of triangles (faces). The edge length of the individual triangles is hereby limiting the smoothness of the resulting surface. All file formats for surface meshes mentioned above allow the representation of the same surface model, the differences consist rather in the way these data are stored in the files. For storing those surface meshes, the *ply* format is the most versatile, as it keeps the ordering of the vertices consistent. The *stl* format, on the other hand,

[7] https://cran.r-project.org/package=shapes.
[8] https://cran.r-project.org/package=geomorph.
[9] http://graphics.idav.ucdavis.edu/research/projects/EvoMorph.
[10] https://www.stratovan.com/products/checkpoint.

Table 7.1 Functions dealing with landmark import and export.

Function name	Purpose
`write.fcsv/read.fcsv`	Reading/writing fiducials (a.k.a landmarks) placed in 3DSlicer[a]
`read.mpp`	Read landmarks placed in meshlab[b]
`readallTPS`	Read landmark data acquired using James Rohlf's tps series[c]
`r2morphoj/` `r2morphologika`	Save landmark data readable for MorphoJ[d] and Morphologika[e]
`read.csv.folder`	Batch import data from multiple csv files stored in the same folder
`readLandmarks.csv`	Import landmark data from csv files

[a]https://www.slicer.org/.
[b]http://meshlab.sourceforge.net/.
[c]http://life.bio.sunysb.edu/ee/rohlf/software.html.
[d]http://www.flywings.org.uk/morphojpage.htm.
[e]https://sites.google.com/site/hymsfine/downloadmorphologica.

references each triangle individually and assigns three vertices per face, explicitly defining their 3D coordinates. This is quite inefficient because the same vertex can be part of multiple triangles, and the resulting vertex ordering is strongly dependent on the software used to process the mesh. Within R, the meshes are stored as objects of class *mesh3d*, as specified by the package *rgl*[11], which is also used for all 3D visualization purposes. This is basically a named list containing the matrices containing the vertex coordinates, faces, and vertex normals.

Example 0.1. Be `mymesh`, a mesh imported into R via one of the functions described above, consisting of k vertices and l faces. Then `mymesh$vb` wil be a $4 \times k$ matrix containing homogeneous coordinates with the first three rows holding the x-y-z coordinates, and the fourth row contains a scaling factor (usually set to 1). The triangles are defined by sets of three indices that define the vertices constituting the face. This information is stored `as` $3 \times l$. matrix in `mymesh$it`.

Morpho contains the function `vert2points` that obtains all vertices from a mesh and stores them in a $k \times 3$ matrix, identical to the convention for landmarks (see above).

Here is an example of how to obtain information about a triangular mesh using both *Morpho* and *Rvcg* and extract the vertices.

[11] https://cran.r-project.org/package=rgl.

```
> data(nose)
> meshInfo(shortnose.mesh)
> myvertices <- vert2points(shortnose.mesh)
```

Plot those vertices:

```
> points3d(myvertices)
```

Batch processing multiple files

For most studies, there are usually multiple files, containing surface and landmark data, to be processed. We are using the example data from the Yacchi sample to demonstrate the power of using R. We assume that we have two files per specimen: one file contains the surface scans stored in the Stanford Polygon format (*.ply*), and the other file holds the landmark data using the *pts* file format used by the Checkpoint software and IDAV Landmark editor. The names of these files only differ in their suffix (*ply* vs. *pts*).

Example 0.2. First we scan the folder containing the Yacchi data for ply files and use the handy `lapply` function to import them all at once and store them in a list called `surfaces`. To avoid any ambiguity, we name content of the resulting list by stripping the file extension and the subfolder prefix from the folder content.

Create a character vector containing the filenames of the surface files:

```
> plyfiles <- list.files("./Data/Yacchi-HF/",full.names = T,
                          pattern = ".ply$")
> surfaces <- lapply(plyfiles, vcgImport)
```

Extract the specimen IDs, and name the surface list:

```
> IDstring <- basename(gsub(".ply","",plyfiles))
> names(surfaces) <- IDstring.
```

The next step is to import the landmarks. To make things consistent, we will use the names of the surface files stored in `plyfiles`, replace the "*.ply*" suffix with a "*.pts*" suffix, and load all data into a list. Again, we name the list according to the specimen IDs.

```
> YacchiPts <- lapply(gsub("ply","pts",plyfiles),read.pts)
> names(YacchiPts) <- IDstring.
```

Now convert the list to an array to be processed by the R-packages *Morpho*, *shapes*, or *geomorph*.

```
> YacchiArray <- list2array(YacchiPts)
```

Now we can use the `checkLM` function to conveniently browse through our data. The function goes through all landmark configurations in the array and renders them. Additionally, it looks for appropriately named surfaces in the specified folder, loads, and renders them (Fig. 7.1):

```
> checkLM(YacchiArray,path="Data/Yacchi-HF/")
```

Dealing with erroneous data

More often than not, researchers have to deal with flawed data. From experience, these issues are most commonly landmarks placed in an inconsistent ordering (mishap by the researcher) or missing landmarks due to incomplete or missing structures (e.g., due to taphonomic processes). In our example data used above, there are both types of issues present. If it is known that the data have both missing and wrongly ordered landmarks, the best way is to do a preliminary imputation of missing landmarks. That way, we already get a good estimate for missing landmarks, which allows us to align the data and to estimate the Procrustes differences between the sample instances to identify outliers more easily.

Imputation of missing landmarks

Morpho is sporting two ways for imputing missing landmarks (Schlager, 2017): `fixLMtps` that performs a weighted nearest neighbor approximation, and `fixLMmirror` uses symmetry to estimate unilaterally missing bilateral landmarks. When the sample consists of specimens with missing structures, the researcher has to decide whether (1) to discard incomplete observations,

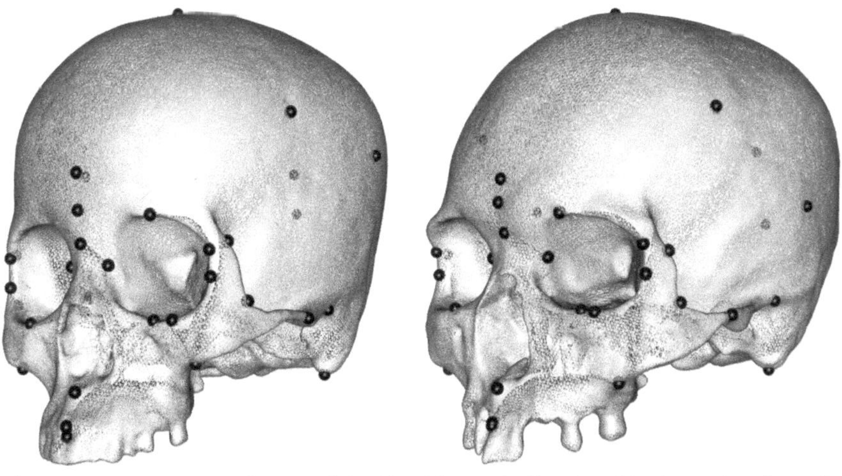

Figure 7.1 First two specimens of the Yacchi sample. Rendered by browsing through the sample using the `checkLM` function from *Morpho*.

(2) use only those landmarks that exist throughout the sample, or (3) estimate the position of missing landmarks. All of those decisions will bias the results in one way or another. Here we decide to impute the missing landmarks as we have 37 landmarks, and small imputation errors regarding single landmarks can be expected to have a rather small effect on the overall outcome.

Example 0.3. In this example, we will use the first function as it is applicable without any prior processing:

```
> YacchiArrayFixed <- fixLMtps(YacchiArray)
```

Now we have a look on which specimens had missing landmarks:

```
> YacchiArrayFixed$check
[1] 3 5 8 9 10 11 13
```

Let us visualize the estimated landmarks in specimen 8 (*2go-2-30_m*). First we plot the surface (as wireframe) and all landmarks:

```
> wire3d(surfaces[[8]],col="white")
> spheres3d(YacchiArrayFixed$out[,,8],col="green")
```

Now emphasize the estimated ones by plotting them in red and a big larger.

```
> spheres3d(YacchiArrayFixed$out[YacchiArrayFixed$checklist[[8]],,8],
            col="red",radius=1.1)
```

Fig. 7.2 shows the estimated landmarks. As the base of the skull is truncated, the estimated landmarks are "hanging in the air," but the positions are quite reasonable.

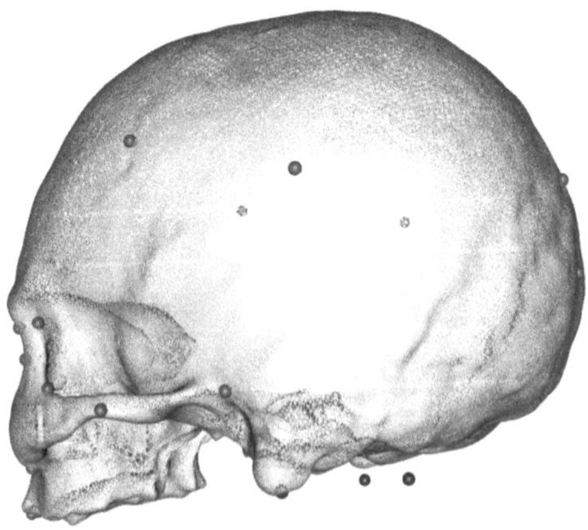

Figure 7.2 Imputed landmarks on specimen *2go-2-30_m*. Red: imputed landmarks; green manually digitized landmarks.

Inconsistently ordered landmarks

Another common occurrence in landmark data are inconsistently ordered landmarks. For performing a proper alignment, it is essential that the order of the landmarks is consistent throughout the sample. If this is not the case, the resulting analyses will be strongly flawed. Using the *Morpho* package, there exist two ways of fixing these issues. An interactive one that is applicable for few mislabeled landmarks using the readily available function `find.outliers`, which is not applicable for badly mislabeled specimens like in the example below, and one shown below that aligns the wrongly labeled configuration with a correct one using an iterative closest point procedure (ICP—see Zhang, 1994). After the alignment, the mislabeled configuration updates is ordered according to the closest landmark on the correct one.

Example 0.4. We start by superimposing all specimens using a Partial Procrustes alignment—because in case of mislabeled landmarks, the scaling factor can be completely wrong.

```
> proc <- procSym(YacchiArrayFixed$out,scale=FALSE)
```

Looking at the distance to the mean, we can see that the first specimen is way off with a Procrustes distance of ~0.87.

```
11-14_f_hf 11-15_m_hf 11-34_m_hf [ ...]
0.87070531 0.08456685 0.09059817 [...]
```

Visualizing the differences (Fig. 7.3A) shows the mislabeling of the landmarks:

```
> deformGrid3d(proc$rotated[,,1],proc$mshape)
```

We now align the mislabeled specimen to the mean shape by their principal axes and refine this estimate using a rigid ICP.

```
> spec1aligned <- pcAlign(proc$rotated[,,1],proc$mshape,
                          iterations=20)
```

In the last step, the correct correspondences are sought by pairing the landmarks of specimen 1 with their counterparts of the mean shape.

```
> index1 <- mcNNindex(spec1aligned,proc$mshape,k=1)
```

This gives us (hopefully) the correct order. After checking this visually,

```
> deformGrid3d(proc$rotated[index1,,1],proc$mshape)
```

We can now update the raw landmark array sorting the landmarks in the correct order.

```
> YacchiArray[,,1] <- YacchiArray[index1,,1]
```

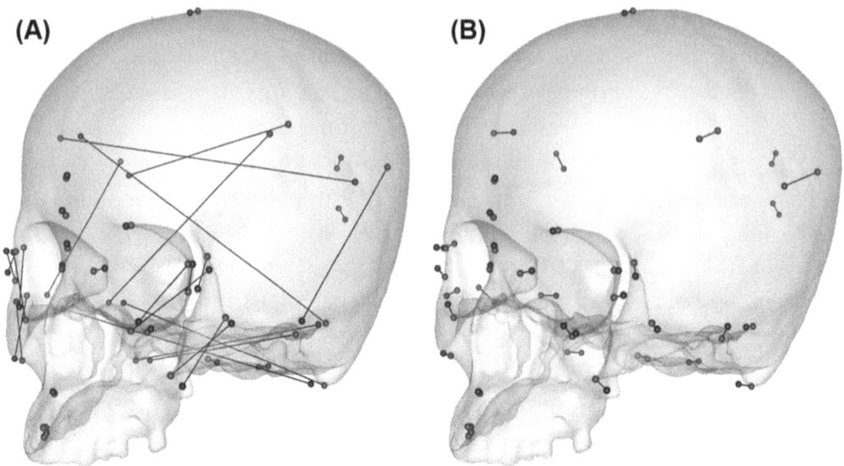

Figure 7.3 (A) Mislabeled landmarks on specimen *11–14_f_h*. Red dots: specimen *11–14_f_h*; blue dots: sample mean shape. (B) The suggested pairings after the closest point search.

Now we redo the imputation (only keeping the actual array)

```
> YacchiFixed <- fixLMtps(YacchiArray)
> YacchiArrayFixed <- YacchiFixed$out
```

Spatial alignment and Procrustes analysis

Removing differences owed to different positions in space and, optionally, scale and reflection, a.k.a. Procrustes superimposition, is an essential prerequisite of statistical shape analysis (Kendall, 1989; Dryden and Mardia, 1998). This means the original data recorded in an *x*-*y*-*z* coordinate system needs to be spatially transformed to make two or more shapes statistically comparable. *Morpho* provides functionality to compute a variety of transformations of which a subset is required for Procrustes superimposition.

The following spatial transformations can be computed in *Morpho*: rigid alignment, similarity transformation (rigid alignment + scaling), affine transformation (rigid alignment + scaling + shearing) as well as TPS interpolation. Additionally, there are functions allowing rotating a 3D object around arbitrary axes in space.

Although the functionality is spread throughout different separate functions (Table 7.2), we concentrate on presenting a simplified interface for computing and applying transformations based on two sets of corresponding coordinates. At first, we look at the transformations that are designed to handle the mapping between two configurations based on landmark information, or more general, between two sets of corresponding points. `computeTransform` operates on $k \times m$ matrices as well as on meshes of class *mesh3d* (assuming correspondence between their vertices). For affine transformations, it returns a square transformation matrix, and for TPS transforms, an object of class *tps* that contains the coefficients used for TPS interpolation, as well as the original landmark coordinates. The resulting transformation can subsequently be applied using `applyTransform` to both matrices and meshes. The option `invert` allows to apply the inverse of the transformation—as there is no trivial inversion of TPS deformations, a TPS transformation will be computed by swapping target and reference coordinates.

Table 7.2 Functions dealing with spatial transformations.

Function name	Purpose
`computeTransform/` `applyTransform`	Wrapper for `rotonto` and `tps3d` to allow for computing and applying rigid, similarity, affine and TPS transformations
`rotonto`	Rotate/scale/translate one set of landmarks onto another
`rotmesh.onto`	Align a mesh based on two landmark configurations
`tps3d`	Deform a set of coordinates or a mesh using a TPS deformation based on two landmark configurations
`rotaxis3d`	Rotate an object around an arbitrary axis in 3D
`rotaxisMat`	Calculate a rotation matrix around an arbitrary axis through the origin in 3D
`rotonmat`	Rotate matrix of landmarks by using a rotation determined by two matrices
`pcAlign`	Align two pointclouds based on their principal axes—optionally with subsequent rigid icp alignment
`ProcGPA`	Perform general Procrustes analysis
`procSym`	Perform general Procrustes analysis, with support for bilateral landmarks, including projection into tangent space and subsequent PCA
`icpmat`	Match two pointclouds using an iterative closest point search

For performing statistical analyses, a sample-wide alignment is needed. The most common method is the generalized Procrustes analysis (GPA) (Kendall, 1989; Dryden and Mardia, 1998).

The functions `ProcGPA` and `procSym` both provide this functionality, also allowing for a variety of other options controlling the transformations, with `ProcGPA` being the workhorse and `procSym` also performing subsequent Euclideanization via orthogonal projection into the tangent space at the sample's mean, followed by a PCA. Additionally, a variety of useful statistics are reported. The most important parameters controlling the alignment are `scale` enabling scaling for minimizing Procrustes distances, `reflection` to allow/prohibit reflections, and `CSinit` to perform an initial scaling to unit centroid size. Additionally, `ProcGPA` allows to assign weights (option `weights`) for each landmark and `centerweight` to allow the center of rotation to be the accordingly weighted centroid. The latter options have to be used with care because changing these weights can lead to significant differences/ bias in subsequent analyses. Especially using only a subset of available landmarks for the superimposition will decrease variability among those landmarks and on the same time increase variability of the remaining landmark coordinates. This effect is owed to the fact that minimizing the Procrustes distance among the landmarks used (or assigned with higher weights) is no longer constrained by the positions of the excluded landmarks (or those with low weights).

Example 0.5. The following example intends to show the effect of restricting the rotation to a locally restricted subset, using only four midfacial landmarks (*Subspinale, Nasion, Dacryon left and right*) in the Yacchi sample to align all data. We then visually compare the per-landmark variability to that of a Procrustes alignment using the entire data set. This is done by plotting the variability (at three standard deviations) using the first five Principal Components.

Alignment using the subset using landmarks 2, 4, 18, and 19:

```
> procSubset <- procSym(YacchiArrayFixed,use.lm=c(2,4,18,19))
```

Alignment using all landmarks:

```
> procFull <- procSym(YacchiArrayFixed)
> pcaplot3d(procSubset,pcshow = 1:5)
> pcaplot3d(procFull,pcshow = 1:5)
```

Fig. 7.4 visualizes the differences: although the variability is much more evenly distributed using the entire data set (apart from the *Euria* that obviously vary a lot due to them being only the broadest part of the cranium),

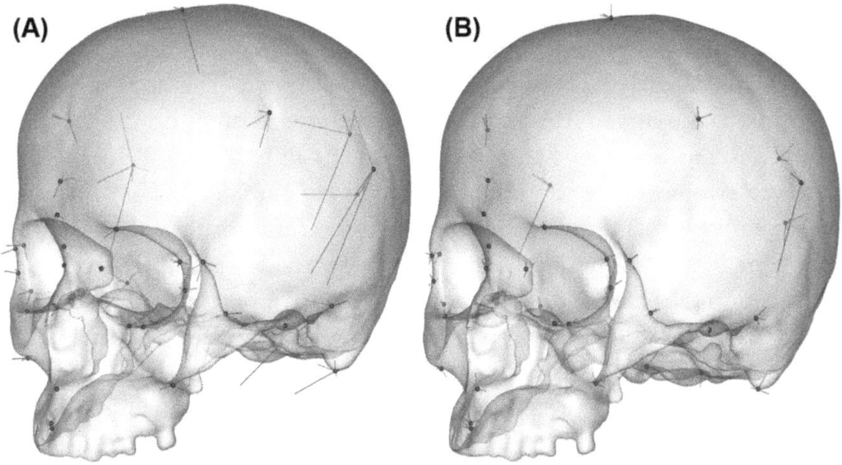

Figure 7.4 (A) Bias in per-landmark shape variability due to different alignment strategies: (A) When only four landmarks are used for the alignment, the variability in those landmarks farther away gets overestimated. (B) When using all landmarks for the alignment, this bias disappears and the landmark variability is more homogeneous.

the alignment based on four landmarks only leads to a strong bias resulting in landmarks to appear more variable, the farther they are away from those four reference landmarks.

Example analysis: assessing measurement error

In most geometric morphometric studies, the superimposed landmark data are processed via a principal component analysis (PCA) or some variation thereof, warp analysis (Bookstein, 1989, 1991), for example. For a more detailed tutorial on these procedures in R, the reader is referred to (Schlager 2017). As with all empirical data, observer error can be a crucial factor when dealing with morphometric data. When recording the data in the same coordinate system (e.g., multiple recordings on the identical CT or surface scan), estimating the per-landmark error is relatively easy. When comparing data recorded by different methods, however, this is often not feasible, because we do not know about the correct alignment. When using a Procrustes alignment, which is a least square minimization procedure, the error will be distributed throughout the entire landmark configuration, and a large error on a single landmark will be mitigated by distributing this difference in the alignment step. As most morphometric analyses deal with assessing variability (patterns), it is more important that the observer error is way below the between-specimens variability. Below we will show an example based on data that were recorded several times on surface scans as well as data recorded on actual skulls using a Microscribe device. The approach is to align the data using a GPA and then run a cluster analysis on the distance matrix (as suggested by Morecroft, et al., 2010; Schlager, 2013). If the observer error is below the interspecimens variation, all versions of each specimen should end up in the same cluster. Unfortunately, the example data contain several missing landmarks. As we want to compare the result on variation throughout the entire sample, we have two options: 1. discard all landmarks missing in at least one specimen or 2. impute the missing landmarks. The following example will show both approaches. In addition to the measurement error assessment, the following example will also show how to extract landmark data from a spreadsheet file and convert it to an appropriate landmark array in R.

Example 0.6. The data used in this example contain four repeated digitizations of landmarks on the surface scans (using different surface processing options) and one digitization on the original skull using a Microscribe device. The data are located in the file "Data/LandmarkCoordAll.csv". *NA* values are encoded by *-999*.

First, the table stored as *csv* file is read into the R workspace, where it is stored as an object of class data.frame.

```
> coord <- read.csv("Data/LandmarkCoordAll.csv")
```

To process the data with *Morpho* (or any other morphometrics package), it has to be converted into an array as specified above (see 3). *Mopho* provides the handy `vecx` function that allows to convert back and forth between matrices and arrays. The first three columns contain information about the data but no coordinates—they are useful to extract the identifiers for the specimens and their digitization.

```
> coord3d <- vecx(coord[,-c(1:3)],byrow = T,revert = T,lmdim = 3)
```

Now the second and third column, containing the specimen identifier and digitization event are concatenated and used to name the array:

```
> ID <- apply(coord[,c(2,3)],1,paste0,collapse="_")

> dimnames(coord3d)[[3]] <- ID.
```

The *NA* values are still encoded as *-999*, so we make a copy of the array and replace them with *NA* values:

```
> coord3dna <- coord3d.
> coord3dna[which(coord3dna == -999)] <- NA
```

Now the missing landmarks are imputed as above (3.3.1):

```
> coord3dnafix <- fixLMtps(coord3dna)
```

Those landmarks that are missing at least in one specimen need to be identified:

```
> missingLM <- sort(unique(unlist(coord3dnafix$checklist)))
```

First a GPA is performed on the data excluding those landmarks that are missing at least in one specimen, then on the data with the missing landmarks imputed:

```
> procPart <- procSym(coord3dna[-missingLM,,])
> procAll <- procSym(coord3dnafix$out)
```

Compute the distance matrices—it is more convenient to use the PC-scores as a PCA only rotates the data:

```
> distsPart <- dist(procPart$PCscores)
> distsAll <- dist(procAll$PCscores)
```

Finally, a cluster analysis is performed and the result is plotted (Fig. 7.5).

```
> clustPart <- hclust(distsPart,method="ward.D")
> clustAll <- hclust(distsAll,method="ward.D")
> plot(clustPart)
> plot(clustAll)
```

When looking at the resulting plots (Fig. 7.5), it can clearly be seen that the landmark configurations digitized on the virtual surface meshes cluster relatively consistent together—apart from some outliers. The landmark data from the Microscribe device, however, form their own cluster, very distinct from the rest of the data. This becomes even more apparent when plotting the first 2 PCs (Fig. 7.6). It is clearly visible that there is a systematic difference (error) regarding the two approaches in digitizing landmark data. To investigate this further, we will look into the between group structure of these data. A between-group PCA can be a useful tool to project this problem into a low-dimensional space (Boulesteix and Strimmer, 2005; Mitteroecker and Bookstein, 2011).

Example 0.7. First the grouping needs to be determined. We distinguish between those digitizations performed with the Stratovan software and those using the Microscribe device.

The next command creates a character vector of the same length as the landmark array and sets all values to "Stratovan"

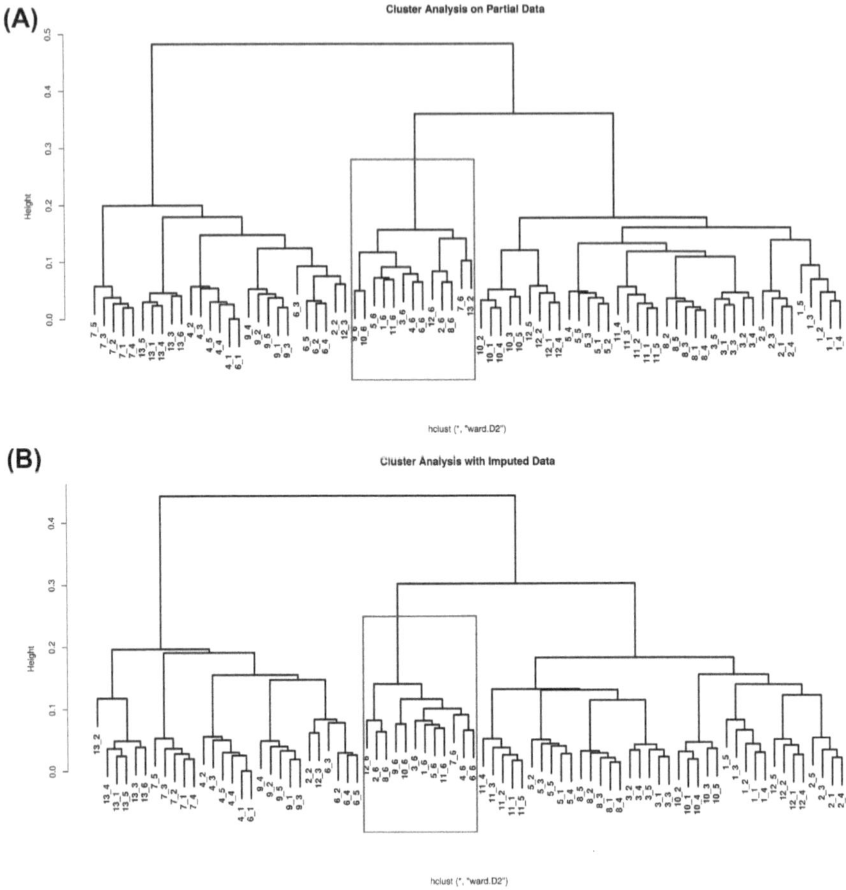

Figure 7.5 Cluster analyses on (A) partial data (with missing landmarks excluded) and (B) with imputed data. Whereas digitizations on the surface meshes cluster (mostly) nicely together, those from the Microscribe device form their own cluster—a clear sign for inconsistent landmark placement.

```
> groups <- rep("Stratovan",dim(coord3dnafix$out)[3])
```

The third column in the data frame contains the information about the landmarking procedure and 6 stands for the Microscribe data. Thus, we replace those instances with the string "Microscribe" and convert the character vector into factors.

```
> groups[which(coord[,3] == 6)] <- "Microscribe"
> groups <- factor(groups)
```

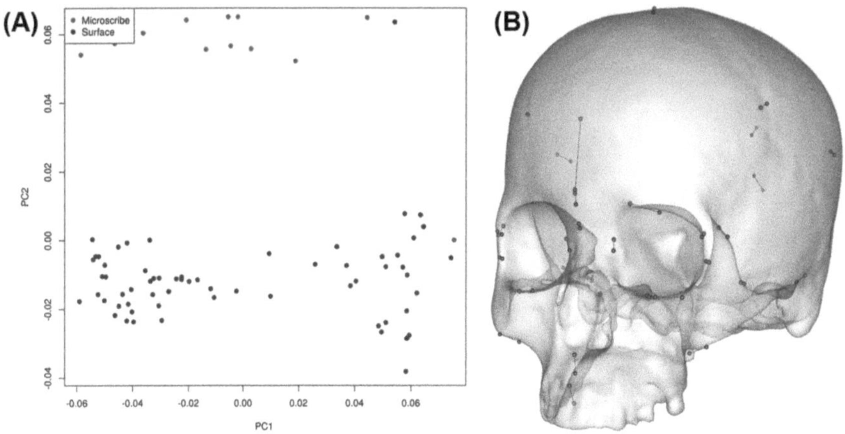

Figure 7.6 (A) Plot of the first two principal components from the partial data. Red dots: Microscribe data; blue dots: data digitized on the surface meshes. (B) Visualization of between-group variability comparing Microscribe to Stratovan data. It indicates that the errors are distributed across most landmarks and cannot be attributed to an accidental misplacement of one single coordinate.

Now run the between-group PCA on the rotated data, and have a look at the resulting classification table:

```
> bgPCA <- groupPCA(procPart$rotated,groups)
> bgPCA
cross-validated classification results in frequencies
            Microscribe Stratovan
Microscribe          12         1
Stratovan             1        64
overall classification accuracy: 97.4359%
```

This shows that the two samples can be separated almost perfectly. To visualize the between-group differences, we construct shapes along the shape trajectory between group means at ± 2 standard deviations of the between-group variability.

Set up the vector holding the between-group PC scores at ± 2 standard deviations:

```
> varbgPC <- c(-2,2)*sd(bgPCA$Scores)
```

Retrieve the shapes and plot them:

```
> micro.vs.stratovan <- showPC(varbgPC, bgPCA$groupPCs,
                                bgPCA$Grandmean)
```

```
> deformGrid3d(micro.vs.stratovan[,,1],micro.vs.stratovan[,,2])
```

The resulting visualization in Fig. 7.6 indicates that errors cannot be attributed to single landmarks—maybe except for the *Glabella* that shows extreme inconsistencies.

Semilandmarks

Since the introduction of semilandmarks on 2D curves (Bookstein, 1997) and their extension to 3D curves and surfaces (Gunz et al., 2005), they have become an indispensable tool for quantifying shape on structures lacking traditional landmarks (Gunz and Mitteroecker, 2013). When digitizing semilandmarks, there is always a considerable amount of uncertainty involved about of the exact position along a curve or on a surface. This uncertainty manifests itself as noise in the data suggesting variance that is simply owed to the lack of homology. For removing this noise, the semilandmarks are allowed to slide along the curves/surfaces minimizing a given metric. For obtaining a linear equation system despite the curved surfaces, the latter are approximated locally. For semilandmarks on surfaces, this approximation is achieved by using tangent planes, orthogonal to the normal vector at that point (Fig. 7.7). For semilandmarks on curves the direction vector of the neighboring points along the curve is used. As the sliding along these approximated surfaces may lead to the coordinates slipping off the actual surface, they are projected back onto the surfaces after each relaxation step.

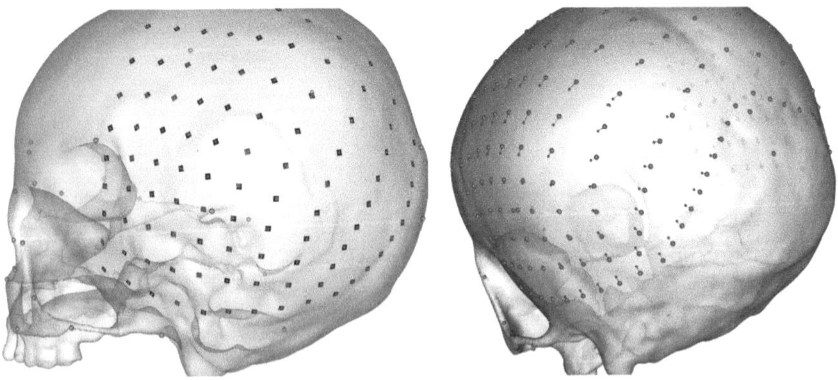

Figure 7.7 Left: Surface with traditional landmarks (cyan spheres) and semilandmarks on surfaces (red spheres). The black squares are the estimated tangent planes at each coordinate. Right: The lines visualize the displacement after the sliding and the blue spheres the final position of the semilandmarks.

The most common metric to be minimized by the sliding is bending energy (of a TPS deformation), but Procrustes distance can also be used. Both metrics have their advantages and disadvantages: Although minimizing Procrustes distance is computationally cheap and can be applied to large amounts of semilandmarks, minimizing bending energy has its limits as the linear equation system based on the bending energy matrix grows quadratically to the amount of semilandmarks involved. For structures with large shape differences, however, minimizing Procrustes distance can lead to unwanted distortions, while the bending energy method ensures a smooth displacement in all cases. It has to be stressed, however, that the homology enforced via this procedure is only valid for the data included in the sliding process.

While function `slider3d` deals with sample wide sliding of 3D semilandmarks, `relaxLM` allows to relax one specific set of semilandmarks against another. For 2D configurations, `procSym` allows semilandmarks to slide along curves. The parameter setup in `relaxLM` and `slider3d` is very similar (Table 7.4).

After setting up the parameters controlling the sliding, the surfaces have to be specified to estimate the tangent planes (via the mesh normals). There are basically three ways to point to the surface meshes in `slider3d`:

1. The meshes are stored on disk (less memory usage for large meshes/large samples), supported file types are *obj*, *stl*, and *ply*.
   a. The `dimnames` of the array holding the coordinates contain the file names (without file extension): the surfaces are automatically loaded by specifying the path to the containing folder using the option `sur.path` and defining the file extension (e.g., *ply*) via the option `sur.type`.
   b. The array is unnamed: the parameter `sur.name` can be used to define a vector containing the surface file names.
2. Meshes are loaded into the workspace as objects of class *mesh3d* (faster but uses more memory):
   - Store them in a list in the same order as the specimens in the array containing the landmark data.

The functionality also caters to cases where no underlying surface information is available:

1. No surfaces are available at all because the data were digitized directly on the physical object (e.g., using a Microscribe device):
   - In the this case, simply do not specify any meshes, the tangent planes will be approximated by estimating per-landmark normals based on

the surrounding semilandmarks—the denser the semilandmarks are placed, the more accurate the normals will be. As there is, for obvious reasons no surface to project the coordinates back onto, it is recommendable to restrict the incremental sliding along the tangent planes using the parameter `stepsize` (Table 7.4).

2. The surfaces are defect, and some of the data are imputed using the methods above but lack underlying surfaces. Surface semilandmarks with the underlying structure missing are relaxed freely in 3D.
   - The indices of the missing landmarks have to be specified per specimen, for an entire sample, the function `createMissingList` creates an appropriate list, and for each specimen with imputed coordinates, a vector containing their indices has to be defined.
   - For `relaxLM`, where only one specimen is addressed, the option `missing` allows to specify a vector with indices of coordinates lacking underlying surface information

The following two subsections provide examples on how to transfer semilandmarks from an atlas to all specimens in the sample and how to run the sliding routines.

Transferring semilandmarks from a template to all specimens in a sample: A simple registration approach

Placing traditional landmarks provides useful information and incorporates biological information and concepts and therefore should preferably performed by a trained expert (Gunz and Mitteroecker, 2013). Placing semilandmarks, however, can be performed in an automated fashion to decrease processing time. For curves, one has to carefully decide: depending on the structure they run along, it is preferable to place them manually; however, the procedure outlined below, also allows for placing them semiautomatically.

Usually, a template specimen is selected (or computed as an average from the sample to avoid individual bias) on which surface landmarks are then placed. Gunz et al. (2005) propose a procedure that simply warps the semilandmarks from the template to the target via a TPS deformation based on the traditional landmarks. This will, however, only work for very simple shapes and only in single-layered meshes. For taking into account more complicated structures, *Morpho* provides basic functionality to perform a more sophisticated registration in a semiautomated and user

Table 7.3 Functions allowing sliding of semilandmarks.

Function name	**Purpose**
`slider3d`	Sample-wide relaxation of semilandmarks
`relaxLM`	Relax reference configuration against target
`procSym`	Relaxation of 2D semilandmarks along curves

friendly fashion (Table 7.3). The main assumptions are as follows: all semilandmarks are placed on the *outside* of an oriented mesh, that is, the faces of the mesh point are oriented consistently, and that the meshes are stored on disk in *ply*, *obj*, or *stl* format. The procedure is outlined in Algorithm 1 (for more details, see Schlager, 2013). Based on a template, the semilandmarks are then transferred to all other specimens. An array will be returned containing complete sets of coordinates, consisting of the transferred semilandmarks and the manually placed landmarks, which can be processed by `slider3d` (see Example 0.9).

In the following example, a set of dense semilandmarks on the cranial vault will be first sampled on the surface using the IDAV Landmark editor on one specimen (Fig. 7.8A). From the GPA on the full data set, we can see that specimen *8–14_f_hf* (at the 12th position in the list/array created above) will be used due to the fact that it is the specimen without

Table 7.4 Important parameters of `slider3d` and `relaxLM`.

Parameter	**Purpose**
`SMvector`	Vector containing indices of landmarks that are allowed to slide. Setting `deselect=TRUE`, the vector contains those landmarks that are ***not*** allowed to slide.
`outlines`	Vector or list of vectors containing the indices of the coordinates that constitute curves; these indices can refer both to semilandmarks as well as traditional landmarks—with the latter being useful to sensibly determine the start and endpoints of curves. For closed curves, the first and last entry must be identical.
`surp`	Vector of all landmarks that are allowed to slide on surfaces.
`bending`	If `TRUE`, bending energy is used as metric, Procrustes distance otherwise.
`stepsize`	For values < 1, this parameter dampens the amount of sliding: Be X the matrix or original positions and D the matrix of displacement vectors from sliding, then the displaced coordinates are $X + stepsize^{*} D$.

```
for all specimens in sample do
    if Curves are placed throughout the sample then
        Relax all curves against template
    end
    Deform template to target via TPS based on those landmarks placed
      throughout the sample (including on semilandmarks on curves if
      available);
    Compute surface normals at semilandmark positions;
    Inflate: Project semilandmarks outward along normals;
    Deflate: Project them back to the closest intersection with the surface;
    Compute deviation of original normals and surface normals at new
      positions;
    for all semilandmarks do
        if deviation of normal directon > π/2 then
            tag coordinate as misplaced;
        end
    end
    Relax semilandmarks against template and allow relaxation of tagged
      semilandmarks in 3D;
    Project semilandmarks on target surface;
end
```

Algorithm 1 Outline of template registration using placePatch

missing data that are closest to the sample mean shape. It is assumed that the files for the specimen generation are stored in the folder "Data/Semilandmarks."

Example 0.8. First, we import the landmarks and the patch defined on *8–14_f_hf:*

```
> template.pts <- read.pts("./Data/Semilandmarks/8–14_f_hf.pts")
```

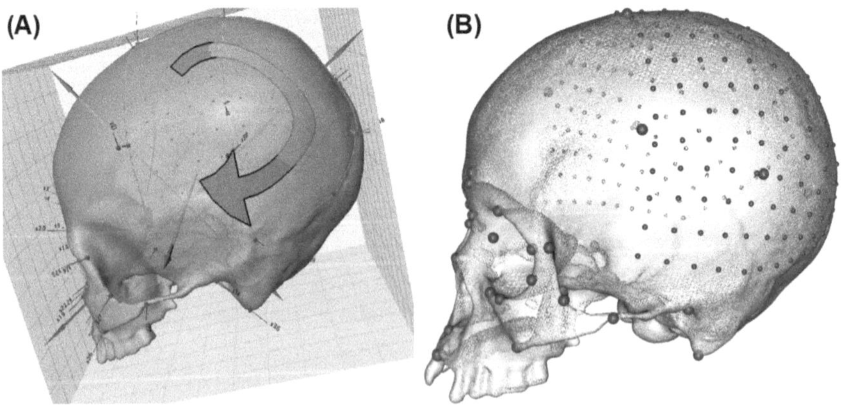

Figure 7.8 (A) Two patches (left and right) placed on the cranial vault of specimen *8–14_f_hf.* (B) Result of `plotAtlas` highlighting the respective type of the defined landmarks and semilandmarks.

Now the template mesh is selected, and we obtain information about the landmark type from their naming:

```
> template.mesh <- surfaces$"8–14_f_hf"
> cinfo <- cExtract(template.pts)
```

Define the fix and semilandmarks:

```
> fix <- cinfo$S
> patch <- c(cinfo$P000,cinfo$P001)
```

Next, the atlas is defined. This can be done conveniently with the `createAtlas` function that is used to define the landmarks present on all specimens and the semilandmarks, defined only on the atlas, which will be transferred to all specimens in the sample. Then we visualize the atlas to check if everything is defined in a sensible fashion (Fig. 7.9B).

```
> atlas <- createAtlas(surfaces[[12]],YacchiArrayFixed[,,12],
                       patch=template.pts[patch,])
> plotAtlas(atlas)
```

Now we run `placePatch`, specifying the path to the surface files and setting some parameters (see Table 7.5)

```
> semiArray <- placePatch(atlas, YacchiArrayFixed,
                          path = "Data/Yacchi-HF/",
                          inflate = 5,rhotol = pi/2)
```

Finally, checkLM allows browsing the data. Defining an atlas, the coordinate type will be highlighted accordingly.

```
> checkLM(semiArray,path="Data/Yacchi-HF/",atlas=atlas)
```

Sliding

After having transferred the semilandmarks on the cranial vault to all the specimens, it is essential to allow the semilandmarks to relax against their sample mean to reduce the noise in the data.

Table 7.5 Functions allowing sliding of semilandmarks.

Function name	Purpose
`createAtlas`	Sets up a template to be used with `placePatch`, defining fix landmarks, manually defined curves and those semilandmarks to be transferred to all specimens in the sample
`placePatch`	Transfer semilandmarks from a template to all specimens in a sample
`checkLM`	Visually inspect the result of `placePatch`

Example 0.9. As the sample under observation includes imputed data, this obviously has no underlying surface mesh. As the sliding process involves reprojection onto the surface, we will have to avoid this for those imputed coordinates. As all the imputed data are anatomical landmarks that are not to slide anyway, this can be achieved by setting `fixRepro=FALSE`.

Again, the variables patch is used to specify the row indices of the semi-landmarks. We already have imported the surfaces into our workspace in the correct order, so we can use those. Otherwise, we would have needed to provide the path to the correct folder.

```
> YacchiSlide <- slider3d(semiArray,SMvector = patch, surp=patch,
                          meshlist=surfaces, iteration=5,tol=0,
                          fixRepro=FALSE)
```

The resulting displacement can be visualized as in Fig. 7.7.

Routines for manipulating triangular meshes

Chapter 2 introduced a protocol for processing triangular surface models generated from the Yacchi example data. This section will present functions to achieve some of those steps in R. The advantage of the scripting language is evident again. As seen above, a function can be run on an entire sample at once using the lapply functions (for lists).

Changing the mesh resolution

There are three possible ways to change the resolution of a mesh: simplification (less triangles), complexification (more triangles) and a complete remeshing of the surface. All three can be accomplished using *Rvcg*. For high quality mesh simplification, `vcgQEdecim` implements a quadric edge collapse decimation, allowing the user to specify same parameters as the GUI of *meshlab* with the standard settings leading to good results in most cases. To increase the resolution of a mesh, i.e., to refine the surface, `vcgSubdivide` allows a triangle subdivision using a butterfly interpolation or loop subdivision scheme (Zorin et al., 2000). To create an entirely new mesh from an existing one, `vcgUniformRemesh` calculates a distance volume and creates a surface at the value zero using a marching cube algorithm.

Example 0.10. This example demonstrates how to simplify (to 20% the amount of its faces), subdivide (until an edge length of one is reached), and remesh an example surface. As an example, again, the first specimen from the Yacchi sample is used (Fig. 7.9).

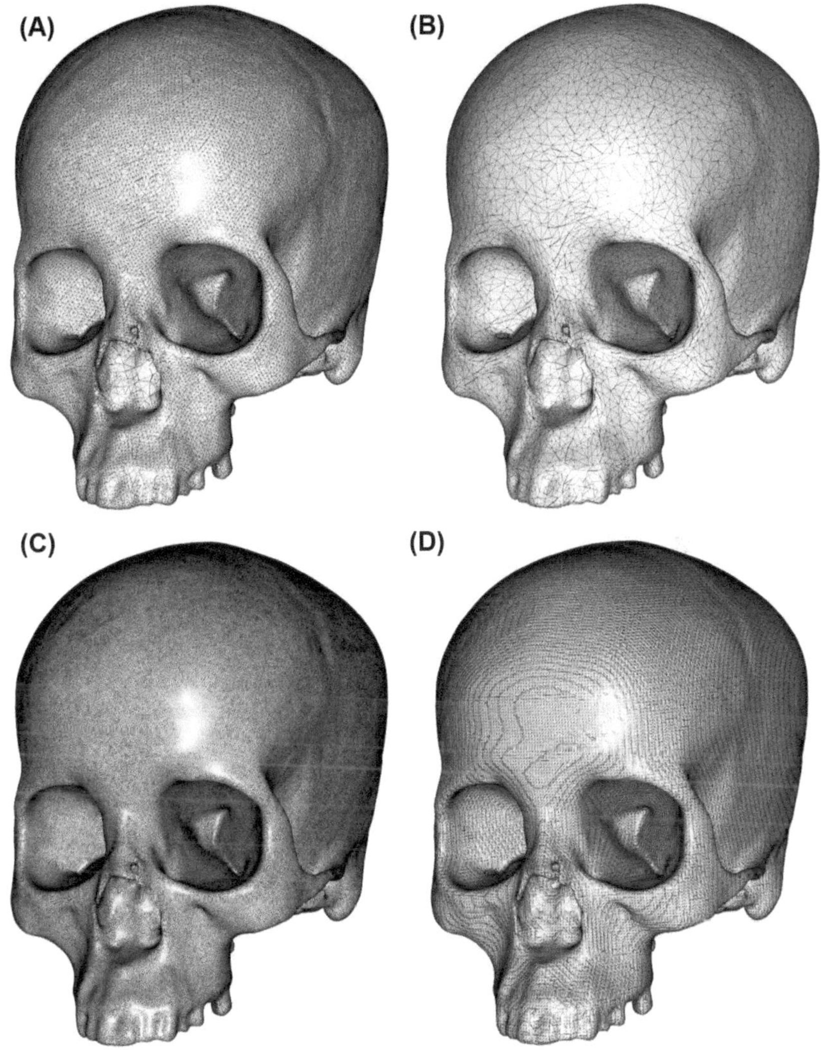

Figure 7.9 Meshing operations in *Rvcg*: (A) original mesh; (B) a mesh decimated to 20% of the amount its original faces; (C) a mesh refined using a loop subdivision scheme optimizing regularity; and (D) a uniformly remeshed surface.

```
> require(Rvcg) #load the Rvcg package.
> origmesh <- surfaces[[1]]
```

Simplify.

```
> decimesh <- vcgQEdecim(origmesh, percent=0.2)
```

Subdivide.

```
> subdivide <- vcgSubdivide(origmesh, type="Loop",
                            looptype="regularity",threshold=1)
```

First we slightly smooth the mesh to fix small-scale irregularities, which can cause issues with the remeshing:

```
> smoothmesh <- vcgSmooth(origmesh)
```

Remesh (this can take a while):

```
> remesh <- vcgUniformRemesh(smoothmesh, voxelSize=1,
                             multiSample = TRUE)
```

Additionally, *Morpho* contains a variety of functions for removing vertices (`rmVertex`), to reorient all faces of a mesh (`invertFaces`), to concatenate multiple meshes into one (`mergeMeshes`), or to align two meshes by their principal axes (`pcAlign`). For analyses dealing with asymmetry, the function `mirror or mirror2plane` can be of interest: the first one mirrors a mesh and tries to align it to the original one using a rigid iterative closest point procedure, whereas the second allows to mirror a mesh at an arbitrary plane, defined by three coordinates on a plane or by one coordinate on a plane and the plane's normal vector.

Cleaning

To clean and smooth surface meshes, *Rvcg* provides three functions that implement a variety of algorithms. `vcgClean` allows for efficient cleaning such as removal of duplicated, unreferenced (i.e., not part of the triangles forming the surface) and nonmanifold vertices as well as duplicated, nonmanifold or degenerate faces. The different cleaning options are coded numerically, and the parameter `sel` allows to specify a vector with multiple selections. Because one operation can cause the creation of another unwanted property—for example merging close vertices can lead to degenerate faces—the option `iterate` will run the function with the selected cleaning operations, until no further cleaning is required. Often, meshes generated from clinical CT data do not consist of manifolds but of a set of unconnected meshes. `vcgIsolated` can either extract the largest component(s) (those above a given diameter/number of faces) or split it into separate disjunct meshes (stored in a list). For smoothing a mesh, `vcgSmooth` provides several algorithms, including common ones such as those proposed by Vollmer et al. (Vollmer et al., 1999) and Taubin (Taubin, 1995).

Virtual mesh scan

Another important task in mesh processing is selecting those parts of interest, for example, cavities such as the endocranium. Doing this manually can be a very labor-intensive task. *Morpho* contains the function virtualMeshScan that performs a virtual scan of the mesh but constrained to predefined points of view. This means all parts of the mesh that are visible from at least one of these point of views will be extracted from the mesh, and the unseen parts will be discarded (for details, see Profico et al., 2018). Here is an example on how to extract the endocast of the Neanderthal specimen *Saccopastore 1* that is part of the example documentation in *Morpho*.

Example 0.11.
```
> SCP1 <- file2mesh(system.file("extdata",
                    "SCP1.ply", package="Morpho"))
> viewpoints <- read.fcsv(system.file("extdata",
                          "SCP1_Endo.fcsv",package="Morpho"))
```

Create a quick (and slightly "dirty") endocast.

```
> quickEndo <- virtualMeshScan(SCP1,viewpoints)
```

Now we visualize the endocast, also rendering the original mesh transparently:

```
> shade3d(quickEndo$visible,col="orange")
> shade3d(SCP1,col = "white",alpha=0.5)
```

Fig. 7.10 shows the results: The endocast is separated from the rest (apart from some parts of the orbits) and can now be analyzed.

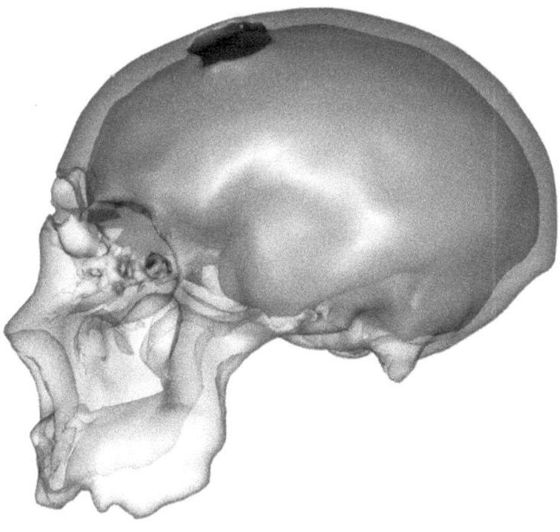

Figure 7.10 Result from extracting the inner surface of the cranial vault using the `virtualMeshScan` function.

References

Bookstein, F.L., 1989. Principal warps: thin-plate splines and the decomposition of deformations. IEEE Transactions on Pattern Analysis and Machine Intelligence 11, 567–585.

Bookstein, F.L., 1991. Morphometric Tools for Landmark Data: Geometry and Biology. Cambridge Univ. Press, Cambridge.

Bookstein, F.L., 1997. Landmark methods for forms without landmarks: morphometrics of group differences in outline shape. Medical Image Analysis 1, 225–243. https://doi.org/10.1016/S1361-8415(97)85012-8.

Boulesteix, A.L., Strimmer, K., 2005. Partial Least Squares: A Versatile Tool for the Analysis of High-Dimensional Genomic Data. http://epub.ub.uni-muenchen.de/1826/.

Dryden, I.L., Mardia, K.V., 1998. Statistical Shape Analysis. John Wiley and Sons, Chichester.

Gunz, P., Mitteroecker, P., 2013. Semilandmarks: a method for quantifying curves and surfaces. Hystrix – the Italian Journal of Mammalogy 24, 103–109. http://www.italian-journal-of-mammalogy.it/article/view/6292.

Gunz, P., Mitteroecker, P., Bookstein, F., 2005. Semilandmarks in three dimensions. In: Slice, D. (Ed.), Modern Morphometrics in Physical Anthropology, Developments in Primatology: Progress and Prospects. Kluwer Academic/Plenum Publishers, Chicago, IL, pp. 73–98. MG.

Kendall, D., 1989. A survey of the statistical theory of shape. Statistical Science 4, 87–120.

Mitteroecker, P., Bookstein, F., 2011. Linear discrimination, ordination, and the visualization of selection gradients in modern morphometrics. Evolutionary Biology 38, 100–114. https://doi.org/10.1007/s11692-011-9109-8.

Morecroft, L., Fieller, N., Dryden, I., Evison, M., 2010. Shape variation in anthropometric landmarks in 3d. In: Computer-Aided Forensic Facial Comparison. CRC Press, pp. 35–52. https://doi.org/10.1201/9781439811344-c3.

Okinawa Prefectural Archaeology Center, 2001. Report No. 6. In: Yacchi Cave, Kanjin-Hara Tombs: The Report on the Archaeological Excavation in Conjunction with the Prefectural Project on Irrigation and Drainage. Okinawa Prefectural Archaeology Center, p. 436 (In Japanese).

Profico, A., Schlager, S., Valoriani, V., Buzi, C., Melchionna, M., Veneziano, A., Raia, P., Moggi-Cecchi, J., Manzi, G., 2018. Reproducing the internal and external anatomy of fossil bones: two new automatic digital tools. American Journal of Physical Anthropology. https://doi.org/10.1002/ajpa.23493.

R Core Team, 2015. R: A Language and Environment for Statistical Computing. R Foundation for Statistical Computing, Vienna, Austria. https://www.R-project.org/.

Schlager, S., 2013. Soft-tissue Reconstruction of the Human Nose: Population Differences and Sexual Dimorphism. Ph.D. thesis. Universitätsbibliothek Freiburg. http://www.freidok.uni-freiburg.de/volltexte/9181/.

Schlager, S., 2017. Morpho and Rvcg – shape analysis in R. In: Zheng, G., Li, S., Szekely, G. (Eds.), Statistical Shape and Deformation Analysis. Academic Press, pp. 217–256.

Schneider, P.J., Eberly, D., 2002. Geometric Tools for Computer Graphics. Elsevier Science Inc., New York, NY, USA.

Taubin, G., 1995. Curve and surface smoothing without shrinkage. In: Computer Vision, 1995. Proceedings., Fifth International Conference on, pp. 852–857. https://doi.org/10.1109/ICCV.1995.466848.

Vollmer, J., Mencl, R., Müller, H., 1999. Improved laplacian smoothing of noisy surface meshes. Computer Graphics Forum 18, 131–138. https://doi.org/10.1111/1467-8659.00334.

Zhang, Z., 1994. Iterative point matching for registration of free-form curves and surfaces. International Journal of Computer Vision 13, 119–152. https://doi.org/10.1007/BF01427149. https://doi.org/10.1007/BF01427149.

Zorin, D., Schröder, P., DeRose, T., Kobbelt, L., Levin, A., Sweldens, W., 2000. Subdivision for Modeling and Animation. In: ACM SIGGRAPH Course Notes, vol. 12.

CHAPTER EIGHT

Considerations in the application of 3DGM to stone artifacts with a focus on orientation error in bifaces

Will Archer[1,2], Darya Presnyakova[3]

[1]Department of Human Evolution, Max Planck Institute for Evolutionary Anthropology, Leipzig, Germany
[2]Department of Archaeology, University of Cape Town, Cape Town, South Africa
[3]Department of Early Prehistory and Quaternary Ecology, University of Tübingen, Schloss Hohentübingen, Tübingen, Germany

Introduction and background

Variability in stone artifact form provides the foundation on which interpretive frameworks in lithic studies are built. Three-dimensional (3D) approximations of stone artifacts, such as 3D outlines and landmark configurations, afford a more detailed means of documenting variability in both artifact shape and size than traditional linear measurements (Shott and Trail, 2010). Such 3D approximations document systematic but subtle aspects of stone artifact variability that may not easily be visible to, or measurable by, lithic analysts. The powerful statistical tools of 3DGM (three-dimensional geometrics morphometrics) are advantageous relative to traditional linear measurements of stone artifacts, as the latter will almost always be correlated with overall object size (Bookstein, 1997). 3DGM, however, enables the retention of information regarding the geometric covariation between large numbers of landmarks on a given artifact, in all steps of analysis. The retention of these complex relationships is generally not possible with linear measurements as the majority of these measures, such as technological length, width, or thickness, are not measuring distances between geometrically homologous features on stone artifacts, and therefore capture the combination of both artifact size and shape together (Iovita, 2010).

The benefits afforded by 3DGM opens the potential for documenting stone artifact manufacture and maintenance behaviours at higher resolution than has been possible within conventional lithic analyses. It is worth

3D Data Acquisition for Bioarchaeology, Forensic Anthropology, and Archaeology
ISBN: 978-0-12-815309-3
https://doi.org/10.1016/B978-0-12-815309-3.00008-5

mentioning that in recent years, the number of available instruments for applying 3DGM to stone artifacts has increased substantially. The freedom afforded by statistical platforms such as R to adapt one's workflows flexibly to the specific features of different artifact forms is useful, if not essential, to developing reliable 3DGM stone artifact routines (Schlager, 2013; Archer et al., 2018).

The adaptation of 3DGM approaches for usage in stone artifact analysis, however, poses several challenges. These arise in comparison with their traditional application in biological research. Unlike many biological organisms, stone artifacts have very few homologous features. Consequently, the analysis of stone artifacts using geometric morphometrics was generally not feasible until the relatively recent development of applying semilandmarks to document curves and surfaces on objects where homologous landmarks are rare or absent (Bookstein, 1997; Gunz et al., 2004; Mitteroecker et al., 2004; Slice, 2007). Using semilandmarks, it is possible to analyze stone artifact types that have technologically or functionally homologous axes in the absence of clearly homologous features (Archer et al., 2018; González-José and Charlin, 2012; Presnyakova et al., 2018). Some artifact forms such as "cores", however, remain complicated to analyze meaningfully with 3DGM due to the lack of technologically homologous axes available to orient them.

Raw data capture

Before conventional transformations (e.g. generalized Procrustes analysis) can be undertaken with stone artifact landmark data, several additional issues require attention in the raw data collection phase. At the outset one is faced with the task of raw data acquisition, which entails largely the scanning or the generation of structure from motion 3D models of stone artifacts. This process involves selecting a method that is both sufficiently detailed to capture the characteristic features of a selected stone artifact type and is efficient in the time required to scan a sample of specimens.

The majority of 3DGM studies on stone artifacts rely on surface scanners to obtain meshes to analyze. Three properties of stone artifacts that cause difficulties for most surface scanners are (a) the transparency, (b) the reflectivity of the raw materials being scanned, and (c) the acuteness of the angles of the targeted artifact edges. In this vein, translucent and glossy raw materials such as quartz and obsidian can be particularly challenging to scan. Low-edge angles on thin artifacts such as blades can further perpetuate the scanning issue. Thus, artifacts with problematic properties can take longer to scan effectively and generally require more postprocessing steps; for instance the filling of holes on mesh surfaces, the reversing of inverted face normals, and the removing of unreferenced and duplicated vertices. Postprocessing steps such as filling holes generally increase the error between the mesh and the morphology of the artifact that is approximated by the mesh. Different coating powders are often provided with the purchase of surface scanners or can be replaced by talcum powder. These powders can be brushed onto the surfaces of objects and are intended to make these surfaces less reflective and therefore easier to scan. However, coating raises the possibility of contaminating archeological materials such as residues on tool edges and therefore is recommended only for experimental (nonarcheological) assemblages. In situations where 3D analysis is not feasible, 2D geometric morphometrics using artifact image analysis may be a suitable alternative (Buchanan and Collard 2007, 2010; Monnier and McNulty, 2010).

Artifact orientation

After scanning, artifact meshes need to be digitized to produce configurations of coordinates or "landmarks." It is critical, however, that all stone artifacts are oriented in three dimensions before landmarking. This is the case even if 2D in contrast to 3D geometric morphometric analysis is intended. Orientation of artifacts in 3D is sometimes overlooked by archeologists in the analysis of artifact types that have few geometrically correspondent features, such as Handaxes and most bifacial point types (hereafter "bifaces"). Bifaces have only tips and, occasionally, bases on which "fixed"—that is, immovable—landmarks can be placed. Flakes, on the other hand, are more complex forms that have distinctive dorsal, ventral, and platform surfaces that can guide the placement of landmarks on geometrically correspondent corners and curves at the intersections of these three surfaces (Archer et al., 2018).

The vector linking the tip and the base of bifaces, that is, the points between which one would typically measure biface length, is often considered a first axis of orientation for specimens in a sample of bifaces (McPherron and Dibble, 1999; Archer and Braun, 2010; Archer et al., 2016). Yet, to make other semilandmarks on bifaces—such as those on the edges and surfaces—comparable across all specimens, orientation requires a second step. Bifaces need to be oriented in a second orthogonal axis before edge landmarks can be digitized. A conventional approach to this issue of biface orientation is to ensure that the more convex face, or alternatively the face with more cortex always faces the same direction relative to the placement of individual landmarks (Lycett et al., 2006; Archer et al., 2015). Although the two surfaces of heavily reduced bifaces often may not retain any cortex at all, they will invariably differ in volume. We discuss below that one method of orienting certain artifacts such as bifaces objectively is to use principal components analysis (PCA).

If one skips the second orientation step discussed above (orientation in the bifacial axis), subsequent landmarks placed on tool edges will not correspond geometrically between specimens and therefore will not be comparable across specimens. In such incorrectly orientated assemblages, the shape variance that is apparent on a PCA, for example, can as easily be underpinned by orientation error as by the hominin behaviors in which we are interested (i.e. when opposing edges and surfaces are being compared as correspondent features between incorrectly and correctly oriented specimens). To illustrate this potential influence of orientation error on geometric morphometrics, here, edge landmark configurations of an assemblage of 1000 bifaces are simulated. These simulated bifaces vary substantially in terms of their lengths and widths. Furthermore, the shapes of the biface edges are varied by fitting Bezier curves to each individual specimen, using a subset of the edge landmarks as control points (Olsen, 2014).

Within this simulated data set, randomly selected cases (sets of individual bifaces) can be selected and can be bilaterally inverted, that is, they can essentially be reflected, a procedure that for ease of reference will hereafter be referred to as "mis-orientation." This specimen-by-specimen procedure is analogous to taking an archeological biface that is correctly oriented, for example, and flipping it over onto its opposing face before digitizing it. Importantly, the effects of mis-orientation on assemblage level biface variability can then be visualized with a bivariate plot of specimen scores from a PCA. In the following paragraphs, the potential consequences of error in initial orientation will be explored in this simulated assemblage of bifaces.

This approach allows one to investigate the effects of orientation error on aspects of asymmetry in an assemblage where one knows exactly what the shape variation should look like (Figs. 8.1A and 8.2). Specifically, a biface assemblage with directional edge asymmetry was generated (note the variability in the upper edges of grey specimens on Fig. 8.1A). Shape variation associated with edge asymmetry is a feature that one would expect to be particularly susceptible to the effects of orientation error. One would expect

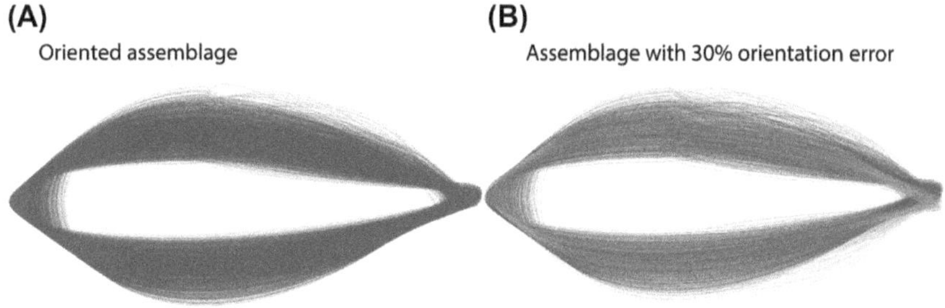

Figure 8.1 The simulated assemblage of 1000 biface edge outlines adjusted for size with Procrustes superimposition, for the original simulated assemblage (A) and the simulated assemblage with added orientation error shown in *red* (B).

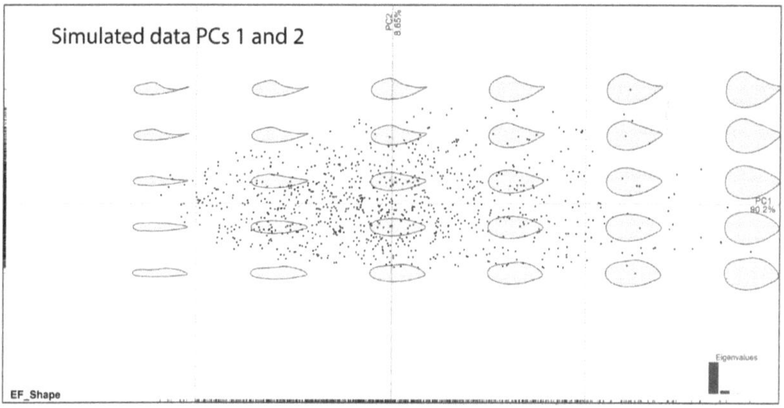

Figure 8.2 Principal components 1 and 2 of the first 8 harmonic coefficients, showing the structure of variability of the correctly oriented simulated biface assemblage.

such assymetry in bifaces where the functional edge, for example, tends to have the same three-dimensional position relative to other geometric features, such as in "Keilmesser" (Weiss et al., 2018). In actual archeological assemblages, where there may be substantial noise in the data, systematic asymmetry in bifaces tends to be more subtle. This simulation is, therefore, an example of the effects of orientation error on an assemblage wherein asymmetry is perhaps unrealistically visible.

To outline the potential effects of orientation error, an elliptical Fourier analyses (EFA) was conducted on the simulated assemblage using functions available in the Momocs and sp R packages (Pebesma and Bivand, 2005; Bonhomme et al., 2014). EFA is a method of decomposing closed curves into sets of coefficients that cumulatively estimate closely, for example, a given artifact shape or set of artifact shapes. The coefficients correspond to harmonics which approach actual artifact shape more closely with each added harmonic. EFA has been used in the analysis of biface and flake shapes (Iovita 2009, 2010, 2011; Iovita and McPherron, 2011; Rezek et al., 2011; Archer et al., 2016).

A PCA of elliptic Fourier transformed coefficients was then visualized to display the major axes of variation in the simulated assemblage, showing the correctly oriented data first (Fig. 8.2). As is the case with many biface collections, the variation between ovate forms and elongate forms is represented along PC1 (i.e., biface elongation: ~91% variance). Systematic "upper-edge" shape variation (or asymmetry) appears to be represented on PCs 2 and 3 (8.65% and 0.92% variance: Fig. 8.3A).

Randomly selected samples of cases were then drawn iteratively from this sample of 1000 bifaces, and their edges were inverted. This inversion was undertaken on samples of cases at 2.5% size intervals (i.e. first n = 25 cases, then n = 50 cases, then n = 75 cases, etc.). These intentionally incorrectly oriented specimens were returned back into the overall assemblage, and the effects on the major components of shape variation were assessed with PCA at each interval.

Importantly, with only 2.5% incorrectly oriented specimens in the data set, the distribution of cases on the PCA already looked substantially different (Fig. 8.3B). By the stage at which this figure reached ~33% (n = 325 cases), the proportion of variance accounted for by asymmetry on PCs 2 and 3 had dropped to negligible amounts (0.59% and 0.1%) and the distribution of specimens on the PCA looked nothing like the distribution of specimens in the correctly oriented assemblage (Fig. 8.3C).

Our simple experiment demonstrates how even marginal artifact orientation error (small numbers of incorrectly oriented specimens) can have substantial effects on assemblage level shape variation. These effects can potentially hide behaviorally meaningful aspects of artifact shape, such as the variation underpinning edge asymmetry in this particular example. In geometric morphometric studies of stone artifacts, therefore, initial orientation is an important consideration at the early stages of data collection (scanning or photographing and landmarking) and is generally difficult to correct retrospectively.

To avoid orientation errors such as the one illustrated with the simulated assemblage above, it is important to orient bifaces in two orthogonal axes (as opposed to just the length axis). One way to do this is to ensure that one of the biface surfaces is oriented (i.e. is facing) in the same direction on all specimens before the edges are landmarked. As mentioned already, one approach

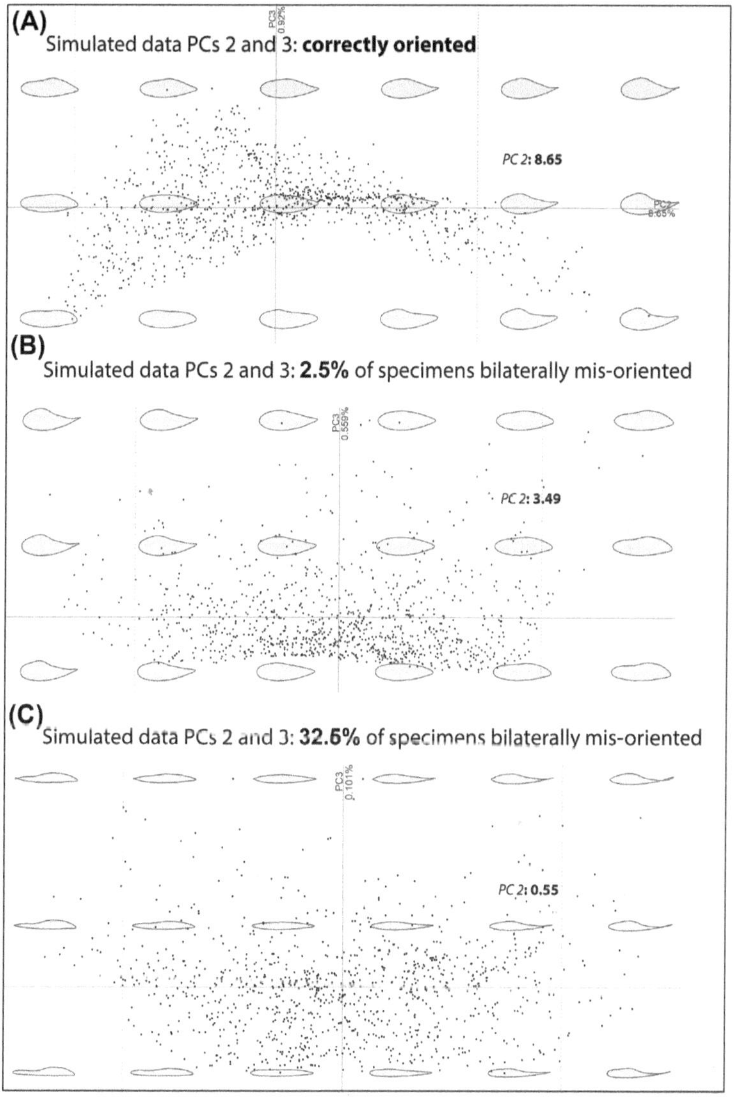

Figure 8.3 Biface shape variation on principal components 2 and 3 for (A) the assemblage of correctly oriented specimens, (B) the assemblage with 25 specimens bifacially inverted or "misoriented," and (C) the assemblage with 325 specimens bifacially inverted.

to establishing this opposition uniformly across all specimens is to ensure, firstly, that the most convex surface in every specimen faces the same direction in bilateral plan before landmarking. However, as many bifacial tools are more or less bifacially symmetrical, determining which of the two faces

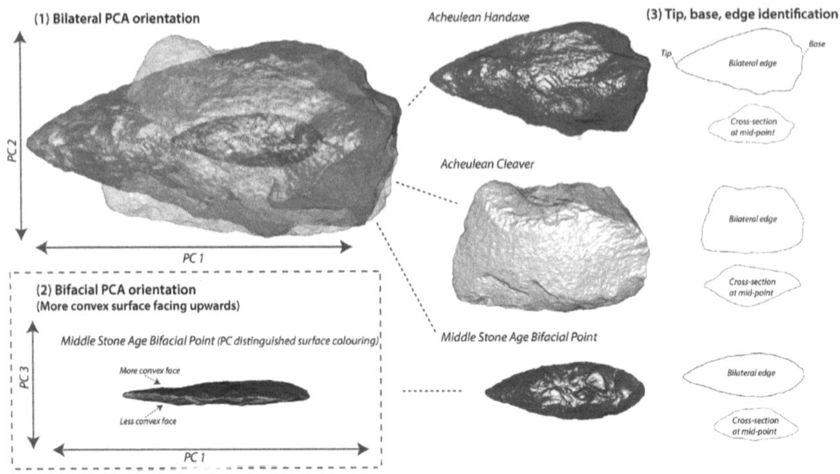

Figure 8.4 Scans of a Handaxe and a Cleaver from the Acheulean deposits at Montagu Cave (1) and a "Still Bay" bifacial point from the Middle Stone Age site of Blombos Cave (2). Both sites are in South Africa. (1) A plot of the scores of artifact mesh vertices on PCs 1 and 2. (2) A plot of the mesh vertices on PCs 1 and 3 demonstrating that artifact bifacial orientation can, if needed, easily be modified by inverting the scores of vertexes on PC3. (3) Polygons of the automatically extracted biface edge landmarks in plan view as well as in cross-sectional view.

is the more convex (i.e., which surface encompasses a greater volume of stone) may not be a trivial task. It is useful, therefore, although not essential, to automate such orientation considerations (Archer et al., 2015) (Fig. 8.4).

PCA is a useful tool for orienting automatically the meshes of certain artifact types, such as bifacial tools, in terms of homologous orthogonal technological axes (i.e. principal components) (Fig. 8.4). Artifact meshes saved as Polygon File Format "PLY" are made up of vertices (points with XYZ coordinates); information on how these vertices are linked up into triangles, and vectors indicating the direction in which these triangles are facing (so-called "normals"), which together approximate an artifact's surface. Using PCA for mesh orientation entails initially undertaking a PCA on the XYZ coordinates of the vertices of each individual mesh in a sample. One can then take the XYZ coordinates of the vertices of each mesh in PCA space (the PC 1–3 scores for each vertex) and write them, along with the other mesh information (triangles, normals), as a newly oriented PLY file. See Archer et al. (2015) for a detailed overview of this orientation process being applied to Middle Stone Age bifacial points.

PCA generally identifies the technological length axis of bifacial tools as the first component of variation, and the edge-to-edge width(s) as the second component (i.e., "PC2"). Similarly, Principal Component 3 ("PC3") identifies variance in bifacial tool thickness, which is approximated by the distance between the two faces of an individual tool. The variance in vertex scores along PC3 can therefore be used to evaluate which of the biface surfaces is more convex on each specimen. In addition, the scores for vertexes on PC3 can then be inverted, if required, so that the most convex surface is oriented in the same direction.

In addition, PCA makes the automatic identification of tool tips, bases, and edges possible in accordance with geometrically correspondent PC axes (Fig. 8.4(3)). For instance, one can identify biface tips and bases simply by looking at the differences between individual vertex scores along PC1. Secondly, in a bivariate plot of vertexes on PCs 1 and 2, a concave hull will identify the entire tool edge accurately on the majority of bifaces.

Placing landmarks

As mentioned already, most stone artifact types have very few homologous features in comparison with biological organisms. A central challenge in applying geometric morphometrics to stone artifacts, therefore, is the paucity of geometrically correspondent locations available on which landmarks can be placed. In this vein, stone artifacts generally need to be digitized using the combination of a small number of fixed landmarks on clearly identifiable common features and many more semilandmarks in between these common features. It is important that these fixed landmarks do not move in subsequent steps of any workflow. Examples of reliable fixed landmarks are the tip and base of bifacial points, or the point of percussion on flake platforms (Archer et al. 2015, 2018).

Semilandmarks can then be placed on "curves" such as geometrically correspondent stone tool edges, as well as on "surfaces" such as flake ventral and dorsal surfaces. Semilandmark placement on curves relies on previously placed fixed landmarks in between which these semilandmarks can slide. These semilandmarks on the curves of stone artifacts equate largely to coordinates on artifact edges. For instance, the semilandmarks on one edge of a biface might slide along that edge between the tip and the base (Fig. 8.5).

As stone artifacts often are highly variable in overall shape, even in a single type of stone tool such as a biface, some specimens within a given assemblage will have relatively more complex edges than others. It is important that these relatively more complex edges have higher initial numbers of

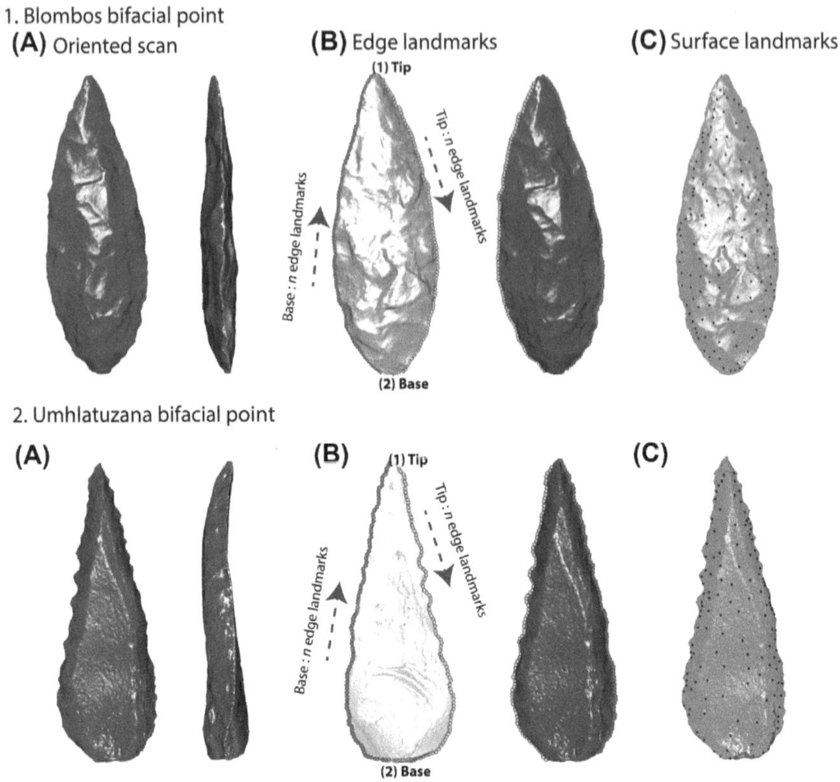

Figure 8.5 Examples of landmark configurations of two different morphologies of Middle Stone Age bifacial points, dating 77–70 ka, from the sites of Blombos Cave (1) and Umhlatuzana (2) in South Africa. (A) The meshes with the two faces segmented, illustrating the more convex (*purple*) and the less convex (*gray*) surface in different colors. (B) The landmarks on the two edges in different colors, which are separated by the tip and base. (C) The surface landmarks on the more convex bifacial surface.

points approximating them than do edges that have a more homogeneous shape. The points initially digitized on stone artifact edges thus serve the purpose only of delineating a vector along which the final (resampled) semilandmarks will be positioned (Fig. 8.5B). If this vector is represented by too few points relative to the complexity of a particular edge, then semilandmarks could "slip off" the edge and onto an artifact surface during resampling, an accident that could introduce substantial error into a data set. There are a number of functions in the Morpho and Geomorph R packages which will undertake resampling and also the sliding of semilandmarks on stone artifact edges (Adams and Otárola-Castillo, 2013; Schlager, 2013).

Placing landmarks on artifact edges may well capture sufficient data to address a particular research question. However, where shape variance is driven more by features of artifact surface morphology—such as an assemblage of flakes wherein variability in the morphology of the bulbs may be important—additional landmarks may be useful (Archer et al., 2018). In such an application, the placement of additional landmarks on flake ventral and dorsal surfaces, for example, may be required (see Fig. 8.5C for an example of surface landmarks in bifacial points).

The procedures needed to place landmarks on artifact surfaces rely heavily on the accurate prior placement of landmarks on the artifact edges. One method of placing landmarks on stone artifact surfaces entails first manually landmarking the surfaces of a single randomly chosen template specimen. It does not matter which specimen in an assemblage is selected to be this template. A biface template may, for example, comprise a configuration of one fixed point on the tip, one fixed point on the base, a set number of evenly spaced landmarks on each edge and a set of manually placed landmarks on each of the two surfaces.

The template configuration of landmarks can then be deformed or "warped," iteratively, onto each of the surfaces of the other bifaces in that assemblage (the "target" specimens). The purpose of this deformation is to approximate the positions of the corresponding surface landmarks on each of the target specimens that, up to this stage, are absent on every specimen but the template itself. This deformation can be challenging, depending on how variable the morphology of the assemblage of target specimens is, and it can be computationally slow if many surface landmarks need to be estimated. The R package "Morpho" describes a series of functions that are extremely useful for undertaking surface landmarking in a stone artifact analysis context (Schlager, 2013).

Conclusion

3DGM offers a powerful set of tools for lithic analysis, which are being adopted by archeologists at a rapidly increasing rate. The ability to document artifacts with landmarks facilitates an unprecedentedly detailed approximation of artifact shape. Using these landmarks, the tools of 3DGM enable lithic analysts to document the complex covariation between large numbers of artifact features in all steps of analysis, to treat the properties of artifact size and shape separately, and to isolate the relationships between different aspects of artifact shape and size. As all phases of stone tool manufacture and maintenance are inherently reductive, the ability to map detailed allometric trajectories in different technologies is of great importance to understand past hominin behaviors.

Currently, the use of 3DGM is inhibited by the time-efficiency of available scanning technologies, and the feasibility of landmarking large collections of stone artifacts. Yet the rapidly increasing capacity of scanning technologies, and the possibility of developing automated landmarking protocols, is making the option of 3DGM more feasible in wider ranges of lithics assemblages and archaeological questions. As the simulated example above demonstrates, however, using 3DGM blindly, even in assemblages of relatively simple artifact forms can quite easily result in error-strewn results. While orientation error, for instance, may have limited effects on certain assemblages, it has the potential to significantly blur behaviorally meaningful variance in others.

Acknowledgments

Thanks to Shannon McPherron for writing the code that simulates the biface landmarks and for continuing discussion. Thanks to Jean-Jacques Hublin and the Max Planck Society for supporting this research.

References

Adams, D.C., Otárola-Castillo, E., 2013. Geomorph: an R package for the collection and analysis of geometric morphometric shape data. Methods in Ecology and Evolution 4 (4), 393–399.

Archer, W., Braun, D.R., 2010. Variability in bifacial technology at Elandsfontein, Western cape, South Africa: a geometric morphometric approach. Journal of Archaeological Science 37 (1), 201–209.

Archer, W., Gunz, P., van Niekerk, K.L., Henshilwood, C.S., McPherron, S.P., 2015. Diachronic change within the Still Bay at Blombos Cave, South Africa. PLoS One 10 (7), e0132428.

Archer, W., Pop, C.M., Gunz, P., McPherron, S.P., 2016. What is Still Bay? Human biogeography and bifacial point variability. Journal of Human Evolution 97, 58–72.

Archer, W., Pop, C.M., Rezek, Z., Schlager, S., Lin, S.C., Weiss, M., Dogandžić, T., Desta, D., McPherron, S.P., 2018. A geometric morphometric relationship predicts stone flake shape and size variability. Archaeological and Anthropological Sciences 10 (8), 1991–2003.

Bonhomme, V., Picq, S., Gaucherel, C., Claude, J., 2014. Momocs: outline analysis using R. Journal of Statistical Software 56 (13), 1–24.

Bookstein, F.L., 1997. Morphometric Tools for Landmark Data: Geometry and Biology. Cambridge University Press.

Buchanan, B., Collard, M., 2007. Investigating the peopling of North America through cladistic analyses of Early Paleoindian projectile points. Journal of Anthropological Archaeology 26 (3), 366–393.

Buchanan, B., Collard, M., 2010. A geometric morphometrics-based assessment of blade shape differences among Paleoindian projectile point types from western North America. Journal of Archaeological Science 37 (2), 350–359.
González-José, R., Charlin, J., 2012. Relative importance of modularity and other morphological attributes on different types of lithic point weapons: assessing functional variations. PLoS One 7 (10), e48009.
Gunz, P., Mitteroecker, P., Bookstein, F.L., 2004. Semilandmarks in three dimensions. In: Slice, D.E. (Ed.), Modern Morphometrics in Physical Anthropology. Kluwer Academic/Plenum Publishers, New York, pp. 73–98.
Iovita, R., 2011. Shape variation in Aterian tanged tools and the origins of projectile technology: a morphometric perspective on stone tool function. PLoS One 6 (12), e29029.
Iovita, R., 2009. Ontogenetic scaling and lithic systematics: method and application. Journal of Archaeological Science 36 (7), 1447–1457.
Iovita, R., 2010. Comparing stone tool resharpening trajectories with the aid of elliptical Fourier analysis. In: New Perspectives on Old Stones. Springer, pp. 235–253.
Iovita, R., McPherron, S.P., 2011. The handaxe reloaded: a morphometric reassessment of Acheulian and Middle Paleolithic handaxes. Journal of Human Evolution 61 (1), 61–74.
Lycett, S.J., von Cramon-Taubadel, N., Foley, R.A., 2006. A crossbeam co-ordinate caliper for the morphometric analysis of lithic nuclei: a description, test and empirical examples of application. Journal of Archaeological Science 33 (6), 847–861.
McPherron, S.P., Dibble, H.L., 1999. Stone tool analysis using digitized images: examples from the Lower and Middle Paleolithic. Lithic Technology 24 (1), 38–52.
Mitteroecker, P., Gunz, P., Bernhard, M., Schaefer, K., Bookstein, F.L., 2004. Comparison of cranial ontogenetic trajectories among great apes and humans. Journal of Human Evolution 46 (6), 679–698.
Monnier, G.F., McNulty, K.P., 2010. Questioning the link between stone tool standardization and behavioral modernity. In: New Perspectives on Old Stones. Springer, pp. 61–81.
Olsen, A., 2014. Bezier: Bezier Curve and Spline Toolkit. URL: http://cran.rproject.org/web/packages/bezier.
Pebesma, E., Bivand, R.S., 2005. Classes and methods for spatial data: the sp package. R News 5 (2), 9–13.
Presnyakova, D., Braun, D.R., Conard, N.J., Feibel, C., Harris, J.W.K., Pop, C.M., Schlager, S., Archer, W., 2018. Site fragmentation, hominin mobility and LCT variability reflected in the early Acheulean record of the Okote Member, at Koobi Fora, Kenya. Journal of Human Evolution 125, 159–180.
Rezek, Z., Lin, S., Iovita, R., Dibble, H.L., 2011. The relative effects of core surface morphology on flake shape and other attributes. Journal of Archaeological Science 38 (6), 1346–1359.
Schlager, S., 2013. Morpho: Calculations and Visualizations Related to Geometric Morphometrics. R package version 0.23 3.
Shott, M.J., Trail, B.W., 2010. Exploring new approaches to lithic analysis: laser scanning and geometric morphometrics. Lithic Technology 35 (2), 195–220.
Slice, D.E., 2007. Geometric morphometrics. Annual Review of Anthropology 36 (1), 261–281.
Weiss, M., Lauer, T., Wimmer, R., Pop, C.M., 2018. The variability of the Keilmesser-concept: a case study from Central Germany. Journal of Paleolithic Archaeology 1 (3), 202–246.

CHAPTER NINE

Conclusions

Beatrix Dudzik[1], Noriko Seguchi[2,3], Anna M. Prentiss[3]
[1]Department of Anatomy, DeBusk College of Osteopathic Medicine, Lincoln Memorial University, Harrogate, TN, The United States of America
[2]Faculty of Social and Cultural Studies, Kyushu University, Fukuoka, Japan
[3]Department of Anthropology, The University of Montana, Missoula, MT, The United States of America

This volume serves as an introductory text for burgeoning researchers and students of biological anthropology and archeology that are interested in learning about the application of geometric morphometric analyses in forensic and bioarcheological contexts. Specifically, this text introduces the reader to the basics of three-dimensional (3D) data, the logistics of and step-by-step tutorials on data collection, and concludes with example analyses and case studies to illustrate how these types of data and associated analyses can be used to address forensic and bioarcheological research questions in novel and meaningful ways.

Each chapter provides clear explanations and introduces the reader to different types of 3D data, to include landmarks and semilandmarks collected with a 3D digitizer, and scan data derived from 3D scanners, CT, and digital mesh models created from scan data. The technology needed to collect these data is described as well as how to pre- and postprocess the data, analyze, and digitally curate. This text serves as a guide for researchers who have access to or interest in 3D data but are not sure where to start or are interested in learning more about the many applications and new technologies that are becoming available. We understand that learning how to work with these types of data can be intimidating and thus this text provides guidelines and case studies to walk the reader through their own analyses.

The utility of working in the field of geometric morphometrics (GM) is wide ranging, as it allows for visualization of similarities and/or differences of the specimens in question, rather than within isolated dimensions of metric differences. In biological anthropology and archeology, GM techniques allow for assessment of morphological variation in several dimensions simultaneously (Marcus and Corti, 1996), which allows for examination of morphology of the skeleton in orientations outside of vertical and horizontal planes (heights, width, breadths) that are used in traditional studies of skeletal metrics. Much of the pivotal biological research in the last several decades

3D Data Acquisition for Bioarchaeology, Forensic Anthropology, and Archaeology
ISBN: 978-0-12-815309-3
https://doi.org/10.1016/B978-0-12-815309-3.00009-7

have focused on plasticity, heritability, and such on the human skull, but geometric morphometric approaches have been used to examine an onslaught of topics within biological and forensic anthropology and bioarcheology.

For example, recent publications within the last 5 years have explored such topics as sexual dimorphism of the cranium and pelvis to improve sex estimation techniques, comparison of metric and GM data for ancestry estimation, shape analysis of joint spaces for age estimation, shape analysis of cranial modifications in archeological samples, as well as using shape analysis to examine growth and development patterns of fetal and adolescent skeletal structures (Campo et al., 2018; Kuzminsky et al., 2016; San-Millán et al., 2017; Small et al., 2018; Spradley and Jantz, 2016; Stull et al., 2014; Rusk and Ousley, 2016).

The first few chapters have outlined the specifics of various types of 3D data and the associated critical technologies. Chapter 1 of this text provided a short introduction to the commonly used types of 3D data, and the technology required to collect it, all of which are expanded on in later chapters. This includes an introduction to 3D coordinate, or landmark, data as well as surface and medical-grade scans such as CT.

Chapter 2 introduces virtual data and the virtual environment in which these types of data can exist. The reader learns the definitions of commonly encountered terminology while also being introduced to the context in which these will be encountered, such as during data collection, pre- or postprocessing, statistical analysis, and so on. Basic information regarding what type of files are to be encountered, and other logistical definitions are also provided. A discussion is presented that describes how an increase in the shape complexity of a 3D object, such as the craniofacial region of a skull compared with the outline of a long bone, will result in a more complex shape outline and thus the data and the data file type will become more detailed and multifaceted.

This chapter also introduces the reader to 3D renderings, which is arguably the most complicated type of data to work with. Open source software packages, such as Meshlab, can be used to produce mesh models, a type of preprocessing that formats the 3D data to allow for other software programs, such as *CloudCompare, Morpheus et al.,* and *Geomagic* that can analyze mesh and point cloud data types. This chapter briefly covers standard alignment and orientation and data collection for different 3D data types, to include CT images, digitized coordinates, and surface scans while also discussing possible sources of error during data collection and postprocessing. A scanning workflow is provided as general guidelines for researchers that are using a 3D surface scanner. The authors also provide an in-depth example of data collection and processing of mesh images captured by a Z-scanner 800 of a collection of archaeological crania from Southern Japan, that details the steps involved in collecting and processing mesh images.

Chapter 3 outlines the realities of working with archaeological skeletal remains and describes protocols for collection of 3D data on fragile and/or archaeological bone. Skeletal preservation can be extremely variable and depends on the environment it was found in, such as the presence of excessive moisture in a burial context, as well as the age, or how much time the specimen has spent in that environment to include the overall age of the archeological site or time since death. A case study is provided describing the fragility of archaeological remains in Japan, due to the acidity of the soil. Different time periods employed different burial practices and inhabited different regions of the archipelago, such as shell-mound burials during the Jomon period, jar-shaped coffins from the Yayoi period, burial mounds from the Kofun period; however, unless remains were preserved in a coastal environment, typically any contact with soil throughout Japan results in poor preservation of skeletal material. These variables are not unique to archaeological sites and burials in Japan but rather should be applied broadly to bioarchaeological environments throughout the world.

It is important for researchers to understand how to safely collect 3D data from fragile as well as highly preserved remains to ensure every precaution is kept ensuring no damage occurs to the skeletal material. Although surface scans and other technologies no longer require physical contact with the material, as is required when measuring with calipers, handling the remains and setting up the material in the right orientation require a well thought-out protocol. This chapter provides alternative approaches to pencil-marking bone, to delineate minimum and maximum lengths and breadths, which are required when using a digitizer. It also introduces a wooden box alternative to the traditional metal tripod used when digitizing crania and when clay pillars cannot be used. The authors describe how to mirror bilateral landmarks if part of the skull is broken or unrecordable, which cannot be used for analyses of asymmetry, but is highly practical for anyone working with remains that are not complete.

Chapters 4–7 provide case studies and work flow charts to walk the reader through working with each type of data described in previous chapters. Chapter 4 addresses how to gather and preprocess coordinate data collected with a digitizer and introduces the reader to the MorphoJ program, a free software package written by Klingenberg (2011). Common statistical analyses used for coordinate data are reviewed.

Chapter 5–6 goes into expert detail describing landmark types and how these can be collected and used to output mesh images. Reproducibility between landmark sets is also covered and a case study that compares coordinate data and 3D surface scans taken from the same skeletal sample is also provided. These chapters also remind readers the importance of research design before data collection fieldwork begins. Along with Chapter 3, these chapters explain that researchers must obtain the necessary information about specific preservation conditions and closely follow the detailed protocols received from curators of the biological material and artifacts for instructions on how to properly handle human remains and what types of data collection methods are allowed. Gathering this background information especially from foreign institutions is important for maximizing the amount of data that can be safely and respectfully recorded from a skeletal collection.

Chapter 7 provides an in-depth tutorial on carrying out common GM analyses in the open source framework, R, which can be used by any user, and is not limited to advanced programmers. The author outlines a step-by-step guide to the downloadable packages Morpho, used for landmark-based shape analyses, and Rvcg2, which is used for mesh-type data. Both of these packages are available to download through CRAN3 repository, which users can search for in R. The author provides a step-by-step example analysis using surface scan data from the Yacchi sample, and all code needed is provided throughout the chapter.

The information and guidelines presented in the majority of the chapters provided, while described in reference to working with human remains, can be adapted to other types of archeological materials. Chapter 8 provides guidelines for 3D geometric morphometric analyses on stone technologies, which have been studied extensively using GM approaches but also present distinct challenges to the researcher that are unique to these types of artifacts.

For example, the majority of GM studies on stone artifacts use surface scanners to produce mesh data, which need to then be digitized to produce the configurations of coordinates, or "landmarks," that approximate the original stone artifacts. Special care must be taken to align all compared specimens in a consistent manner that provides orientation in three dimensions to allow for landmark and semilandmark data to be recorded. Furthermore, the researcher must ensure that surface sides all face a uniform direction, to account for the convexity and concavity of the artifact, something that is typically not a factor in analyses of biological materials that normally exhibit high levels of symmetry.

Despite these unique challenges, many of the statistical analyses of stone artifacts correspond to those described in previous chapters, to include principal component analysis that can be carried out using shape analysis packages such as Morpho and Geomorph available in R.

Future directions

As geometric morphometric software, new statistical approaches and public databases such as 3D-ID (Slice and Ross, 2009) continue to become more readily available, the way that researchers look at human morphology and archeological material artifacts will become more dynamic and more accessible. Our hope is that this volume provides a user-friendly guide to researchers, academics, and students to assist in the somewhat daunting task of learning how to work with these types of data. Shape analysis provides an avenue for interdisciplinary collaborations, and much of the statistical programs required are free and/or open sourced, which aids in the access for all types of users, be it seasoned academic or new student. As new computational approaches are developed, how anthropologists and archaeologists view and analyze morphology and the etiologies behind patterns and trends will continue to be expanded on.

References

Campo, E.J.E., López-Lázaro, S., Rodríguez, C.L.M., Aguilera, I.A., López, M.C.B., 2018. Specific-age group sex estimation of infants through geometric morphometrics analysis of pubis and ischium. Forensic Science International 286, 185–192.

Klingenberg, C.P., 2011. MorphoJ: an integrated software package for geometric morphometrics. Molecular Ecology Resources 11, 353–357.

Kuzminsky, S.C., Tung, T.A., Hubbe, M., Villaseñor-Marchal, A., 2016. The application of 3D geometric morphometrics and laser surface scanning to investigate the standardization of cranial vault modification in the Andes. Journal of Archaeological Science: Report 10, 507–513.

Marcus, L.F., Corti, M., 1996. Overview of the new, or geometric morphometrics. In: Advances in Morphometrics. Springer, Boston, MA, pp. 1–13.

Rusk, K.M., Ousley, S.D., 2016. An evaluation of sex-and ancestry-specific variation in sacral size and shape using geometric morphometrics. American Journal of Physical Anthropology 159 (4), 646–654.

San-Millán, M., Rissech, C., Turbón, D., 2017. Shape variability of the adult human acetabulum and acetabular fossa related to sex and age by geometric morphometrics. Implications for adult age estimation. Forensic Science International 272, 50–63.

Slice, D., Ross, A.H., 2009. 3D-ID: Geometric Morphometric Classification of Crania for Forensic Scientists.

Small, C., Schepartz, L., Hemingway, J., Brits, D., 2018. Three-dimensionally derived inter-landmark distances for sex estimation in intact and fragmentary crania. Forensic Science International 287, 127–135.

Spradley, K.M., Jantz, R.L., 2016. Ancestry estimation in forensic anthropology: geometric morphometric versus standard and nonstandard interlandmark distances. Journal of Forensic Sciences 61 (4), 892–897.

Stull, K.E., Kenyhercz, M.W., L'Abbé, E.N., 2014. Ancestry estimation in South Africa using craniometrics and geometric morphometrics. Forensic Science International 245, 206-e–1.

Index

'*Note:* Page numbers followed by "f" indicate figures, "t" indicate tables and "b" indicate boxes.'

E

F

G

H

I

J

L

FSC
www.fsc.org
MIX
Papier | Fördert gute Waldnutzung
FSC® C083411

Kolibri 360 GmbH
Ferdinand-Jühlke-Straße 7
99095 Erfurt, Deutschland
produktsicherheit@kolibri360.de